BIBLICAL
CRITICISM
ON TRIAL

BIBLICAL CRITICISM ON TRIAL

How Scientific is "Scientific Theology"?

ETA LINNEMANN

Robert Yarbrough, trans.

kregel
PUBLICATIONS

Grand Rapids, MI 49501

Originally published as *Bibelkritik auf dem Prüfstand: Wie wissenschaftlich ist die »wissenschaftliche Theologie«?*
© 1990 by Eta Linnemann
VTR, Nürnberg, Germany

Biblical Criticism on Trial: How Scientific is "Scientific Theology"?

English Translation © 2001 by Eta Linnemann

Published by Kregel Publications, a division of Kregel, Inc., P.O. Box 2607, Grand Rapids, MI 49501. For more information about Kregel Publications, visit our Web site: www.kregel.com.

ISBN 0-8254-3088-7

Printed in the United States of America

1 2 3 / 05 04 03 02 01

CONTENTS

Foreword   10
   To my readers   10
   To my critics   12

Translator's Preface   15

Chapter One: The Lost Gospel of Q—Fact or Fantasy?   18
   A. What is Q?   20
   B. What can we know for sure about Q?   21
   C. The origin of Q   23
   D. What about the Synoptic Gospels?   25
   E. What about Thomas?   28
   F. Q: the Lost Gospel—Fact or Fantasy?   30

Chapter Two: Another Look at the Synoptic Problem   42
   A. Supplement to the quantitative analysis of Mark's
      gospel   42
   B. Vocabulary in identical words of parallel verses that is not
      relevant for literary dependence   44
   C. The Synoptics and the Septuagint   47
   D. Does Mark's gospel reflect a more primitive level of
      language than the gospels of Matthew and Luke?   50

E. Isn't there, nevertheless, literary dependence among the Synoptic Gospels? The arguments of Robert H. Stein   52

F. The synoptic structure of Mark's gospel   61

Chapter Three: Pauline Authorship and Vocabulary Statistics   74

A. Word lists and vocabulary statistics as proof of authenticity   74

B. Word occurrence in the Pauline letters—the presupposition for objective statistical argumentation in questions of genuineness   86

Chapter Four: "Inauthentic" New Testament Writings: Scientific Findings or a Witch Trial?   100

A. Linguistic argumentation   102

   1. Hapax legomena as evidence for inauthenticity   102

   2. Word lists of typical terms whose occurrence speaks against authenticity   106

   3. Word lists of typical terms whose absence speaks against authenticity   109

   4. Lists of stylistic distinctives whose absence or presence speaks against authenticity   110

B. Literary dependence   113

   1. The Epistle to the Ephesians   113

   2. Second Thessalonians   118

   3. Second Peter   122

C. Historical placement   126

   1. The Epistle to the Ephesians   126

   2. The Pastoral Epistles   128

   3. The Epistle of James   132

   4. First Peter   134

   5. Second Peter   136

   6. The Epistle of Jude   137

D. Theological classification   138

   1. The Epistle to the Ephesians   140

   2. The Epistle to the Colossians   142

3. Second Thessalonians 148
4. The Pastoral Epistles 150
E. Description of phenomena with expressions that can be neither objectified nor quantified 152
   1. The Epistle to the Ephesians 152
   2. The Epistle to the Colossians 152
   3. Second Thessalonians 152
   4. The Pastoral Epistles 153
   5. The Epistle of James 154
   6. First Peter 156
F. Results 157

Chapter Five: The Quantitative Structure of the Vocabulary of the New Testament 164
A. Absolute quantities in the entire New Testament and in individual New Testament writings 164
   1. Singles and multies 164
   2. Hapax legomena, *mia-graphē* legomena, and *polygraphē* legomena 166
   3. The monos 167
B. The relative quantities: solos, partials, and completes—the parallel structure in the Scripture groups 167
C. The importance of the quantitative structure for comparison of vocabulary in writings or groups of writings demonstrated by examples 168
   1. Structural analysis of Markan vocabulary 168
   2. Quantitative investigations of the vocabulary of Paul's letters 169
D. Factors that are important for the quantitative structure of the vocabulary of a writing 174
   1. The author 174
   2. The addressee 174
   3. Theme 174
   4. Range 175
   5. The author's circumstances 175
E. Summary 175

Chapter Six: Evangelical and Historical-Critical Theology   177

A. The foundations   177

  1. The concept of "theology" is not used univocally but equivocally   177

  2. The roots of historical-critical theology   178

  3. Evangelical theology—what it is, and what it should be   179

B. The implementation   182

  1. Historical-critical theology = scientific theology? Claim and reality   182

  2. Evangelical theology and the claim to scientific character   188

C. A new beginning   190

  1. Theological thinking rooted in God's Word and oriented toward the triune God   190

  2. Scholarly labor as brotherly service   190

  3. Theological work that is faithful to the Bible is independent in the way it poses its questions as well as in its methods   191

  4. Theological work that is faithful to the Bible as critical assessment of historical-critical theology's supporting pillars   193

D. A new concept   194

  1. Solidarity and division of labor   195

  2. Weighing research projects and considering priorities   195

  3. Personal contribution to the international research structure   197

    a. General   197

    b. Biblical theology   198

      (1) Attaining independence in dating   198

      (2) Basic investigation into questions of introduction   198

      (3) New Testament   199

      (4) Research of comparative material from the history of religion   200

c. Church history   203
4. Realization of solidarity through transparency and
   information   205

Chapter Seven: Results   210

Bibliography   212

Index   214

FOREWORD

*"How can the wise teach what is wise when they reject
the word of the Lord?"* —Jer. 8:9

*"For the Lord gives wisdom, and from his mouth come
knowledge and understanding."* —Prov. 2:6 NIV

*"Stop listening, my son, to instruction which makes you
stray from the words of knowledge."* —Prov. 19:27

To my readers

This book is part of a New Testament apologetic that obeys God's
Word in Jude 3 "to contend for the faith that was once for all entrusted
to the saints" (NIV). The battle is being waged against biblical criticism, which is institutionalized as historical-critical theology or—as
it erroneously characterizes itself—historical-critical method. It claims
exclusive and complete validity as "scientific theology" and, at least
in Germany, dominates not only the theology departments of the universities but also church training centers and even the religious instruction in schools, right down to the primary-school level. In addition
it enjoys worldwide distribution and is powerfully championed not
only in Europe but also in Asia, Africa, and America.

Biblical criticism disputes the claim of Holy Scripture to be God's
revelation, the inspired Word of God. In this way it destroys faith,

although it would neither intend nor admit to that. But as a German hymn asks, "If your Word is no longer valid, on what can faith be founded?"

In Germany preaching based on biblical criticism has emptied the churches, because few people see any reason for attending worship when they are offered only the stones of arbitrary personal opinion rather than the bread of the Word of God. Biblical criticism has brought on a decay of values: historical-critical theology considers it untenable to teach adolescents that the Ten Commandments are God's binding instructions. Instead of taking to heart "whatever is noble" and "whatever virtue there may be" (Phil. 4:8), it has disparaged honesty, punctuality, hard work, and the like as mere secondary virtues, holdovers from a Prussian mentality that should no longer be upheld. In addition some streams of historical-critical thinking popularize the Communist slogan that owning property is thievery. The alleged decay of values is therefore in fact an utter destruction of values, brought about not single-handedly but with the substantial assistance of historical-critical theology.

It is true that God's inspired Word needs no defense. What needs defending is the access to it that biblical criticism has obstructed. That is the task of Old and New Testament apologetics: "The weapons we fight with are not fleshly but divinely powerful for the destruction of strongholds; we demolish specious reasonings and every lofty pretension that opposes the knowledge of God, and take every thought captive to the obedience of Christ" (2 Cor. 10:4–5).

The effort of the battle is exerted for those whose access to God's Word has been blocked by biblical criticism: it is for the victims and not the perpetrators. I am acutely aware that this runs completely against the trend of the times. The person who objects that it is still fruitful to win biblical critics with love in academic discussion can take up that task himself; that is not my calling. I know from personal experience that the move from criticism of the Bible to trust in the Bible does not occur through arguments that consider the intellectual presuppositions of the Bible critic in such a way that he can accept those arguments. The way from biblical criticism to biblical faith runs through the narrow gate, through conversion to Jesus Christ, God's

Son, our Lord, who redeemed us through his blood shed on Golgotha's cross, who "was delivered over to death for our sins and was raised to life for our justification" (Rom. 4:25).

The fascination with historical-critical theology, to which many evangelicals have unfortunately more or less succumbed, lies in its claim to be scientific. It is considered necessary to respect scientific results. But what goes unnoticed is that these "results" are often nothing more than unproven hypotheses that are forcefully declared to be facts once they have found broad agreement.

The last thing I have in mind is to support faith in God's Word through scientific arguments. But I would like to show those who have diverged from simple faith in God's Word, or who stand in danger of doing this, impressed by the exclusive and complete validity claimed by biblical critics for their "scientific theology," that they are exchanging their birthright for a mess of pottage. May the Lord help many to abandon a futile path and others to follow the right path with more conviction and assurance.

I offer my thanks to all who have contributed to the formation of this book with their intercession.

To my critics

In this book too, as in an earlier one,[1] I have used the method of objectification through quantification, without going into statistical investigation in the technical sense. I lack the requirements for this, and the biggest share of my readers would lack the necessary technical understanding. Anyone who would like to see such investigation can carry it out personally on the basis of the data provided elsewhere in this book. My concern is to make it possible for the reader to test my results. It is not least for that reason that I have continued to use the more easily affordable statistical study by Morgenthaler.[2]

After careful reflection, in the area of "inauthentic" New Testament writings (chapter four), I have not extended the discussion to the broad spectrum of monographs on this question but have restricted myself to the discussion typical in the field of New Testament Introduction. An introduction to Old or New Testament does not present its own new investigations but reports on the state of research and passes along what has found general recognition. It is the manual which the student draws on in order to be prepared for exams. He or she can ignore individual monographs, but the introduction must be heeded. A recognized and established introduction shows what historical-critical theology presents to its students as binding. Here you can take historical-critical theology at its word; evasion is not possible. What an individual author writes can be set aside as not normative, but what the introduction says, stands.[3]

The chapters of this book belong to some degree in the area of basic research, which directly sets forth New Testament data and works through the results. On the other hand, historical-critical presentations are analyzed and critically investigated. For neither aspect of the research is it necessary to consult the whole spectrum of relevant literature. For the non-New Testament specialist, it would serve little purpose to incorporate the critical discussion found in this literature. And yet I will not deny that a critic is justified in finding fault with my omission of this literature. Nevertheless, I submit that someone on the far side of seventy years old must set priorities. For that reason I could also not confer deserved honor on some evangelical authors who have arrived at results similar to those of my own.

It would certainly have been right and easy to go into the relevant contributions of Guthrie or Carson-Moo-Morris.[4] But I did not do this because only a very few of my German readers have access to these books, and extensive quotations from them would have disrupted the flow of thought.

May this book, despite acknowledged weaknesses, render a service, and may young scholars see themselves summoned to carry on and supplement the work in the same spirit. In this way they will discover the innovations contained in no small measure herein, innovations that I deeply hope will be incorporated into biblically sound investigation of the New Testament.

All honor belongs to the Lord alone!

Endnotes

1. Eta Linnemann, *Is There a Synoptic Problem?* trans. R. Yarbrough (Grand Rapids: Baker, 1992), to be checked against the newest edition

of *Gibt es ein synoptisches Problem?* 4th ed. (Nürnberg: Verlag für Theologie und Religionswissenschaft, 1999).

2. Robert Morgenthaler, *Statistik der Neutestamentlichen Wortschatzes*, 4th ed. (Zürich: Gotthelf Verlag, 1992).

3. An exception is Trilling's monograph, since Schnelle refers to it instead of presenting the arguments himself.

4. Donald Guthrie, *New Testament Introduction,* 4th ed. (Downers Grove: InterVarsity, 1990); D. A. Carson, Douglas J. Moo, and Leon Morris, *An Introduction to the New Testament* (Grand Rapids: Zondervan, 1992).

Translator's Preface

I WOULD LIKE TO thank Dennis Hillman, Stephen Barclift, and others at Kregel Publications for their willingness to publish Dr. Linnemann's latest book in this English-language version.

Stephen L. Kline performed valuable, speedy, and expert service editorially. His excellent command of German saved the translator from a number of miscues. He also made many of my technically correct but literarily opaque renderings transparent. I am grateful for his thoroughness and diligence.

At a professional meeting some months ago I was verbally accosted by a fellow scholar who complained that Dr. Linnemann's views are so controversial, and so rawly expressed, and such an embarrassment to scholarly evangelicals, that they should never have been translated. Since I have been Linnemann's primary translator into English in recent years,[1] this could reasonably be regarded as a personal attack.

I prefer to regard it as a sign of the growing pains of Christian scholarship in certain quarters. George Marsden is among many who have called attention to the stern test faced by those who enter today's marketplace of ideas (or should we say ideologies) with the resolve to contribute to contemporary learning wherever possible—but to articulate a Christian perspective wherever appropriate.[2] Readers must judge whether Linnemann errs on the side of prophecy rather than scholarly inquiry.[3] What cannot be denied is that she is willing, on both theological and documentary grounds, to challenge an academic hegemony which, especially in her native Germany, has largely despoiled Christian witness in church and society. It is unlikely that the English-speaking world has remained so impervious to the censuring and warping of Christian inquiry and expression that Linnemann's challenges have nothing to teach us here.

Her background and calling are unique, and it may be tempting to discount the outlook she reflects because of its religious zeal and sometimes abrasive edge. Further, her results may be less definitive than she appears to believe. But these things are equally true of the views of those she criticizes. There seems to be a double standard at work: Those with iconoclastic Enlightenment or postmodern convictions regarding first-century historiography and theology can be as myopic and dismissive of confessional readings as they wish and still be regarded as scholarly and critical, while someone like Linnemann, who for the sake of argument adopts many of the same methods as the iconoclasts but is informed by different premises, is marginalized for her myopia and dismissive tone.[4] Thomas C. Oden has called attention to "biblical believers who are assigned pariah roles in Scripture courses" in university religion departments and mainline seminaries.[5] Something analogous may be detected in the reception accorded Linnemann's post-conversion writings by colleagues in the guild—sometimes even those who share her evangelical theological convictions.

Readers who are able to show the deficiencies of this book's arguments and conclusions on empirical grounds can and should do so. Linnemann has lived in the milieu of academic disputation her entire adult life. She deserves and expects no less. But it is to be hoped that colleagues would think twice about assessing her work primarily from the standpoint of those on the bandwagon she criticizes. In a day when both prophecy and learning seem to be increasingly rare (cf. 1 Sam. 3:1),[6] anyone who contributes substantively to the understanding of biblical criticism's origin, character, claims, and legitimacy deserves a place at the discussion table. Linnemann undoubtedly contributes. How substantively will be determined most effectively by readers with the wisdom, maturity, and perhaps also the political courage, not to tune out her message prematurely.

—Robert W. Yarbrough
Trinity Evangelical Divinity School

Endnotes

1. Her first post-conversion book, *Historical Criticism of the Bible: Methodology or Ideology?* (Grand Rapids: Kregel, 2001), summarizes her defection from the largely anti-Christian perspective in which she was trained and which she promulgated as a professor in the German university. Her subsequent volume, *Is There a Synoptic Problem?* (Grand Rapids: Baker, 1992) critiques the two-source, Marcan priority theory of Synoptic Gospel origins, a theory she had believed and taught for decades.

2. George M. Marsden, *The Outrageous Idea of Christian Scholarship* (New York/Oxford: Oxford University Press, 1997).

3. For an investigation of whether Linnemann's post-conversion publications constitute an aid or an obstruction to scholarship, see my essay "Eta Linnemann: Friend or Foe of Scholarship?" in *The Jesus Crisis*, ed. Robert L. Thomas (Grand Rapids: Kregel, 1998), 158–84.

4. For a discussion of reviews, many of them highly critical, of Linnemann's prior two English-language works, see previous note.

5. Thomas C. Oden, "So What Happens after Modernity? A Postmodern Agenda for Evangelical Theology," in *The Challenge of Postmodernism*, ed. David S. Dockery, 2d ed. (Grand Rapids: Baker, 2001), 194.

6. Salutary for contemplating the larger picture of North American communities whose learning and faith are in trouble are John H. Leith, *Crisis in the Church: The Plight of Theological Education* (Louisville: Westminster John Knox, 1997); Iain H. Murray, *Evangelicalism Divided: A Record of Crucial Change in the Years 1950–2000* (Edinburgh/Carlisle, Pa.: Banner of Truth, 2000).

## Chapter One

THE LOST GOSPEL OF Q— FACT OR FANTASY?

IMAGINE FLYING TO A nonexistent island on an airplane that has not yet been invented.[1] Even if this impossible trip were to take place during the thirteenth month of the year, it would not be as fantastic as the tale of the so-called lost gospel Q and the earliest church, recently christened as scientific certainty by some New Testament scholars.

The story of Q (short for the German *Quelle* [source]) is not exactly hot off the press. It began over a century and a half ago. At that time it was part of the "two-source" theory of gospel origins. In the wake of Enlightenment allegations that the gospels were historically unreliable, it was suggested that their origins were instead primarily literary in nature. Matthew and Luke, the theory went, composed their gospels not based on historical recollection but using the dual sources of Mark and a hypothetical document called Q.

The theory was not without its difficulties, and it is no wonder that many Anglo-Saxon scholars—B. F. Westcott (1825–1901) would be a good example[2]—as well as formidable German-speaking authorities like Theodor Zahn (1838–1933) and Adolf Schlatter (1852–1938) declined to embrace it. But it gained ascendancy in Germany, and to this very hour it enjoys a virtual monopoly there and widespread support in many other countries.

According to my earlier research it was Siegfried Schulz who gave renewed impetus to the recent study of Q.[3] It was in Schulz that I first encountered the new ideas about Q:

> ... Q is a source collection, written in Greek, of words and deeds of Jesus. In terms of tradition history Q is not a unity. Primitive tradition, obviously Palestinian, that is to a large extent identical with the proclamation of the historical Jesus, must be distinguished from less primitive and then still more recent Q-materials which belong to the hellenistic-Jewish Christian stage of the tradition in Syria. This entire tradition-historical process, with its transition from the Palestinian-Jewish Christian church tradition to the hellenistic-Jewish church tradition, was then later brought to completion by a single edition.[4]

This process is supposed to have taken place "in the time frame of about A.D. 30–65."[5]

Subsequently I became aware that in some ways Schulz had been scooped by the slightly earlier study of James M. Robinson and Helmut Koester.[6] But it is only recently that a phalanx of studies by Robinson, Koester, John Kloppenborg, Arland Jacobsen, and Burton Mack have in effect expanded on Schulz's work.[7] In the end Q's formation gets broken down into four stages: Proto-Q1, Q1, Proto-Q2, and Q2—each described in detail without the slightest attempt to furnish proof. To save this house of cards from collapse, the so-called Gospel of Thomas is currently being pressed into service to give Q ostensible support.

The cumulative weight of these studies is captured in Stephen J. Patterson's statement that the importance of Q for understanding Christian beginnings should not be underestimated. Mack is surely right in asserting that a better understanding of Q will require a major rethinking of how Christianity came to be. Together with the Gospel of Thomas, Q tells us that not all Christians chose Jesus' death and resurrection as the focal point of their theological reflection. They also show that not all early Christians thought apocalyptically.[8]

Patterson is enamored enough of Mack to quote him favorably on a further point that he (wrongly[9]) claims most New Testament scholars share:

> Q demonstrates that factors other than the belief that Jesus was divine played a role in the generation of early Jesus and Christ movements. . . . [As a result] the narrative canonical gospels can no longer be viewed as the trustworthy accounts of unique and stupendous historical events at the foundation of the Christian faith. The gospels must now be seen as the result of early Christian mythmaking. Q forces the issue, for it documents an earlier history that does not agree with the narrative gospel accounts.[10]

Now we discover the truth: Q is the lever used to pry the Christian faith out of its biblical moorings. Not the gospels but Q must be faith's new anchor, since Q is earlier than the gospels and does not agree with them. Q settles the matter.

Poor Christianity. Are sackcloth and ashes in order because we have followed the wrong gospels, overlooking the real sole authority, Q? Or is it rather time to bar the enthronement of a false gospel, following Paul's counsel and God's Word: "If anyone is preaching to you a gospel contrary to that which you received, let him be accursed" (Gal. 1:9)?

A. What is Q?

The rhetoric used by Patterson and Mack is telling: "Q originally played a critical role"; "Q demonstrates"; "Q forces the issue"; "Q calls into question"; "Q tells us."[11] But assuming for the sake of argument that Q ever existed in the first place, isn't it just a hypothetical source, a lost piece of papyrus, an inanimate object? But Patterson and Mack's language make a dead thing into a commanding personal authority. This is the stuff of fairy tales.

It seems that so-called New Testament science—despising God's Word in the gospels as "the result of early Christian mythmaking"— has created a new myth. Thus we now have not only the imaginary figure Q but also Q's storied people:

The remarkable thing about the people of Q is that they were not Christians. They did not think of Jesus as a messiah or the Christ. They did not take his teachings as an indictment of Judaism. They did not regard his death as a divine, tragic, or saving event. And they did not imagine that he had been raised from the dead to rule over a transformed world. Instead, they thought of him as a teacher whose teaching made it possible to live with verve in troubled times. Thus they did not gather to worship in his name, honor him as god, or cultivate his memory through hymns, prayers, and rituals. They did not form a cult of the Christ such as the one that emerged among the Christian communities familiar to readers of the letters of Paul. The people of Q were Jesus people, not Christians.[12]

If we want to avoid following "cleverly devised tales" (2 Pet. 1:16), then it is preferable to leave such fantasies behind and turn to the facts.

B. What can we know for sure about Q?

Ancient sources give not the slightest hint that such a source ever existed. Among the early church fathers there is not even a rumor of a lost gospel. The earliest information about the gospels of Matthew and Mark is furnished by Papias (ca. A.D. 110), who states that Matthew "compiled τὰ λόγια (the oracles) in the Hebrew [or Aramaic] dialect."[13]

Papias had shortly beforehand used the expression τὰ λόγια with respect to Mark: "[Mark] wrote . . . the things said or done by the Lord . . . but not so as to give a comprehensive presentation of the Lord's words."[14]

In Papias's usage "the oracles" (τὰ λόγια) are parallel with τὰ ὑπὸ τοῦ Χριστοῦ ἢ λεχθέντα ἢ πραχθέντα (the things either said or practiced by Christ). Since Papias in his statement about Mark used the word λόγια to mean the same thing as words and deeds, the expression, used by the same writer only a few lines later, cannot be understood exclusively as words if the rules of logic mean anything—even if that is the general meaning of the term. It must be taken in Matthew precisely as *pars pro toto* (a part for the whole), having the same signification as in Mark. Until the nineteenth century, Papias's statement about τὰ λόγια was rightly taken to refer to Matthew's gospel.

Papias does not say something like this: The author of the familiar Logia is the apostle Matthew. Rather, he says of the renowned apostle Matthew, whom he had already named as a disciple of Jesus in his prologue, that he wrote in a Hebrew dialect [or Aramaic]. However, no ancient church writer ever said anything about a book having this title, much less such a book written by the apostle Matthew. This includes writers who express themselves quite particularly regarding non-canonical gospels and related literature, writers like Irenaeus, Origen, Eusebius, Epiphanius, and Jerome.[15]

According to Zahn, "a title which translated into Greek τὰ λόγια, or rather, if it had been a title, used λόγια without the article, would have been incomprehensibly enigmatic."[16] We haven't the least motive for suspecting that such a book ever existed. In the ancient church there was never any distinction made between a book by Matthew with the title *logia* and Matthew's gospel. Only one book by Matthew was known, and that was the gospel. There was also never any mention that Matthew's gospel (or some other gospel) was produced with the assistance of the use of sources.

There is no text-critical reference to Q. Not even the fragment of an individual manuscript is extant. And yet this so-called lost gospel was allegedly so widely disseminated that Matthew and Luke, and possibly even Mark, possessed copies of it independently of each other.

Paul never mentions Q, although he could hardly have been ignorant of a document that had such virulent influence and championed a faith so contrary to his own. He would not have known the four canonical gospels, but there is no reason why he should not have known Q if it existed in the decades prior to their appearance.

Q allegedly developed between A.D. 30 and 65. It still existed when Matthew and Luke wrote, commonly regarded as the last quarter of the first century. It is supposed to have been so widespread that they each had copies. Is this possible in the light of Paul's writings? These three decades would have given Paul ample time to encounter Q. If the Q people were the earliest "Jesus movement," they must have comprised the church in Jerusalem. Peter and Barnabas, coming from there, could have known Q and would have introduced Paul to it in Antioch in the early 40s. Paul would have encountered it and the "Jesus people" at the latest around A.D. 49 at the Jerusalem Council (Acts 15). Are we to believe that this Council was content to quibble over the question of the validity of the Jewish law for Gentile Christians, as Luke reports, when Paul was "mythologizing" the gospel, claiming Jesus to be God's Son, while the Q people held him to be no more than a sage?

If in fact "the people of Q were Jesus people, not Christians," conflicts would have been inevitable. How could these conflicts have left no trace in Acts or any of Paul's letters? How could Paul have written to the Corinthians that he delivered to them what he had received— "that Christ died for our sins according to the Scriptures" (1 Cor. 15:3)—if the atonement at the cross was only a brand-new, mythological idea, not accepted by the earlier followers of Jesus, who "did not regard his death as a divine, tragic, or saving event"?[17]

Either Paul, "called as an apostle by Jesus Christ by the will of God" (1 Cor. 1:1), is a liar, or the current crop of Q theorists is spinning yarns. We have to choose.

In sum, Q's existence cannot be corroborated from manuscript evidence, Paul's letters, or the known history of the early church. Q and the Q people are a historical fiction, no more real than the man in the moon. It would be intellectually irresponsible to rethink Christian faith based on such a tale.

C. The origin of Q

Q was unheard of until the beginning of the nineteenth century. At first it was nothing but a hypothesis, a supposition that Matthew and Luke might independently have taken their common material from a single written source.

Schleiermacher (1768–1834) got the modern ball rolling by misinterpreting the Papias quote cited above. By ignoring the context of Papias's statement and the gospels' historical background, and paying attention only to the lexical meaning of the word λόγια, he took Papias to be claiming that Matthew had written a document consisting of Jesus-sayings. Later, someone else composed a gospel that contained this document.[18] Unfortunately for Schleiermacher, τὰ λόγια here means "what the Lord Jesus said or did," not just "sayings."[19]

Schleiermacher proposed that Matthew wrote only the sayings, not the gospel itself that bears his name, a view lacking support in both ancient church tradition and Matthew's gospel. There were simply no grounds for distinguishing between the gospel and some sayings source. If one were to sort out all the "sayings," the result would not resemble what is called Q today. For Q does not contain all the "sayings" found in Matthew's gospel, nor does it consist merely of "sayings."

Christian Hermann Weisse (1801–1866), founder of the two-source theory, was the first to build on Schleiermacher's error.[20] Contrary to Schleiermacher, Weisse claimed the sayings source as a source for Luke's gospel as well, misusing Schleiermacher's authority, who had argued the opposite.[21] And so the infamous Q made its debut in the theological world. We likewise have Weisse to thank for the invention of the Lachmann fallacy,[22] which wrongly asserts that Lachmann proved that Mark was the source for Matthew and Luke, when in fact Lachmann had said the opposite. The world-renowned two-source theory, the basis for perhaps 40% of so-called New Testament science today,[23] was therefore founded on both (Schleiermacher's) error and (Weisse's) lie.

What was known for sure about the alleged sayings source behind Matthew and Luke? "The name [Q]. And what else? Nothing! How did one come to know its content and its wording? There was no other way than to infer it. From what? From the gospels of Matthew and Luke, as both allegedly have employed the 'sayings' as a source."[24]

To construct Q one has to take the material common to Matthew and Luke that they do not also share with Mark. The result is a potpourri—not only "sayings" in the pure sense, but also apophthegmata, parables of all sorts, and even a miracle report. Not only Jesus' sayings but also words of John the Baptist show up. Further, the so-called Q, which started as a "sayings source," excludes much of the same kind of material that it includes, material found in both Matthew and Luke. Is it going too far to maintain that the Q hypothesis is anything but convincing?

D. What about the Synoptic Gospels?

Doesn't thorough examination show that Matthew and Luke both rely on sources—i.e., written documents—for their information? Concerning Mark as an alleged source, I have already answered this question in my book *Is There a Synoptic Problem?* My results showed that there is no evidence that Matthew and Luke were literarily dependent on Mark. Nothing prevents the conclusion that the three synoptics could have arisen independently.[25]

Let us now examine Q using the same methods. To avoid defining Q myself, I follow Siegfried Schulz's *Griechisch-deutsche Synopse der Q-Überlieferungen,*[26] correcting the Greek text only as needed to conform to Nestle-Aland[27].

Similarities in content

We concede the obvious at the outset, that—besides the pericopes that Matthew and Luke have in common with Mark—there is common material which they share with each other. But similarity in content is in itself no proof for literary dependence. It could be caused by the same event: one of Jesus' sayings, for instance, reported independently by several different persons who heard it. In other words, similarities might have been historically, not literarily, transmitted.

Similarities in literary sequence

The same holds true here: It is as apt to have been transmitted historically as literarily. In any case the differences in the order of the alleged Q-material as it crops up in Matthew and Luke are enormous. Only 24 of Schulz's 65 pairs of parallels, or 36.9%, occur within a distance of less than two chapters of each other, and only 5 of those (7.69%) occur in the same point of the narrative flow in Matthew as in Luke (or vice versa). It takes a robust imagination to suppose that in spite of such differences the pericopes claimed for Q based on similarities in literary sequence owe their origin to a common source. But imagination is no substitute for evidence, and guesses whether Matthew or Luke diverged from Q's sequence in any given passage do not prove that Q existed.

Quantitative synoptic comparison

The main test for the existence of Q, and "the only safe test for literary dependence,"[27] is identity in actual wording. When we test Q using the principles explained in my earlier book,[28] the results are revealing. Please bear with me as I cite some statistics, the only way I know to arrive at sound results in this matter.

In the 65 pairs of parallels alleged to make up Q (see table 1 at the end of this chapter), the number of words in Q's Matthean form amount to 4319, in Luke's 4253. The number of identical words in parallel verses is 1792, or 41.49% of Matthew's Q portion and 42.13% of Luke's. This material consists mainly of sayings of Jesus, which usually possess a high degree of conformity within the Marcan pericopes. This had led me to project that the number of identical words in the alleged Q material might run 80% or so, but I admit I was surprised when it turned out to be only about 42%. The material breaks down as follows. For a graphic presentation of the following paragraphs, see table 2 at the end of this chapter.

In 34 passages, which comprise 26% of the 130 supposed Q pericopes,[29] *the number of identical words in parallel passages is less than 25%*. The number of words in these passages is 1110 in Matthew, or 26% of his Q material, and 1269 in Luke, or 30% of his.[30]

In 53 passages,[31] or 41% of Q, *the number of identical words in parallel passages is between 25% and 49.9%*. The number of words in these passages is 1702 in Matthew, or 39% of his Q material, and 1491 in Luke, or 35% of his.

In 29 passages of the 130, or 22% of Q, *the number of identical words in parallel passages is between 50% and 74.9%*. The number of words in these passages is 1054 in Matthew, or 24% of his Q material, and 1063 in Luke, or 25% of his.

In 14 passages (6 in Matthew and 8 in Luke), or 11% of the passages that are supposed to constitute Q, *the number of identical words in parallel verses is between 75% and 100%*. The number of words in these passages is 453 in Matthew, or 10% of his Q material, and 430 in Luke, or 10% of his.

Of the 130 passages, 67 (53% of Q) contain less than 50 words. For sake of comparison, the easily memorized Psalm 134 has 43 words; Psalm 117 has 27.[32] Thirty-nine passages (30% of Q) contain 50–99 words. For comparison: Psalm 100 has 79 words; Psalm 121 has 108.

In other words, 106 of the 130 Q passages (82%) are less than 100 words in length. Is it preposterous to suggest that Jesus' disciples, who sat at his feet and were sent out in his name for three years' time, could have preserved such reminiscences, which assumed varied shapes in the telling, by memory? Is a hypothetical written document needed, or even reasonable, to account for Matthew and Luke's overlap?

I have counted all the rest of the Q passages, too. Ten contain 100–149 words; twelve contain 150–199 words; one contains 202 words; and two, or just one pair of parallels, contains 250–300 words.

From these tabulations we can say: the longer the passage, the smaller the number of identical words and the bigger the amount of differences. (See Table 3 at the end of this chapter.) In the longest alleged Q passage, the parable of the talents (Matt. 25:14–30), only 20% of its words (60 out of 291) are identical with the Lucan parallel. Of the 60 identical words, 9 are *and*, 7 are articles, and 6 are pronouns scattered throughout the pericope. So 22 of the 60 (37% of the words) are meaningless for establishing literary dependence. This leaves only 38 words out of 291 that Q-theorists must rely on to establish literary dependence. Most of the identical words (47 of 60, or 78%) occur in direct speech.

The differences, however, between Matthew and Luke in this passage outnumber the 60 identical words by far. They even outnumber the 291 words in Matthew. In all, they add up to 310, or 107% when compared to Matthew's 291 words!

The one passage with 100% identical wording, Matt. 6:24 (cf. Luke 16:13), consists of 27 words. This is one fewer than the tiny Psalm 117 and not even half as much as the Great Commission, Matt. 28:18b–20, which many know by heart.

The longest passage in the 75%–100% category above contains just 78% identical words. The whole passage is about the length of Psalm 1, again a text that many know by heart. It is not hard to imagine accounts of this length being committed to memory in the oral culture of Jesus' day.[33]

Result

There is no conclusive evidence for the alleged Q in Matthew and Luke. There are not even noteworthy facts that speak in favor of such a hypothesis. Rather, the difficulties of the hypothesis are legion. The content of Q does not correspond to what it is supposed to be; the differences in the order of passages lead into a morass of purely subjective auxiliary explanations that cannot be verified. Neither the similarities in content of the pericopes nor the percentages of identical wording present argue for literary dependence, since the differences are much more numerous than the similarities.

The Q hypothesis does not solve a problem but is rather a source of problems—which then require additional hypotheses to remedy.

The gospel data do not comprise a problem if we are willing to abide by what the data along with the documents of the early church tell us: The gospels report the words and deeds of our Lord Jesus. They do this partly through direct eyewitnesses (Matthew, John) and partly by those who were informed by eyewitnesses (Mark, Luke).[34] In that case the similarities as well as the differences are just what one expects from eyewitness reminiscence.

In a word: There is no conclusive evidence for the use of an alleged source Q in Matthew and Luke. At best Q is an unnecessary hypothesis that has never functioned in a satisfactory manner.

E. What about Thomas?

The Gospel of Thomas plays a big role in the recent debate about Q. Patterson writes:

> Scholars took a long time deciding just what Q was. The sheer fact of its nonexistence was no small problem—and an obvious opening for Q skeptics. In recent years, however, resistance to the idea of Q has largely disappeared as the result of another amazing discovery: a nearly complete copy of the non-canonical Gospel of Thomas.[35]

The Gospel of Thomas is a recollection of sayings of Jesus. . . . The Gospel of Thomas shows that a gospel without a passion narrative is quite possible. . . . A theology grounded on Jesus' words, without any particular interest in his death, is no longer unthinkable. . . . The Gospel of Thomas which also has little interest in Jesus' death and resurrection, in effect forced this reevaluation.[36]

Together with the Gospel of Thomas, Q tells us that not all Christians chose Jesus' death and resurrection as the focal point of their theological reflection.[37]

Does the Gospel of Thomas indeed prove how Q, allegedly the oldest gospel, was shaped—consisting mainly of sayings, with no Passion or Easter reports?

Let me answer with another question. If a young man is leading a rock band, does this prove that a deceased person of his grandfather's generation played rock music, too? Of course not, even if it were known that the deceased was a musician.

The Gospel of Thomas is mentioned or quoted by some church fathers in the first decades of the third century. Recent scholarship dates its earliest possible original composition at about A.D. 140 (though the only complete manuscript is a Coptic translation dating from around A.D. 400). Even if this hypothetical dating is correct, that is more than seventy years after our canonical gospels. By that time the true gospels and the very expression *euangelion* (gospel) were well established; understandably, a new creation like Thomas, with its ostensible collection of Jesus sayings, would try to traffic in this good name by claiming the "gospel" title. But nothing here supports the theory that Thomas was a model for, or even a co-competitor of, Q in the A.D. 35–65 time span.

The Gospel of Thomas is not just "noncanonical." Every church father who ever mentioned it called it heretical or gnostic. From a gnostic writing we cannot expect interest in Jesus' death and resurrection, since gnosticism repudiates both as the early church understood them. So how can a heretical writing rightly be taken as the prototype for constructing canonical ones?

It is important to recall here that an actual "Q gospel" *sans* Passion and Easter narratives does not exist. It is rather extracted from Matthew and Luke—which in every form known to us *do* contain the Passion and Easter material.

William R. Farmer has recently suggested why the heretical Gospel of Thomas is being pushed to play so large a role in reconstructing early Christianity:

> Because *Thomas* is a late-second to fourth-century document, by itself it could never be successfully used to lever the significance of Jesus off its New Testament foundation. Similarly, the sayings source Q, allegedly used by Matthew and Luke, by itself could never be successfully used to achieve this result. But used together, as they are by a significant number of scholars, *Thomas* and Q appear to reinforce one another.[38]

You cannot erect a playing-card house with a single card. You might lean two cards together as long as no wind blows. But can you live in such a house?

F. Q: the Lost Gospel—Fact or Fantasy?

The answer to our initial question is now clear. As a modest hypothesis undergirding the two-source theory, Q turns out to be based on an error. It has been promoted without thorough examination. When actually put to the test, it proves untenable.

Q, used in connection with the Gospel of Thomas to rethink how Christianity arose, is nothing but fantasy. The same goes for the literary shuffling used to discern its various layers. Such totally subjective arrangements, depending on dubious suggestions about the historical background, amount to novelistic trifling with early Christian origins. Since this product of fantasy is out of sync with the history of earliest Christianity, it is then maintained in all seriousness that this history must be entirely rewritten.

So why are earnest scholars willing to indulge in such fantasies? Farmer writes,

> At issue today is whether the death of Jesus should be regarded as an unnecessary or an essential part of the Christian message. . . . The trend among New Testament scholars who follow the *Thomas-Q* line is to represent Jesus as one whose disciples had no interest

in any redemptive consequence of his death and no interest in his resurrection.[39]

Farmer's critical assessment is borne out in Stephen J. Patterson's essay, particularly in the closing sentences:

Heresy

> Together with the Gospel of Thomas, Q tells us that not all Christians chose Jesus' death and resurrection as a focal point of their theological reflection. The followers of Jesus were very diverse and drew on a plethora of traditions to interpret and explain what they were doing. With the discovery of the Lost Gospel, perhaps some of the diversity will again thrive, as we rediscover that theological diversity is not a weakness, but a strength.[40]

The motive is clearly perceptible: Unbelief is demanding equal rights within the Christian church. Q (with Thomas's aid) gives a biblical basis for persons who do not accept Jesus as the Son of God and who reject his atoning death on the cross and deny his resurrection. Then, in copyright-infringement fashion, these same scholars combine their newly minted biblical basis with early church diversity to justify calling themselves "Christians" despite their aberrant convictions.

By trumpeting the claims that today's new Q Christians are in sync with earliest historical origins, and that traditional Bible believers hallow "the result of early Christian mythmaking," they lay down an effective smoke screen that enables them to keep their posts as ostensible professors of Christian origins and leaders of the church.

But we are not obliged to follow "cleverly devised tales" (2 Pet. 1:16). The canonical gospels exist. Q does not. The heretical, second-century Gospel of Thomas is not binding on us. Whether on historical or theological grounds, there is no reason to give up the canonical gospels as the original and divinely inspired foundation for our faith.

Endnotes

1. I adapt the title for this chapter from *Fact or Fantasy: The Authenticity of the Gospels* (Worthing, England: Walter, 1980), in honor of its author, David C. C. Watson. This chapter appeared earlier in *Jahrbuch*

für die evangelikale Theologie 9 (1995): 43–61 and in English in *Trinity Journal*, n.s., 17 (1996): 3–18. An abridged version of this article appeared in *Bible Review*, August 1995.

2. B. F. Westcott, *An Introduction to the Study of the Gospels*, 7th ed. (London: Macmillan and Co., 1888). Westcott comments (p. xii): "My obligations to the leaders of the extreme German schools are very considerable, though I can rarely accept any of their conclusions."

3. Siegfried Schulz, *Die Spruchquelle des Evangelisten* (Zürich: Theologischer Verlag, 1972).

4. See Siegfried Schulz, *Griechisch-deutsche Synopse der Q-Überlieferungen* (Zürich: Theologischer Verlag, 1972), 5f.

5. Ibid.

6. *Entwicklungslinien durch die Welt des frühen Christentums* (Tübingen: J. C. B. Mohr [Paul Siebeck], 1971).

7. James M. Robinson, "The Sayings of Jesus: 'Q,'" *Drew Gateway* (fall 1983); Helmut Koester, *Ancient Christian Gospels: Their History and Development* (Philadelphia: Trinity Press International, 1990); John Kloppenborg, *The Formation of Q* (Philadelphia: Fortress, 1987); Arland Jacobsen, *The First Gospel* (Missoula, Mont.: Polebridge, 1992); Burton Mack, *Q—The Lost Gospel* (San Francisco: Harper, 1993).

8. Stephen J. Patterson, "Q—The Lost Gospel," *Bible Review* 9, no. 5 (October 1993): 34–41, 61–62 (here 62). Subsequent references to this article will be given as *BR* plus the page number(s).

9. See Craig Blomberg, "Where Do We Start Studying Jesus?" in *Jesus under Fire*, ed. Michael J. Wilkins and J. P. Moreland (Grand Rapids: Zondervan, 1995), 17–50, esp. 19–25.

10. *BR,* 40, quoting Mack, 8, 10.

11. Ibid., 38, 40, 41 (bis), 62.

12. Ibid., 40 (Patterson quoting Mack, 4f.).

13. Quoted in Lindemann and Paulsen, *Die Apostolischen Väter, griechisch-deutsche Parallelausgabe* (Tübingen, 1992), 294–95.

14. Ibid.

15. Theodor Zahn, *Einleitung in das Neue Testament*, vol. 2 (Leipzig: A. Deichert'sche Verlagsbuchhandlung, 1924), 262.

16. Ibid., 261.

17. Arland Jacobsen, *The First Gospel*, 4, as cited in *BR*, 40.
18. Cf. Hans Herbert Stoldt, *History and Criticism of the Marcan Hypothesis* (Macon, GA: Mercer University Press, 1980), 48.
19. See Gerhardt Kittel, *"logion,"* in *Theological Dictionary of the New Testament*, vol. 4, trans. by Geoffrey Bromiley (Grand Rapids: Eerdmans, 1967), 141.
20. Cf. Stoldt, *History and Criticism*, 50.
21. Ibid.
22. Ibid., 146–49, esp. 148.
23. Cf. Eta Linnemann, *Is There a Synoptic Problem? Rethinking the Literary Dependence of the First Three Gospels*, trans. R. W. Yarbrough (Grand Rapids: Baker, 1992), 68–70.
24. Stoldt, *History and Criticism*, 50.
25. Linnemann, *Is There a Synoptic Problem?* 155–91.
26. See note 4 above.
27. John Wenham, *Redating Matthew, Mark and Luke: A Fresh Assault on the Synoptic Problem* (London: Hodder and Stoughton, 1991), 54.
28. Linnemann, *Is There a Synoptic Problem?* 111–17.
29. One hundred thirty comes from the 65 pairs times 2. Twenty-six percent comes from dividing 34 by 130. Percentages are rounded to the nearest whole number whenever possible.
30. The basis for these figures is 4319, the total of Q words contained in Matthew, and 4253, the total number of Q words contained in Luke.
31. Since we are analyzing pairs, it may seem strange not to have an even number here. But we are putting Matthew's or Luke's individual passages into one of four percentage categories: 1–24.9%, 25%–49.9%, 50%–74.9%, or 75–100%. So, for example, Matt. 6:9–13 (the Lord's Prayer) shares 26 identical words with its counterpart in Luke 11:1–4. These 26 words are 43% of Matthew's total of 61 words, but 59% of Luke's total of 44 words. In this case the two components of the "pair" in view fit into different percentage categories. This pattern repeats itself in about a dozen of the 65 pairs. And that is why we get 53 passages, an odd number, in the 25–49.9% category, or 29 passages in the 50–74.9% category. Despite this complication we still get an accurate picture of the overall verbal correspondence between and among Matthean and Lucan passages alleged to reflect the common Q source.

32. Word counts for the psalms are from the *New American Standard* version.

33. Cf. Linnemann, *Is There a Synoptic Problem?* 182–85.

34. Ibid., 185–88. For fuller discussion and citations see D. A. Carson, Douglas J. Moo, and Leon Morris, *An Introduction to the New Testament* (Grand Rapids: Zondervan, 1992), 66–74, 92–95, 113–15, 138–57. See also Hans-Joachim Schulz, *Die apostolische Herkunft der vier Evangelien* (Freiburg: Herder, 1994).

35. *BR*, 35.

36. Ibid., 36.

37. Ibid., 62.

38. *The Gospel of Jesus: The Pastoral Relevance of the Synoptic Problem* (Louisville: Westminster/John Knox, 1994), 3f.

39. Ibid., 3.

40. *BR*, 62.

41. According to Schulz, *Griechisch-deutsche Synopse der Q-Überlieferungen* (numbers added).

#	Matthew	Luke	Pericope
	Table 1. Pericopes That Make Up Q[41]		
1	10:32	12:8	The prophecy concerning confession and denial of Jesus
2	5:3, 4, 6	6:20b, 21	The Beatitudes
3	6:9–13	11:1–4	The Lord's Prayer
4	23:25, 23, 6–7a, 27, 4, 29–31, 13	11:39, 42–44, 46–48, 52	Woes upon the Pharisees
5	5:18	16:17	The apocalyptic limits of the law of Moses
6	5:32	16:18	The rigorous prohibition of divorce
7	5:39–42	6:29f.	The radical resignment of one's own rights
8	5:44–48	6:27f., 35b, 32–35a, 36	The command to love one's enemy
9	7:12	6:31	The golden rule
10	6:19–21	12:33f.	The admonition not to gather worldly riches
11	7:1–5	6:37f., 41f.	The admonition not to judge others
12	6:25–33	12:22–31	The admonition not to be anxious
13	10:28–31	12:4–7	The admonition against wrong fears
14	7:7–11	11:9–13	Encouragement to pray
15	4:1–11	4:1–13	The temptation of Jesus
16	11:2–6	7:18–23	The question of John the Baptist
17	12:22–28, 30	11:14–20, 23	The Pharisees' blasphemy
18	11:25–27	10:21f.	The revelation-saying

#	Matthew	Luke	Pericope
19	11:7–11	7:24–28	Jesus' tribute to John
20	8:5–13	7:1–10	Jesus heals a centurion's servant
21	12:32	12:10	The sin against the Holy Spirit
22	12:38–42	11:29–32	The sign of Jonah
23	10:34–36	12:51–53	Christ divides men
24	11:12f.	16:16	Taking the kingdom by force
25	24:43f.	12:30f.	The parable of the burglar
26	24:45–51	12:42b–46	The parable of the good and the wicked servant
27	24:26–28, 37–41	17:23f., 37, 26f., 30, 34f.	The Q-apocalypse
28	25:14–30	19:12–27	The parable of the talents
29	13:11f.	13:18f.	The parable of the mustard seed
30	13:33	13:20f.	The parable of the leaven
31	7:13f.	13:23f.	The admonition of the narrow porch
32	7:24–27	6:47–49	The parable of the two foundations
33	7:16–20; 12:33–35	6:43–45	The parable of the tree and the fruit
34	18:15, 21f.	17:3f.	The admonition to forgive
35	8:11f.	13:28f.	The heathens coming into the kingdom of God
36	19:28	22:28–30	The apocalyptic judgment on the twelve
37	23:34–36	11:49–51	The sophia-logion
38	23:37–39	13:34f.	The saying concerning Jerusalem

#	Matthew	Luke	Pericope
39	11:21–24	10:13–15	The woe against the Galilean towns
40	3:7–12	3:7–9, 15–18	John the Baptist preaches judgment
41	11:16–19	7:31–35	The parable about "this generation" with explanation
42	18:12–14	15:4–7	The parable of the sheep gone astray
43	22:1–10	14:15–24	The parable of the dinner
44	9:37f.; 10:16, 9–10a, 11–13, 10b, 7f., 14f.	10:2–12	The disciples sent out
45	13:16f.	10:23f.	The blessedness of the disciples
46	5:25f.	12:57–59	Agreement with one's accuser
47	7:22f.	13:26f.	The rejection of the false disciples
48	7:21	6:46	Against those who call Jesus Lord but don't obey him
49	10:38	14:27	Discipleship in cross-bearing
50	8:19–22	9:57–60	On following Jesus
51	10:19f.	12:11f.	Confession before the synagogues
52	10:39	17:33	Life-keeping and life-losing
53	10:37	14:26	Hatred on behalf of Jesus
54	10:24f.	6:40	Pupil and teacher
55	23:12	14:11; 18:14	Exaltation and humiliation
56	5:11f.	6:22f.	Beatitude of the insulted
57	10:40	10:16	Admonition to listen to the disciples

#	Matthew	Luke	Pericope
58	6:24	16:13	Warning not to serve two masters
59	10:26f.	12:2f.	What is hidden shall become revealed
60	17:20	17:3f.	Faith accomplishes miracles
61	6:22f.	11:34–36	The parable of the eye
62	5:13	14:34f.	The parable of the salt
63	15:14	6:39	The parable of the blind, leading the blind
64	5:15	11:33	The parable of the lamp on the lampstand
65	12:43–45	11:24–26	The warning against the return of the evil spirit[41]

Table 2 below: The numbers under the column headed "#" correspond to the numbers of the 65 pericopes listed in Table 1 above.

For each pericope, the words of the Greek text were counted and the results tabulated as seen below. For example, in #1 below, Matthew's Gospel contains 40 words in the first alleged "Q" percicope, Matthew 10:32. Luke's corresponding pericope (Luke 12:8) contains 38 words. If you compare Matthew and Luke, you will find 12 identical words. This figure is listed under the "Identical" heading below. Finally, those 12 words are 30.00% of Matthew's 40 words and 31.58% of Luke's 38 words; each percentage figure is listed in the two far right hand columns of the table.

Table 2. Quantitative Comparison of the Alleged Q-Material in Matthew and Luke					
#	Matthew	Luke	Identical	Matthew	Luke
1	40	38	12	30.00%	31.58%
2	28	22	10	37.71%	45.45%
3	61	44	26	42.62%	59.09%
4	196	158	64	32.65%	40.51%
5	27	15	1	3.70%	6.67%

#	Matthew	Luke	Identical	Matthew	Luke
6	23	17	7	30.43%	41.18%
7	49	34	7	14.29%	20.59%
8	83	115	27	32.53%	23.48%
9	23	11	7	30.44%	63.64%
10	49	36	11	22.45%	39.56%
11	82	106	55	67.05%	51.89%
12	186	160	102	54.84%	63.75%
13	61	72	25	40.98%	34.72%
14	74	85	59	79.73%	69.71%
15	184	203	48	26.09%	23.65%
16	63	104	41	65.08%	39.42%
17	138	133	82	59.42%	61.65%
18	69	75	49	71.02%	65.33%
19	94	94	73	77.66%	77.66%
20	165	187	64	38.79%	34.23%
21	33	21	10	30.30%	47.62%
22	68	41	22	32.55%	53.66%
23	42	57	8	19.05%	14.04%
24	28	19	6	21.43%	31.58%
25	39	34	28	71.80%	82.35%
26	111	102	80	72.07%	78.43%
27	124	122	46	37.10%	37.71%
28	291	257	60	20.62%	23.35%
29	50	40	18	36.00%	45.00%
30	23	24	12	52.17%	50.00%
31	44	29	5	11.36%	17.24%
32	95	83	21	22.11%	25.30%
33	63	63	26	41.27%	41.27%
34	53	31	6	11.32%	19.35%
35	43	47	9	20.93%	19.15%
36	38	43	12	31.58%	27.91%
37	72	58	21	29.17%	36.21%
38	56	53	46	82.14%	86.79%
39	78	49	44	56.41%	89.80%

#	Matthew	Luke	Identical	Matthew	Luke
40	134	157	105	78.36%	66.88%
41	65	76	44	67.69%	57.90%
42	64	81	10	15.63%	12.35%
43	161	180	7	4.35%	3.89%
44	189	186	61	32.28%	32.80%
45	36	38	23	63.89%	60.53%
46	43	58	10	23.26%	12.35%
47	42	29	4	9.52%	13.79%
48	25	11	2	8.00%	18.18%
49	15	15	7	46.66%	46.66%
50	70	77	51	72.86%	66.23%
51	35	35	11	31.43%	31.43%
52	17	15	7	41.18%	46.67%
53	23	37	4	17.39%	10.81%
54	28	14	11	39.29%	78.57%
55	10	11	4	40.00%	36.36%
56	35	51	11	31.43%	21.57%
57	13	19	7	53.85%	36.42%
58	28	29	28	100.00%	96.55%
59	36	36	24	66.67%	66.67%
60	31	34	6	19.36%	17.65%
61	45	63	30	66.67%	47.62%
62	26	29	11	42.31%	37.93%
63	15	15	5	33.33%	33.33%
64	20	20	8	40.00%	40.00%
65	67	55	51	76.12%	92.73%
Total	4319	4253	1792	41.69%	42.13%

Identical words less than 25% in 34 passages of 130 = 26.15%
　　　　17 passages in Matthew　　= 1110 words or 25.70% of his material
　　　　17 passages in Luke　　　= 1269 words or 29.84% of his material

Identical words 25–49.90% in 53 passages of 130 = 40.76%
　　　　27 passages in Matthew　　= 1702 words or 39.41% of his material
　　　　26 passages in Luke　　　= 1491 words or 35.06% of his material

Identical words 50–74.90% in 29 passages of 130 = 22.30%
   15 passages in Matthew = 1054 words or 24.40% of his material
   14 passages in Luke   = 1063 words or 24.99% of his material

Identical words 75–100.00% in 14 passages of 130 = 10.76%
   6 passages in Matthew = 453 words or 10.49% of his material
   8 passages in Luke   = 430 words or 10.11% of his material

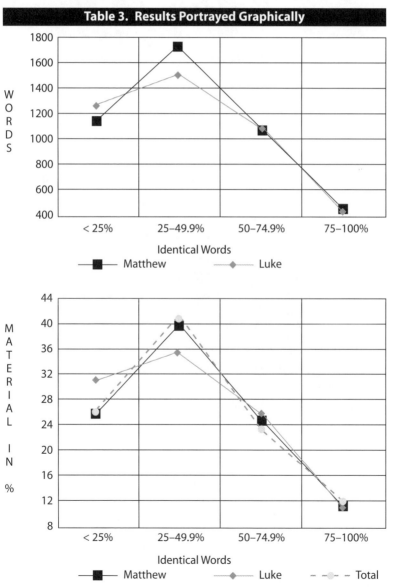

Table 3. Results Portrayed Graphically

## Chapter Two

ANOTHER LOOK AT THE SYNOPTIC PROBLEM

A. Supplement to the quantitative analysis of Mark's gospel

In the fourth edition of my *Gibt es ein synoptisches Problem?* [English *Is There a Synoptic Problem?*],[1] I considered all the Markan pericopes that could be meaningfully analyzed with a quantitative synoptic comparison. The results were as follows: the sixty-six pericopes that could be meaningfully investigated amount to 6450 words, or 57.28% of Mark's gospel.

- 1433 words (22.21% of the 6450 words) are completely identical in Matthew/Mark/Luke.
- 1218 words (18.88% of the 6450 words) are completely identical in Matthew/Mark.
- 803 words (12.44% of the 6450 words) are completely identical in Mark/Luke.
- 352 words (5.45%) are completely identical in Matthew/Luke.

For supplementation and control I have now incorporated those ten Markan pericopes in which the cross references at first glance indicate a lack of parallelism.[2] **Their word count comes to 1175, or 10.45% of the number of words in Mark's gospel.**

With the above investigations, 7625 words—67.72% in relation to the number of words in Mark—have been covered. The remaining forty pericopes (3635 words, 32.28% of the number of words in Mark's gospel) cannot be incorporated, because they lack parallels with one or even both of the other synoptic gospels. Of the ten investigated pericopes, encompassing 1175 words, the number of words that are completely identical are:

- Matthew/Mark/Luke: 106 words (9.02% of the 1175 words)
- Matthew/Mark: 410 words (34.89% of the 1175 words)
- Mark/Luke: 74 words (6.30% of the 1175 words)
- Matthew/Luke: 29 words (2.47% of the 1175 words)
- The differences between Mark and Matthew came to 1320 words, or 112.34% of the 1175 words.
- The differences between Mark and Luke came to 1651 words, or 140.51% of the 1175 words.

For comparison, in the thirty-eight pericopes of my cross-sectional investigation covering 3945 words, the differences came to:

- between Mark and Matthew, 3761 words (95.34% of the 3945 words);
- between Mark and Luke, 3964 words (100.48% of the 3945 words).

In the seventy-six pericopes (containing 7625 words occurring in all three synoptic gospels), parallel verses are completely identical to the following extents:

- 1526 words Matthew/Mark/Luke   (20.01%)
- 1628 words Matthew/Mark   (21.35%)
- 874 words Mark/Luke   (11.46%)
- 376 words Matthew/Luke   (4.03%)

These numbers surely do not speak for literary dependence of the Synoptic Gospels, especially since a portion of the words is conditioned by the content of the pericopes, while an additional part consists of a language's basic words that any author must use to communicate.

B. Vocabulary in identical words of parallel verses that is not relevant for literary dependence

On the basis of my observations, I remarked in the first edition of my *Is There a Synoptic Problem?* that a portion of the completely identical words in the pericopes investigated are "basic words of the language without which sentences cannot be formulated."[3] These are referred to in the Basic Words tables below. In his treatise "The Tenability of Synoptic Independence"[4] André Verkaik has pursued this matter. Since this work has not yet been published, I share the results below. The numbers relate to the thirty-five passages that I investigated in my first pass through the material. They cover thirty-eight of Aland's pericopes.

Basic Words I			
Greek word or part of speech	Matt./Mark/Luke	Matt./Mark	Mark/Luke
Καί ("and")	84	70	46
Articles	127	90	55
Pronouns	118		

Based on my own research, I have supplemented these figures, which provides the figures for Matthew/Luke and the listing of the pronouns in Matthew/Mark and Mark/Luke. I also extend the pericope of Mark 9:2–8 to include verses 9–10, following Aland's division. The result then looks like this:

Basic Words II				
Greek word or part of speech	Matt./Mark/Luke	Matt./Mark	Mark/Luke	Matt./Luke
Καί ("and")	84	71	46	3
Articles	127	93	55	17
Pronouns	118	79	61	11

In addition, I have computed the basic words for the twenty-eight pericopes that I investigated in my second pass through the material:

Basic Words III				
Greek word or part of speech	Matt./Mark/ Luke	Matt./Mark	Mark/Luke	Matt./Luke
Καί ("and")	60	34	30	8
Articles	86	72	39	24
Pronouns	51	32	31	21

The number of basic words in the pericopes that can be meaningfully investigated comes to:

Basic Words Totals				
Greek word or part of speech	Matt./Mark/ Luke	Matt./Mark	Mark/Luke	Matt./Luke
Καί ("and")	144	105	76	11
Articles	213	165	94	41
Pronouns	169	111	92	32
Totals:	**526**	**381**	**262**	**84**

Of the 6450 words of the pericopes that can be meaningfully investigated, we see that basic words make up a sizable percentage of the words that are completely identical:

	Matt./Mark/ Luke	Matt./Mark	Mark/Luke	Matt./Luke
Identical words:	1420	1218	800	347
Basic words:	526	381	262	84
	37.04%	31.28%	32.75%	24.20%

Of the 1420 words in Matthew/Mark/Luke that are completely identical, only 824 words (1420–526), or 13.86%, remain relevant in relation to the 6450 words. On the average, the number of basic words amounts to not quite a third (33.10%) of the words that are fully identical in the pericopes relevant for investigation that are shared by any two or three of the gospels. If one brackets out the agreements between Matthew and Luke, which speak indeed not for but against literary dependence in the gospels, then the number of basic words comes to 1169. Divided by the sum of 3438 words, that comes to 34.00%. **In other words, this result does not speak in favor of literary dependence of the Synoptic Gospels.**

For the sake of completeness, we should include the ten pericopes in which the cross references at first glance indicate a lack of parallelism (see above). In a range of 1175 words, the numbers of matches are:

Matthew/Mark/Luke: 106 words
Matthew/Mark: 410 words
Mark/Luke: 74 words
Matthew/Luke: 29 words

Within these numbers, the number of basic words looks like this:

Basic Word Totals in Ten Additional Pericopes				
Greek word or part of speech	Matt./Mark/ Luke	Matt./Mark	Mark/Luke	Matt./Luke
Καί ("and")	10	35	7	1
Articles	17	62	10	5
Pronouns	16	52	7	1
Totals:	**43**	**149**	**24**	**7**
	40.57%	**36.64%**	**32.43%**	**24.13%**

The sum of basic words in all investigated pericopes comes to:

Basic Word Totals in All Investigated Pericopes			
Greek word or part of speech	Matt./Mark/ Luke	Matt./Mark	Mark/Luke	Matt./Luke
Καί ("and")	154	140	83	12
Articles	230	227	104	46
Pronouns	185	163	99	33
Totals:	**569**	**530**	**286**	**91**
In relation to	1526	1628	874	376
Yields:	37.28%	32.55%	32.72%	24.20%

Excluding the agreements between Matthew and Luke, the average comes to 1385 words out of 4028 (34.38%).

Including the data from Matthew/Luke, the average comes to 1476 words out of 4404 (33.51%). In every case, basic words make up about a third of the common vocabulary.

The incorporation of pericopes that lack parallelism does not push percentages in the direction of favoring literary dependence among the Synoptic Gospels, a theory which the evidence continues to speak against and not for.

C. The Synoptics and the Septuagint

The similarities in vocabulary of the Synoptic Gospels are alleged to prove their literary dependence. It is not taken into account that there are other grounds that can explain these similarities.

The entire common vocabulary of Matthew, Mark, and Luke encompasses 839 words. Of these, 793 occur in the Septuagint. In other words, with the exception of 46 words, the authors of the Synoptic Gospels were already familiar with their entire common vocabulary from the Greek edition of the Bible. This means that 94.52% of the words that all three authors use could have been used independently of each other. None of them was required to borrow them from one of the other writers.

While in general 1199 (22.04%) of the 5439 words of the New

Testament vocabulary are lacking in the Septuagint, only 46 (5.48%) of the 839 words of the Synoptic Gospels are not found there. These are numbers that give pause. If the 46 words are looked at closely, one discovers that 22 of them, nearly half, are names, the knowledge of which did not have to be passed along by literary dependence (see below, "Names in the Common Synoptic Vocabulary"). Ten words are terms that may be presupposed to have been generally known in the first century A.D., at least in Judea and Galilee; they are terms indigenous to the historical period (see below, "Contemporary Terms"). That leaves 14 of the 839 words, or 1.67% (see below, "Words common to all three synoptic gospels but absent from the Septuagint"). Whatever the results of investigation of their common occurrence among the synoptics, this is not a proof for literary dependence! Apart from a negligible exception, the similarities of vocabulary in the three synoptic gospels are sufficiently explained by the observation that 94.52% of their common vocabulary was familiar to them from the Septuagint and independently of each other, and another 1.19% were generally used terms of the historical period. The knowledge of the places and personal names that make up 2.62% of the words may be presumed to have been present in the congregations anyway, since they were directly linked to the events.

Names in the Common Synoptic Vocabulary

Place names (with variants)	Personal names
Ἀριμαθαία ("Arimathea")	Ἀλφαῖος ("Alphaeus")
Βηθανία ("Bethany")	Ἀνδρέας ("Andrew")
Βηθσαῖδα ("Bethsaida")	Βαραβᾶς ("Barabbas")
Βηθφαγή ("Bethphage")	Βαρθολομαῖος ("Bartholemew")
Γαλιλαῖος ("Galllee")	Ζεβεδαῖος ("Zebedee")
Γεννήσαρετ ("Gennesaret")	Ἡρώδης ("Herod")
Ἰσκαριώτης ("Iscariot")	Ἡρωδίας ("Herodias")
Μαγδαλήνη ("Magdalene")	Θωμᾶς ("Thomas")
Ναζαρέτ ("Nazareth")	Ἰάκωβος ("James")
	Μαθθαῖος ("Matthew")
	Πέτρος ("Peter")
	Πιλᾶτος ("Pilate")

Comtemporary terms	
βάπτισμα ("baptism")	σαδδουκαῖος ("Sadducee")
βαπτιστής ("baptizer")	σταυρός ("cross")
δηνάριον ("denarius")	τελώνης ("tax collector")
καῖσαρ ("Caesar")	τελώνιον ("tax office")
λεγιών ("legion")	φαρισαῖος ("Pharisee")

Words common to all three synoptic gospels but absent from the Septuagint

1. ἀσπασμός ("greeting")	8. μόδιος ("peck-measure")
2. γαμίζειν ("to marry")	9. οἰκοδεσπότης ("head of household")
3. γεέννα ("hell")	10. πρωτοκαθέδρια ("seat of honor")
4. διαβλέπειν ("to see clearly")	11. πρωτοκλισία ("place of honor")
5. διακονεῖν ("to serve, minister")	12. σινάπις ("mustard seed")
6. δυσκόλως ("hardly, with difficulty")	13. σκύλλειν ("to trouble, annoy")
7. ἐπιγραφή ("inscription")	14. συμπνίγειν ("to choke")

For critical control I investigated those words of Mark's vocabulary that are lacking in Matthew as well as in Luke.[5] Of the 184 words that fit this description, 51 (27.72%) are not found in the Septuagint. This is 5.68% more than the amount of New Testament vocabulary that in general is absent from the Septuagint (22.04%). In comparison with the list of 831 words that occur in all three synoptic gospels, the difference comes to 22.30%. To put it differently, those words that occur in all three synoptic gospels can to a very high degree (94.58%) be attested in the Septuagint; those words peculiar to Mark are attested in the Septuagint to a much lower degree (72.28%).

In order to be exact, it should also be considered that Morgenthaler in his Septuagint columns expressly shows the words that are found only in the Apocrypha as well as those that are found only in Aquila, Symmachus, and Theodotion. In the list of those words that Matthew, Mark, and Luke have in common, 17 are found in the Apocrypha, and 3 are found in Aquila, Symmachus, and Theodotion. Together that makes 20, which out of 831 is no more than 2.41%. Even if one does not take these into account, there still remain 766 of the words common to all three synoptics, or 92.18%, that are fully attested in the Septuagint.

Of the 184 words that occur in neither Matthew nor Luke, 12 are found only in the Apocrypha and 6 only in Aquila, Symmachus, and Theodotion. 18 restricted occurrences of 184 make 9.78%. Thus, that leaves from this list 115 words or 62.50% that are covered by the Septuagint. The difference between both lists at this point comes to 29.68%, nearly 30%, which is too considerable to be neglected.

D. Does Mark's gospel reflect a more primitive level of language than the gospels of Matthew and Luke?

In Udo Schnelle's *The History and Theology of the New Testament Writings*, "linguistic and material improvements made by both Matthew and Luke" are taken as "a further indication of the priority of Mark."[6] I have already gone into this in pages 48–53 of my *Gibt es ein synoptisches Problem?*[7] for the relevant section in Schnelle is pretty much identical to the corresponding section of Strecker and Schnelle's *Einführung in die neutestamentliche Exegese* with which I was interacting. Yet there are still a few things to be said regarding this claim.

Schnelle regards the use of the simple rather than the compound form as more primitive language;[8] I leave to the side whether that is generally warranted. Of course it is easy to find examples in which Mark uses the simple form of a word and Luke uses the compound. For good reason, however, Schnelle does not bring Matthew's gospel into the discussion, although it, just like Luke's, is supposed to distinguish itself from Mark's by more elevated language. In order to arrive at a grounded verdict, one must investigate the use of compound verbs in all three gospels. Again I make use here of Morgenthaler's *Statistik des Neutestamentlichen Wortschatzes* because it is readily accessible in German-speaking circles.

There are 1036 compound verbs in the New Testament, formed using one of seventeen prepositions. Some facts:

- Matthew has 242. That is 14.31% of his vocabulary of 1691 words.
- Mark has 239. That is 17.77% of his vocabulary of 1345 words.
- Luke has 240. That is 20.44% of his vocabulary of 2055 words.

The number of compound verbs in comparison to overall vocabulary in Mark is therefore 3.46% higher than in Matthew and 2.67% lower than in Luke.

Whoever maintains, on the basis of the lower number of compound verbs, that the Greek of Mark is inferior to that of Luke, should also admit that by the same criterion the Greek of Matthew is inferior to that of Mark.

The number of compounds in Luke is in other respects relatively high; this may be seen by comparing Luke with Paul. Paul has only 461. Related to his vocabulary of 2645 words, that is 17.43%. If the percentage of compounds relative to vocabulary were evidence for quality of language, the quality of Mark's Greek would be slightly superior to that of Paul!

In the entire New Testament vocabulary of 5436 words, according to Morgenthaler, there are 1036 compound verbs. That is 19.06%.

There are 91 compound verbs with two prepositions in the New Testament, or 1.67% of the entire vocabulary. In the Synoptic Gospels, we find that

- Matthew has 8 out of a vocabulary of 1691; that is 0.47%.
- Mark has 10 out of a vocabulary of 1345; that is 0.74%.
- Luke has 20 out of a vocabulary of 2055; that is 0.97%.

That means that Mark has 0.27% more two-preposition compounds than Matthew and 0.23% fewer than Luke. Care is well advised in denigrating Mark on this account, since Matthew is even more open to criticism.

In this connection we should not overlook the list of 184 words in Mark's vocabulary that are apparently absent from Matthew and Luke. Of these 184, no fewer than 51 are compound verbs. That is 27.72%. Among these one even finds three double compounds, or 1.63% of the list, negligibly lower than the New Testament average but considerably higher than the percentage found in the vocabulary of the Synoptic Gospels generally.

If we compare this with the vocabulary common to all three synoptic gospels, we must conclude that among the 839 words there are only 122 compound verbs, no more than 14.54%.

Whoever wishes to support the priority of Mark by referring to the lower number of compound verbs found in Mark should be consistent. He or she should also draw the conclusion that Mark has a more advanced level of language than Matthew. But that does not fit at all with the idea of the two-source theory.

We therefore state: Once we investigate comprehensively, that is, scientifically instead of just plucking out individual examples from Luke that support the point being argued (i.e., that Luke's language is superior to Mark's), then it becomes clear that the argument does not prove what it claims to. The evidence does not show that Mark is more primitive in language than Matthew and Luke and therefore must be older than both and must be seen as their source.

In passing we should note that even if it could be shown that Mark's gospel contains more primitive language, that would still not prove that it was a source for Matthew and Luke. It would merely support the conclusion that a portion of the differences (which in fact speak against the assumption of Mark's being a source) thereby lose weight, because they can be explained as improvements in language. But that is only possible under the prior assumption that it has already been proven or at least, with rigorous arguments, shown to be probable, that Matthew and Luke used Mark as a source and therefore are literarily dependent on his gospel.

E. Isn't there, nevertheless, literary dependence among the Synoptic Gospels? The arguments of Robert H. Stein

Anyone venturing to speak about the Synoptic Problem among evangelicals in the USA is constantly referred to the book by Robert H. Stein, *The Synoptic Problem: An Introduction* (Grand Rapids: Baker, 1994).[9] Part one is subtitled "The Literary Relationship of the Synoptic Gospels," and the first chapter is "The Literary Interdependence of the Synoptic Gospels." His arguments, which I now take up in turn, focus on agreement in wording, agreement in narrative order, and agreement in parenthetical material.

Agreement in Wording

Three synoptic pericopes are presented to the reader in English (!) and five are displayed schematically (30–32) in order "to demonstrate the close agreement in wording between the synoptic Gospels" (33 n. 2).

The literary dependence is not proven *but presupposed* as already given. This dependence is *to be observed* in pericopes that were *selected* because they were taken to be best suited to demonstrate literary dependence. They were not drawn from a representative cross-section of the synoptic data. The rule is derived from the exception!

Passages laid out schematically by Stein (30–32):

- Mark 10:13–16: 64 words (35 of them words of Jesus), 23 words fully identical in Matthew/Mark/Luke
- Mark 12:18–27: 170 words (70 of them words of Jesus), 59 words fully identical in Matthew/Mark/Luke
- Mark 13:5–8: 54 words (50 of them words of Jesus), 32 words fully identical in Matthew/Mark/Luke

Passages alluded to in footnote 2, page 33 of Stein:

- Mark 1:40–45: 99 words (24 of them words of Jesus), 31 words fully identical in Matthew/Mark/Luke
- Mark 2:1–12: 197 words (60 of them words of Jesus), 52 words fully identical in Matthew/Mark/Luke
- Mark 8:34–9:1: 135 words (122 of them words of Jesus), 62 words fully identical in Matthew/Mark/Luke
- Mark 11:27–33: 127 words (36 of them words of Jesus), 57 words fully identical in Matthew/Mark/Luke
- Mark 12:1–12: 181 words (155 of them words of Jesus), 53 words fully identical in Matthew/Mark/Luke

In sum: 1027 words (552 of them [53.75%] words of Jesus), 369 words (35.93%) fully identical in Matthew/Mark/Luke.

For comparison: of the 6450 words in the synoptics that can be meaningfully investigated, 1420 words, or 22.01% of Matthew/Mark/Luke, are completely identical!

By an intentional choice of pericopes favoring his own hypothesis, Stein gives his readers the impression that there is literary dependence between the Synoptic Gospels. After presenting readers with the first three of these pericopes (see above) for color coding, he poses the question, "How are we to explain the obvious similarities in wording that we find in these passages?" (33). He refers to a first possible answer as "they agree because they are dealing with history!" (ibid.). But he mentions this, it seems, only for the purpose of repudiating it immediately as "less than satisfactory" (ibid.). He cites three reasons for this rejection (33).

1. The historical explanation does not explain why at times the accounts do not agree exactly, unless we assume that perfect agreement means exact historical reproduction and that imperfect agreement or lack of agreement means that we do not have exact historical reproduction, i.e., that we are talking about different sayings and actions of Jesus.

Stein operates here with a false dichotomy: either the agreement is perfect or the historical account is not exact. What evangelical wishes to deny the gospels' historical exactness? He will rather set the historical question aside and buy into the theory of literary dependence. But he has thereby fallen into a trap and made an unnecessary concession. Perfect agreement in wording is indeed required as proof of literary dependence, but not as evidence for reference to the same historical event. It is normal for eyewitnesses to diverge from each other in their formulations, but that is not to be expected when several make use of the same written primary source. Even the dubiously obtained findings of Stein's three specially selected pericopes listed above (Mark 10:13–16; 12:18–27; 13:5–8), in which only 114 of 288 words (39.58%) are completely identical, do not serve to make literary dependence of the Synoptic Gospels credible.

2. "A second problem that this [historical] explanation encounters is that whereas Jesus spoke and taught primarily in Aramaic, these agreements in wording are in Greek!"

The 22.01% completely identical words in the Greek text of the three synoptic gospels pose no threat to the assumption that their similarities go back to the words and deeds of Jesus, i.e., are historically based. I have already gone into this question in my *Is There a Synoptic Problem?*[10]

    a. All three synoptic gospels are written in "translation Greek": the linguistic fixing of the words and deeds of Jesus occurred completely in Aramaic.

    b. The use of the Septuagint in the Greek-speaking Christian congregations had to lead to assimilations in language.

    c. It is to be expected that a common Christian vocabulary in the Greek language very soon took shape.

3. Against the historical explanation, Stein raises the third question of "why, when John reports a similar incident or saying in the life of Jesus, there is little or no exactness present in the wording." But this is no problem at all when one considers that the similarities are historically based, for it is normal for eyewitness reports to show divergences in wording. The percentage of words that are identical between John and the synoptics is, however, less than that between the synoptics themselves, and the similarities as a rule relate to only one of these, so that John has a word in common alternately with Matthew, Mark, or Luke. But on the one hand, both differences as well as similarities of personality, education, and orientation come into play in the linguistic fixing of events; on the other hand, the similarities in wording among the synoptics are too few to justify acceptance of literary dependence.

Agreement in Narrative Order

Stein writes: "Another impressive area of agreement between the synoptic Gospels involves the common order of the events recorded in them" (34).

In this connection I refer first to my investigation of narrative sequence (*akoluthia*) in my *Is There a Synoptic Problem?*[11] But let us now attempt a more thorough assessment of Stein's argumentation specifically. He lays out three lists and draws from them the conclusion that a common sequence can be detected. "It is apparent that although an Evangelist may at times depart from the common order of the accounts, he nevertheless always returns to the same order" (34).

With "it is apparent," Stein presupposes what needs to be proved, namely that a common order exists, from which an Evangelist can diverge and to which he can return. Stein's three lists do not yield this finding. They are arbitrarily constructed. By setting forth just three lists chosen expressly to prove a point, and not investigating the Synoptic Gospels in their entirety, those parts of the gospels in which a common order is less observable than elsewhere remain out of consideration from the outset. Within the lists, sections that do not stand in the same order are mixed with others in such a way that because of this optical illusion only the careful observer gains the correct impression that one can speak of an "agreement in order" only in a very restricted sense. The examples, which are supposed to show that the Evangelist diverges from a common order and returns to it, are set forth as circular proofs, a "method" dear to practitioners of historical-critical theology when there is a dearth of proof for its assertions:

> For example, even after Luke adds his large insertion of teaching material in 9:51–18:14, he immediately then picks up the departed order at Luke 18:15. (34)

When Stein maintains that Luke "departs" from and again "picks up" or "adds" something to the order, he presupposes what needs to be proved, namely that this order lay complete before him. But the unprejudiced observer will note the considerable differences between the gospels of Mark and Luke: in this passage Luke lacks three Markan pericopes and contains instead no fewer than sixty-four pericopes that one will seek in vain in Mark or which at most—in individual cases—are found in a different place. One might add that a modest agreement can be observed: four pericopes occur in the same order in Mark and Luke. But that is too few to establish literary dependence.

Things are similar with the same order of three miracle stories in Matthew, which are found there in an entirely different place than in Mark. Thus Stein finds it necessary to warn the reader: "Whereas attention is sometimes focused upon the variations in the order of the gospel events, we must not lose sight of the rather impressive agreement in order as seen in the examples given above" (34).

Stein repudiates the assumption that this agreement could be conditioned by the chronological sequence of the events in Jesus' life with the incorrect assertion that the differences would then mean that the evangelists at times give a varying historical sequence. Eyewitness reports of a lengthy sequence of events, however, are as a rule not without gaps; it is not to be expected that *every* witness will pass along *all* that took place completely. The *differences* that result by no means indicate that the eyewitnesses *contradict* each other regarding the sequence of the historical events. The return to agreement following previous nonagreement in sequence can just as easily be historically as literarily based. It can therefore not serve as proof for literary dependence.

As a further argument against the assumption that the narrative order is historically based, Stein must resort to the alleged topical arrangement:

> It is clear that Mark sees the parables of Mark 4:3–32 as a summary collection and not a chronology of consecutive parables that Jesus taught in a single day. (36)

I have already taken up this question elsewhere.[12] Only half of Mark's parables are found in chapter four; the rest are distributed over three other chapters (2, 12, 13). Had it been his intention to create a topical arrangement, then he would have placed them all in one context. The four parables in Mark 4:3–32 take up no more than sixty-two lines in Nestle-Aland[27] and could be expounded in a quarter of an hour, or at most a half hour. Jesus would not have needed a whole day to speak them.

In Matthew too the parables are distributed throughout the entire gospel. Only seven, just a third, are found in Matthew 13, 109 lines in Nestle-Aland[27]. That is at most material for one hour; a part of it is spoken however not to the crowd by the sea but to the disciples alone. Only two of Luke's twenty-nine parables are parallels to the sermon by the sea in Mark 4.

The old assertion that the parable chapter of Mark 4 along with its synoptic parallels is proof of topical arrangement in the gospels does not stand up to scrutiny. It is no truer for being constantly repeated.

> It is also clear that certain materials in the Gospels seem to be grouped together according to subject matter, for between Mark 1:23 and 2:12 we have five miracles of healing, interrupted at 1:35–39 by a summary. (36f.)

The situation looks different than what Stein presents. Following two miracles at different venues, the synagogue and Peter's house, 1:32–34 provides the summary of the healing of sick in the evening. The short report regarding Jesus' departure from Capernaum (1:35–38) and the subsequent summary in 1:39 of his travel activities in Galilee are not the interruption of a collection of miracle stories but, with their historical-geographical orientation, evidence that Mark did not have such a collection before him. The cleansing of the leper is associated with this travel activity in Galilee, while the healing of the lame man is placed in Capernaum. Such particulars are not to be expected in a collection made on the basis of content or type.

Of the eighteen miracle stories in Mark's gospel, then, three are found in chapter one, the third one being clearly demarcated geographically from the other two. In chapter two an additional one comes into view, again clearly demarcated by a change in locale. The other fourteen are distributed across nine additional chapters. There can be no talk of a topical arrangement.

Finally Stein claims that ". . . from Mark 2:13 to 3:6 we have a collection of controversy stories" (37).

If it had been Mark's concern to set forth the types of accounts he used as collections, then he would not have distributed the controversy stories across six chapters (2, 3, 7, 8, 11, 12). We find no more than four controversy stories in 2:13–3:6, set in various venues, though geographic specifics are lacking. In view of these findings, there is no justification for speaking of a thoroughgoing topical arrangement that owes its existence "to topical rather than chronological [i.e., historical] considerations" (37).

Agreement in Parenthetical Material

Stein writes:

> One of the most persuasive arguments for the literary interdependence of the synoptic Gospels is the presence of identical parenthetical material, for it is highly unlikely that two or three writers would by coincidence insert into their accounts exactly the same editorial comment at exactly the same place. (37)

Let us view his four examples.

1. Mark 13:14/Matthew 24:15: ὁ ἀναγινώσκων νοείτω ("let the reader understand").

Since there is a scriptural tie here to the prophecy in Daniel 11:31, expressly noted in a few manuscripts (A and others), the reference is not to the reader of the gospel text. The parenthetical aside is not the redactional remark of the gospel writer but a component of Jesus' discourse. That is, he distinguishes between those listening to him, the disciples, and those who in coming days will see what 13:14 is talking about. The parenthesis could therefore well have been transmitted independently by various eyewitnesses[13] and is no proof of literary dependence between Matthew and Mark.

2. Mark 2:10: λέγει τῷ παραλυτικῷ ("he says to the paralytic")
   Matthew 9:6: τότε λέγει τῷ παραλυτικῷ ("he says then to the paralytic")
   Luke 5:24: εἶπεν τῷ παραλελυμένῳ ("he spoke to the paralytic")

If Jesus in his actual discourse did begin addressing a different individual—directly recognizable during the occurrence—this would need to be reflected in a written account. All three Evangelists could have recognized this necessity and shaped their accounts accordingly. The differences in formulation argue in favor of this. The assumption of literary dependence is not required to account for the data.

3. Mark 5:8: ἔλεγεν γὰρ αὐτῷ ἔξελθε τὸ πνεῦμα τὸ ἀκάθαρτον ἐκ τοῦ ἀνθρώπου. ("Then he said to it: 'Come out from this man, you unclean spirit.'")
   Luke 8:29: παρήγγειλεν γὰρ τῷ πνεύματι τῷ ἀκαθάρτῳ ἐξελθεῖν ἀπὸ τοῦ ἀνθρώπου. ("For he had commanded the unclean spirit to come out from the man.")

Of the eleven words contained in the Markan parenthesis, only three, slightly more than one-fourth, are identical with Luke. This is much lower agreement than on average between these gospels. One of the identical words is an article. Even if one does not count the twenty-two words that Luke has in the parallel verse and sticks only to the parenthetical material, the number of differences still comes to eight. The dissimilarity is therefore much greater than the exact similarity—that does not speak in favor of literary dependence. The fact that the parenthesis is there does not in and of itself suffice to warrant maintaining such dependence. The parenthetical transmission in Mark and Luke of the exorcism Jesus performed, partially simultaneous with the outcry of the demon, could have arisen, with the evangelists or with the eyewitnesses from whom they took over the pericope, as a solution to the problem posed for narration by the complexity of details of the original situation.

4. Mark 15:10: ἐγίνωσκεν γὰρ ὅτι διὰ φθόνον παραδεδώκεισαν αὐτὸν οἱ ἀρχιερεῖς. ("For he knew that the high priests had delivered him over out of jealousy.")
   Matthew 27:18: ᾔδει γὰρ ὅτι διὰ φθόνον παρέδωκαν αὐτόν. ("For he knew that they had delivered him over out of jealousy.")

Of the nine words in Mark's parenthesis, five are identical with Matthew, and the number of differences comes to only four. Yet this negligibly above-average percentage of similarity cannot establish literary dependence. Moreover, the parenthesis cannot be removed from the context of the pericope in Mark 15:6–14.

Of the 107 words in Mark, one finds fully identical: Matt./Mark/ Luke 10, Matt./Mark 30, Mark/Luke 3, and Matt./Luke 3.

The number of differences between Matthew and Mark comes to 132; between Mark and Luke, 142. The pericope belongs to those containing lower-than-average parallelism overall.

In three of the four examples, the parenthetical material assembled by Stein is not present in all three synoptics but in only two of them. His twenty-six words, which in relation to the full range of Mark's 11,260 words amount to only 0.23%, yield no proof of literary dependence. Nor do the agreements in wording or in order. Stein's attempt (42f.) to claim Luke 1:1–4 for his cause cannot bear the weight he places on it, either. That "Luke clearly had available written materials on the life and teaching of Jesus" (42) is not established by what Luke writes there; that is mere assertion.[14]

Evidence for literary dependence of the Synoptic Gospels is not furnished by Robert H. Stein's book.

F. The synoptic structure of Mark's gospel

Below we enumerate the results of careful analysis of each of Mark's 116 pericopes (as listed in Aland's *Synopsis Quattuor Evangeliorum*, 594–96). Results are summarized at the end of the tabulations.

Markan Pericope in Aland's *Synopsis*	Number of Words in Markan Pericope	Parallel(s) with Matthew and/or Luke, or between Matthew and Luke (if any)	Differences between Mt/Mk and Mk/Lk
1:1	7	No parallels with Luke	
1:2–6	92	Completely identical: Mt/Mk/Lk 3 Mt/Mk 23 Mk/Lk 6 Mt/Lk 0	Mt/Mk 137, Mk/ Lk 184
1:7–8	31	Completely identical: Mt/Mk/Lk 13 Mt/Mk 2 Mk/Lk 8 Mt/Lk 31	Mt/Mk 50, Mk/ Lk 71
1:9–11	53	Completely identical: Mt/Mk/Lk 13 Mt/Mk 12 Mk/Lk 7 Mt/Lk 2	Mt/Mk 83, Mk/ Lk 42
1:12–13	30	No parallels with Matthew and Luke	
1:14a	12	Completely identical: Mt/Mk/Lk 3 Mt/Mk 1 Mk/Lk 2 Mt/Lk 0	Mt/Mk 9, Mk/ Lk 12
1:14b–15	23	Completely identical: Mt/Mk/Lk 0 Mt/Mk 5 Mk/Lk 0 Mt/Lk 0	Mt/Mk 24, Mk/ Lk 32
1:16–20	82	No parallels with Luke	
1:21–22	31	No parallels with Matthew	
1:23–28	93	No parallels with Matthew	
1:29–31	44	Completely identical: Mt/Mk/Lk 8 Mt/Mk 6 Mk/Lk 10 Mt/Lk 0	(1:29–34) Mt/Mk 96, Mk/ Lk 10
1:32–34	46	Completely identical: Mt/Mk/Lk 1 Mt/Mk 7 Mk/Lk 8 Mt/Lk 0	See directly above.

1:35–38	48	No parallels with Matthew	
1:39	15	No parallels with Luke	
1:40–45	99	Completely identical: Mt/Mk/Lk 31 Mt/Mk 5 Mk/Lk 7 Mt/Lk 2	Mt/Mk 79, Mk/ Lk 98
2:1–12	197	Completely identical: Mt/Mk/Lk 52 Mt/Mk 18 Mk/Lk 26 Mt/Lk 8	Mt/Mk 157, Mk/ Lk 223
2:13–17	109	Completely identical: Mt/Mk/Lk 36 Mt/Mk 24 Mk/Lk 10 Mt/Lk 5	Mt/Mk 69, Mk/ Lk 82
2:18–22	119	Completely identical: Mt/Mk/Lk 49 Mt/Mk 24 Mk/Lk 22 Mt/Lk 2	Mt/Mk 70, Mk/ Lk 103
2:23–28	108	Completely identical: Mt/Mk/Lk 41 Mt/Mk 10 Mk/Lk 15 Mt/Lk 2	Mt/Mk 122, Mk/ Lk 69
3:1–6	95	Completely identical: Mt/Mk/Lk 15 Mt/Mk 22 Mk/Lk 22 Mt/Lk 1	Mt/Mk 97, Mk/ Lk 103
3:7–12	103	No parallels with Matthew	
3:13–19	95	Completely identical: Mt/Mk/Lk 8 Mt/Mk 8 Mk/Lk 25 Mt/Lk 1	Mt/Mk 99, Mk/ Lk 93
3:20–21	28	No parallels with Matthew and Luke	
3:22–27	98	Completely identical: Mt/Mk/Lk 20 Mt/Mk 22 Mk/Lk 2 Mt/Lk 62	Mt/Mk 146, Mk/ Lk 208
3:28–30	43	No parallels with Luke	

3:31–35	85	Completely identical: Mt/Mk/Lk 19 Mt/Mk 28 Mk/Lk 1 Mt/Lk 5	Mt/Mk 69, Mk/ Lk 82
4:1–9	151	Completely identical: Mt/Mk/Lk 37 Mt/Mk 44 Mk/Lk 9 Mt/Lk 3	Mt/Mk 91, Mk/ Lk 91
4:10–12	52	Completely identical: Mt/Mk/Lk 9 Mt/Mk 2 Mk/Lk 11 Mt/Lk 7	Mt/Mk 163, Mk/ Lk 42
4:13–20	145	Completely identical: Mt/Mk/Lk 16 Mt/Mk 36 Mk/Lk 21 Mt/Lk 3	Mt/Mk 125, Mk/ Lk 147
4:21–25	74	No parallels in Matthew	
4:26–29	60	No parallels in Matthew and Luke	
4:30–32	57	Completely identical: Mt/Mk/Lk 57 Mt/Mk 8 Mk/Lk 6 Mt/Lk 12	Mt/Mk 54, Mk/ Lk 49
4:33–34	25	No parallels in Luke	
4:35–41	118	Completely identical: Mt/Mk/Lk 12 Mt/Mk 12 Mk/Lk 13 Mt/Lk 10	Mt/Mk 113, Mk/ Lk 134
5:1–20	325	Completely identical: Mt/Mk/Lk 40 Mt/Mk 14 Mk/Lk 77 Mt/Lk 0	Mt/Mk 310, Mk/ Lk 274
5:21–43	373	Completely identical: Mt/Mk/Lk 28 Mt/Mk 21 Mk/Lk 64 Mt/Lk 8	Mt/Mk 373, Mk/ Lk 392
6:1–6a	125	No parallels in Luke	

6:6b–13	106	Completely identical: Mt/Mk/Lk 17 Mt/Mk 13 Mk/Lk 13 Mt/Lk 8	Mt/Mk 133, Mk/ Lk 106
6:14–16	54	Completely identical: Mt/Mk/Lk 5 Mt/Mk 9 Mk/Lk 13 Mt/Lk 3	Mt/Mk 54, Mk/ Lk 59
6:17–29	247	No parallels in Luke	
6:30–31	42	No parallels in Matthew	
6:32–44	195	Completely identical: Mt/Mk/Lk 41 Mt/Mk 42 Mk/Lk 11 Mt/Lk 13	Mt/Mk 170, Mk/ Lk 226
6:45–52	139	No parallels in Luke	
6:53–56	72	No parallels in Luke	
7:1–23	361	No parallels in Luke	
7:24–30	129	No parallels in Luke	
7:31–37	115	No parallels in Matthew and Luke	
8:1–10	146	No parallels in Luke	
8:11–13	47	No parallels in Luke	
8:14–21	106	No parallels in Luke	
8:22–26	80	No parallels in Matthew and Luke	
8:27–30	75	Completely identical: Mt/Mk/Lk 23 Mt/Mk 18 Mk/Lk 5 Mt/Lk 4	(8:27–33) Mt/Mk 182, Mk/ Lk 111
8:31–33	69	Completely identical: Mt/Mk/Lk 14 Mt/Mk 26 Mk/Lk 6 Mt/Lk 5	See directly above.
8:34–9:1	135	Completely identical: Mt/Mk/Lk 62 Mt/Mk 19 Mk/Lk 18 Mt/Lk 3	Mt/Mk 83, Mk/ Lk 74

9:2–10	157	Completely identical: Mt/Mk/Lk 43 Mt/Mk 44 Mk/Lk 6 Mt/Lk 8	Mt/Mk 129, Mk/ Lk 204
9:11–13	52	No parallels in Luke	
9:14–29	270	Completely identical: Mt/Mk/Lk 21 Mt/Mk 21 Mk/Lk 20 Mt/Lk 2	Mt/Mk 292, Mk/ Lk 280
9:30–32	47	Completely identical: Mt/Mk/Lk 7 Mt/Mk 5 Mk/Lk 8 Mt/Lk 3	Mt/Mk 39, Mk/ Lk 67
9:33–37	85	Completely identical: Mt/Mk/Lk 15 Mt/Mk 5 Mk/Lk 9 Mt/Lk 2	Mt/Mk 117, Mk/ Lk 89
9:38–41	73	No parallels in Matthew	
9:42–50	149	No parallels in Luke	
10:1	25	Completely identical: Mt/Mk/Lk 1 Mt/Mk 12 Mk/Lk 0 Mt/Lk 1	Mt/Mk 27, Mk/ Lk 40
10:2–12	128	No parallels in Luke	
10:13–16	64	Completely identical: Mt/Mk/Lk 23 Mt/Mk 6 Mk/Lk 24 Mt/Lk 1	Mt/Mk 48, Mk/ Lk 25
10:17–22	110	Completely identical: Mt/Mk/Lk 38 Mt/Mk 11 Mk/Lk 30 Mt/Lk 3	Mt/Mk 92, Mk/ Lk 46
10:23–31	171	Completely identical: Mt/Mk/Lk 45 Mt/Mk 33 Mk/Lk 23 Mt/Lk 7	Mt/Mk 137, Mk/ Lk 113

10:32–34	73	Completely identical: Mt/Mk/Lk 11 Mt/Mk 19 Mk/Lk 4 Mt/Lk 4	Mt/Mk 54, Mk/ Lk 83
10:35–45	190	No parallels in Luke	
10:46–52	123	Completely identical: Mt/Mk/Lk 21 Mt/Mk 6 Mk/Lk 33 Mt/Lk 1	Mt/Mk 104, Mk/ Lk 105
11:1–10	164	Completely identical: Mt/Mk/Lk 37 Mt/Mk 22 Mk/Lk 28 Mt/Lk 17	Mt/Mk 172, Mk/ Lk 183
11:11	21	No parallels in Luke	
11:12–14	55	No parallels in Luke	
11:15–17	65	Completely identical: Mt/Mk/Lk 18 Mt/Mk 20 Mk/Lk 3 Mt/Lk 0	Mt/Mk 30, Mk/Lk 48
11:18–19	32	No parallels in Matthew	
11:20–26	101	No parallels in Luke	
11:27–33	125	Completely identical: Mt/Mk/Lk 57 Mt/Mk 22 Mk/Lk 11 Mt/Lk 7	Mt/Mk 63, Mk/Lk 86
12:1–2	181	Completely identical: Mt/Mk/Lk 53 Mt/Mk 35 Mk/Lk 36 Mt/Lk 19	Mt/Mk 211, Mk/Lk 148
12:13–17	106	Completely identical: Mt/Mk/Lk 30 Mt/Mk 30 Mk/Lk 17 Mt/Lk 2	Mt/Mk 75, Mk/Lk 79
12:18–27	170	Completely identical: Mt/Mk/Lk 59 Mt/Mk 34 Mk/Lk 22 Mt/Lk 3	Mt/Mk 112, Mk/Lk 147

12:28–34	153	Completely identical: Mt/Mk/Lk 18 Mt/Mk 6 Mk/Lk 8 Mt/Lk 9	Mt/Mk 158, Mk/Lk 157
12:35–37a	56	Completely identical: Mt/Mk/Lk 27 Mt/Mk 6 Mk/Lk 4 Mt/Lk 4	Mt/Mk 67, Mk/Lk 33
12:37b–40	51	Completely identical: Mt/Mk/Lk 7 Mt/Mk 2 Mk/Lk 29 Mt/Lk 2	Mt/Mk 216, Mk/ Lk 180
12:41–44	75	No parallels in Matthew	
13:1–2	40	Completely identical: Mt/Mk/Lk 7 Mt/Mk 5 Mk/Lk 0 Mt/Lk 2	(13:1–8) Mt/Mk 90, Mk/ Lk 114
13:5–8	93	Completely identical: Mt/Mk/Lk 37 Mt/Mk 24 Mk/Lk 9 Mt/Lk 4	See directly above.
13:9–13	97	Completely identical: Mt/Mk/Lk 13 Mt/Mk 37 Mk/Lk 9 Mt/Lk 2	Mt/Mk 69, Mk/ Lk 129
13:14–20	116	Completely identical: Mt/Mk/Lk 25 Mt/Mk 57 Mk/Lk 0 Mt/Lk 2	Mt/Mk 53, Mk/ Lk 154
13:21–23	37	Completely identical: Mt/Mk/Lk 2 Mt/Mk 23 Mk/Lk 1 Mt/Lk 3	Mt/Mk 60, Mk/ Lk 61
13:24–27	71	Completely identical: Mt/Mk/Lk 19 Mt/Mk 30 Mk/Lk 1 Mt/Lk 2	Mt/Mk 48, Mk/ Lk 91

13:28–32	87	Completely identical: Mt/Mk/Lk 40 Mt/Mk 35 Mk/Lk 4 Mt/Lk 2	Mt/Mk 14, Mk/ Lk 53
13:33–37	65	No parallels with Matthew and Luke	
14:1–2	34	Completely identical: Mt/Mk/Lk 5 Mt/Mk 12 Mk/Lk 5 Mt/Lk 0	Mt/Mk 58, Mk/ Lk 31
14:3–9	124	No parallels with Luke	
14:10–11	30	Completely identical: Mt/Mk/Lk 6 Mt/Mk 7 Mk/Lk 6 Mt/Lk 2	Mt/Mk 33, Mk/ Lk 42
14:12–17	106	Completely identical: Mt/Mk/Lk 21 Mt/Mk 19 Mk/Lk 27 Mt/Lk 1	Mt/Mk 80, Mk/ Lk 86
14:18–21	76	Completely identical: Mt/Mk/Lk 14 Mt/Mk 40 Mk/Lk 4 Mt/Lk 0	Mt/Mk 46, Mk/ Lk 86
14:22–25	69	Completely identical: Mt/Mk/Lk 15 Mt/Mk 34 Mk/Lk 4 Mt/Lk 1	Mt/Mk 31, Mk/ Lk 141
14:26–31	87	No parallels in Luke	
14:32–42	181	Completely identical: Mt/Mk/Lk 14 Mt/Mk 98 Mk/Lk 1 Mt/Lk 7	Mt/Mk 102, Mk/ Lk 236
14:43–52	140	Completely identical: Mt/Mk/Lk 34 Mt/Mk 52 Mk/Lk 2 Mt/Lk 10	Mt/Mk 138, Mk/ Lk 175

14:53–65	222	Completely identical: Mt/Mk/Lk 17 Mt/Mk 84 Mk/Lk 3 Mt/Lk 3	Mt/Mk 165, Mk/ Lk 399
14:66–72	128	Completely identical: Mt/Mk/Lk 24 Mt/Mk 26 Mk/Lk 10 Mt/Lk 9	Mt/Mk 100, Mk/ Lk 154
15:1	23	Completely identical: Mt/Mk/Lk 0 Mt/Mk 7 Mk/Lk 0 Mt/Lk 2	Mt/Mk 29, Mk/ Lk 32
15:2–5	48	Completely identical: Mt/Mk/Lk 34 Mt/Mk 12 Mk/Lk 3 Mt/Lk 2	Mt/Mk 50, Mk/ Lk 91
15:6–14	105	Completely identical: Mt/Mk/Lk 10 Mt/Mk 30 Mk/Lk 3 Mt/Lk 3	Mt/Mk 132, Mk/ Lk 142
15:15	20	Completely identical: Mt/Mk/Lk 0 Mt/Mk 7 Mk/Lk 0 Mt/Lk 2	Mt/Mk 55, Mk/ Lk 28
15:16–20a	63	No parallels in Luke	
15:20b–21	25	Completely identical: Mt/Mk/Lk 6 Mt/Mk 3 Mk/Lk 3 Mt/Lk 1	Mt/Mk 21, Mk/ Lk 21
15:22–26	55	Completely identical: Mt/Mk/Lk 6 Mt/Mk 16 Mk/Lk 2 Mt/Lk 0	Mt/Mk 51, Mk/ Lk 71
15:27–32a	72	Completely identical: Mt/Mk/Lk 3 Mt/Mk 52 Mk/Lk 0 Mt/Lk 0	Mt/Mk 39, Mk/ Lk 104

15:32b	7	Completely identical: Mt/Mk/Lk 1 Mt/Mk 5 Mk/Lk 0 Mt/Lk 0	Mt/Mk 6, Mk/ Lk 72
15:33–39	106	Completely identical: Mt/Mk/Lk 13 Mt/Mk 45 Mk/Lk 6 Mt/Lk 3	Mt/Mk 111, Mk/ Lk 134
15:40–41	43	Completely identical: Mt/Mk/Lk 3 Mt/Mk 16 Mk/Lk 1 Mt/Lk 4	Mt/Mk 41, Mk/ Lk 50
15:42–47	101	Completely identical: Mt/Mk/Lk 13 Mt/Mk 16 Mk/Lk 8 Mt/Lk 6	Mt/Mk 101, Mk/ Lk 134
16:1–8	136	Completely identical: Mt/Mk/Lk 10 Mt/Mk 19 Mk/Lk 7 Mt/Lk 1	Mt/Mk 212, Mk/ Lk 220
16:9–20	171	No parallels in Matthew and Luke	

Quantitative Analysis of the Synoptic Gospels—
Concluding Observations:

- Mark's gospel is made up of 116 pericopes.
- 40 Markan pericopes, comprising 3635 words, have no parallel in Matthew and/or Luke. That is 32.28% of the entirety of Mark's gospel.
- Only 76 Markan pericopes, comprising 7625 words, occur in Matthew and/or Luke. That is 67.72% of the entirety of Mark's gospel.
- Of the 7625 words in parallel verses, the number of words that are fully identical are:

In Mt/Mk/Lk	1539 words	or 20.19%
In Mt/Mk	1640 words	or 21.51%

In Mk/Lk   877 words   or 11.50%
In Mt/Lk   381 words   or 5.00%

- The differences in verses that are parallel are:
  In Mt/Mk   7256 words   or 95.16%
  In Mk/Lk   8217 words   or 107.76%

- The 1539 identical words contain a high percentage of linguistic base-words (copula, articles, and pronouns):
  The identical words of Mt/Mk/Lk contain 569 base words or 36.97%.
  The identical words of Mt/Mk contain 530 base words or 32.32%.
  The identical words of Mk/Lk contain 286 base words or 32.61%.
  The identical words of Mt/Lk contain 91 base words or 23.88%.

- The identical words of Mt/Mk/Lk contain only 970 words of significance; that is only 12.72% of the 7625 words of the synoptic pericopes.

These results are no evidence for literary dependence among the Synoptic Gospels.

Endnotes

1. Eta Linnemann, *Gibt es ein synoptisches Problem?* 4th ed. (Nürnberg: Verlag für Theologie und Religionswissenschaft, 1999).
2. Cf. "Conspectus Locorum Parallelorum Evangeliorum," in K. Aland, *Synopsis Quattuor Evangeliorum* (Stuttgart: Deutsche Bibelgesellschaft, 1996).
3. Eta Linnemann, *Is There a Synoptic Problem?* trans. R. Yarbrough (Grand Rapids: Baker, 1992), 128.
4. André Verkaik, "The Tenability of Synoptic Independence," Free University Amsterdam, August 1995, Appendix H: Basic Vocabulary in 35 Representative Pericopes, 203–8.
5. See Linnemann, *Is There a Synoptic Problem?* 133–34.
6. Udo Schnelle, *The History and Theology of the New Testament Writings*, trans. M. E. Boring (Minneapolis: Fortress, 1998), 168.

7. Cf. Linnemann, *Is There a Synoptic Problem?* 51–56.

8. In Greek, compound verbs are words formed from a basic verb to which is added one or more prepositional prefixes. E.g., a "simple" form for expressing "I come, I go" is *erchomai;* a compound form would be *exerchomai* (I come out, I go out).

9. Parenthetical page numbers in this section refer to Stein's book.

10. Ibid., 163–65. Cf. 4th German edition, 152–53.

11. Ibid., 83–95. Cf. 4th German edition, 77–85.

12. Ibid., 165n., 166f. Cf. 4th German edition, 153–55.

13. See Jakob van Bruggen, *Marcus*, 2d ed., 1988, 405–12 ("Marcus 13 en de Profetien van Daniel").

14. Cf. Linnemann, *Is There a Synoptic Problem?* 190f.

## Chapter Three

Pauline Authorship and Vocabulary Statistics

A. Word lists and vocabulary statistics as proof of authenticity

From Schleiermacher to Schnelle, from the beginning of the nineteenth century to the end of the twentieth, the genuineness of New Testament writings or segments of them has been called into question through vocabulary tabulations. On the one hand, collections of words are set forth that would allegedly be expected if the pretended author were the actual author, while on the other hand, lists are laid down of those words that allegedly do not belong to his vocabulary. This statistical argument is, to be sure, only one of several, but its weight is not to be underestimated. It has the advantage of appearing to be objective, whether it is applied to language usage or to literary style.

Would anyone risk adducing purely stylistic arguments against the genuineness of a biblical book without attempting to support those arguments through statistical proofs based on vocabulary? Would anyone dispute the genuineness of a biblical book using historical considerations alone, without possessing the slightest literary support? Probably not. An assessment of statistical argumentation in relation to vocabulary could, therefore, not only bring such argumentation into question but also ultimately show that the entire business of calling New Testament writings inauthentic is untenable. Even if such an assessment clears just one of the arguments out of the way, it will have been worth it.

Historical-critical theology serves up the arguments against the genuineness of biblical writings in deceptive wrappings that make the content seem greater and weightier than it is in reality. Unfortunately a portion of these wrappings have also been compliantly adopted and sold to others by some evangelical theologians. But others have provided the valuable service of tearing them off and showing us how much, or rather how little, they conceal.

The authenticity question plays an important role in various areas of the science of New Testament Introduction. One of these areas is the three Pastoral Letters, which we will now examine as an example of how vocabulary arguments are used.

As in the case with other New Testament writings, it is urged against the genuineness of the Pastoral Letters that they lack Paul's typical vocabulary and instead use one that is atypical. A list of about two dozen such words appears impressive—but only until one checks to see if they stand up to scrutiny.

Udo Schnelle cites twenty-four "characteristic terms for the theology of the Pastorals" (see List 1 below, p. 92, in conjunction with the following discussion).[1] Three of these terms, εὐσέβεια ("godliness"), μῦθος ("myth, fable"), and ὑγιαίνω ("to be sound or healthy [in teaching]") occur only in the Pastorals. Four others, διδασκαλία ("instruction"), ἐπιφάνεια ("appearance"), καθαρός ("clean"), σωτήρ ("savior") occur there primarily. But Schnelle lists another word εἰρήνη ("peace"), which occurs in the Pastorals only four times, yet in the other ten Pauline letters thirty-nine times. And consider these ratios: 4:53 (δικαιοσύνη ["righteousness"]), 20:84 (λόγος ["word"]), 35:142 (πίστις ["faith"]), 6:71 (δόξα ["glory"]), 7:139 (πνεῦμα ["spirit"]), to name only the most prominent examples.

"The Pastorals manifest considerable differences from the theology of the undisputed Pauline letters," Schnelle declares.[2] (See List 2 below, p. 92) "Lacking are concepts such as the 'righteousness of God,' 'freedom,' 'cross,' 'son of God,' and 'body of Christ.' . . . [T]he antithesis 'flesh/spirit' does not occur at all."[3]

Nothing is said here of the fact that δικαιοσύνη θεοῦ ("righteousness of God") occurs only in Romans (eight times) and 2 Corinthians (once), while ἐλευθερία ("freedom") is to be found in Romans, 1 Corinthians, and 2 Corinthians (two times each), and in Galatians (four times)—but otherwise not at all. Υἱὸς θεοῦ (Son of God) or its equivalents are admittedly found seven times in Romans, twice in 1 Corinthians, and four times in Galatians, but on the other hand they occur only a single time in 2 Corinthians, Ephesians, Colossians, and 1 Thessalonians, and are totally absent in Philippians, 2 Thessalonians, and Philemon. One will search in vain for σταυρός ("cross") in Romans and 2 Corinthians, nor is the word found in the Thessalonian letters or Philemon. The word occurs, in fact, only ten times in the thirteen Pauline letters. Σῶμα Χριστοῦ is found only once in Romans, three times in 1 Corinthians, eight times in Ephesians, once in Philippians, and five times in Colossians. Σάρξ occurs in contrast to πνεῦμα thirteen times in Romans and seven times in Galatians, but apart from that only once in each of the following: 1 and 2 Corinthians, Colossians, and—in 1 Timothy!

It is possible to postulate a great deal, but untested recollection sometimes leads into error. In order for statistics to be conclusive, they have to be correct!

In historical-critical introductions to the New Testament, the impression is created that a typical Pauline vocabulary exists which is present in all genuine letters and is lacking only in the Pastorals. This impression is, however, a deception.

Morgenthaler gathers together sixty words that he considers to be distinctly Pauline. But these are not—as one might expect—New Testament words found only in Paul. They are rather words that occur in most New Testament writings and accordingly are to be found in most of Paul's letters. Their relative frequency in Paul primarily results from the fact that the content of thirteen writings goes into the numbers establishing Paul's usage.

Even of these selected sixty words, only seventeen occur in all Pauline writings. If we leave Philemon to the side, the number rises to twenty-one. If both Philemon and the Pastorals are set aside, there still remain no more than thirty words—just half of the alleged distinctly Pauline vocabulary—in each of the remaining letters. Again setting Philemon and the Pastorals aside, you will look in vain for the rest of these words in one, two, three, or even five other Pauline letters. Precisely those eight distinctly Pauline words that are lacking in all three Pastoral letters are also absent in other Pauline letters (see List 3 below, p. 93).

If one compares the frequency of occurrence of the distinctly Pauline words in the individual letters, it is striking that as a rule, they are crucial words in one of the three large Pauline epistles. Something like half of them are concentrated in one letter, and the remainder are also not evenly distributed. With the distinctly Pauline words, we are therefore by no means dealing with words that regularly occur in the Pauline corpus and are evenly spread throughout. Were that the case, it would be fully justified to expect to find them in every genuine Pauline letter. However, the eight distinctly Pauline words that are absent from all three pastorals occur a total of 382 times in Paul. On the average each word occurs forty-eight times, and then these forty-eight occurrences are spread among thirteen letters. Even if the distribution corresponded evenly with the word stock, shorter epistles would have to lack certain words, there being too few to go around. The lack of these words in the Pastorals, therefore, settles absolutely nothing as far as the question of genuineness is concerned.

It appears more impressive when the genuineness of the Pastorals is disputed by pointing out that entire word groups characteristic of Paul are absent from the Pastorals. But this objection, too, impresses only until it is scrutinized more closely (see List 4 below, p. 94): Ἀποκαλύπτειν ("to reveal") and ἀποκάλυψις ("revelation") are found thirteen times each in Paul; that makes twenty-six words out of a total of 32,303. Ideally the word groups would be found twice each in the thirteen Pauline letters. But since the distribution is heaviest in Romans (3 + 3), 1 Corinthians (3 + 3), Galatians (2 + 2), and 2 Thessalonians (3 + 1), six Pauline letters apart from the Pastorals are left entirely without these words.

The word group based on ἐνεργεῖν ("to effect") boasts a total of thirty occurrences: seven in Ephesians; five in 1 Corinthians; four in Galatians; three times each in Philippians, Colossians, and 2 Thessalonians; twice in 2 Corinthians; and once in Romans and Philemon. It is true that with respect to this word group the Pastorals come away empty-handed, but with the sort of proportions involved, not a lot can be made of this.

Καυχᾶσθαι ("to boast"), etc., is lacking in the Pastorals; isn't that a weighty consideration? No, for of the fifty-five occurrences, forty-seven are concentrated in the three large epistles (Romans eight times, 1 Corinthians ten times, 2 Corinthians twenty-nine times). The rest are distributed among Galatians (three times), Philippians (three times), and finally Ephesians and 1 Thessalonians (once each).

The word group περισσεύειν ("abound, cause to abound"), etc., has forty-eight occurrences. Of these, twenty-two are concentrated in 2 Corinthians, seven in 1 Corinthians, six in Philippians, five in Romans, four in 1 Thessalonians, and exactly one in both Ephesians and Colossians. Six Pauline letters lack any occurrence whatsoever.

Ὑπακούειν ("to obey"), etc., is absent from the Pastorals; is that not of considerable significance? No, the word group in Paul consists of only twenty-two occurrences, eleven of which are found in Romans. That leaves only three occurrences in 2 Corinthians, two each for Ephesians and Colossians, one each for Philippians and Philemon. Seven epistles do not contain the word, among them 1 Corinthians. Outside the Pauline letters this word group is, by the way, attested only fourteen times.

Φρονεῖν ("to think"), etc., is lacking in the Pastorals. There are however only thirty-three occurrences in all of Paul's writings, of which fifteen are in Romans and ten in Philippians. First Corinthians contains three, 2 Corinthians two, and three additional Pauline letters one each (Ephesians, Galatians, Colossians). Six epistles do not contain the word.

Words occurring far fewer times than those cited above are pressed into service to argue that a non-Pauline conception of eschatology and of the church underlies the Pastorals. Such words, occurring as few as eight, six, or five times—or even just one time—are used as a basis for weighty theories! Παρουσία ("presence, arrival"), the word said to indicate the actual Pauline eschatological outlook, does occur fourteen times in Paul, but only in five epistles: 1 Corinthians (twice), 2 Corinthians (twice), Philippians (twice), and both 1 and 2 Thessalonians (four times each). It isn't even found in Romans!

Of these fourteen occurrences, six (1 Cor. 16:17; 2 Cor. 7:6, 7; 10:10; Phil. 1:26; 2:12) have no connection with the return of Jesus. In an additional passage (2 Thess. 2:8) the word παρουσία is directly connected with ἐπιφάνεια, allegedly its conceptual opposite. That leaves one of the six occurrences of ἐπιφάνεια out of consideration. Second Timothy 1:10 and Titus 3:4 use ἐπιφάνεια to refer to the First Coming, leaving only the occurrences of ἐπιφάνεια in 1 Tim. 6:14 and 2 Tim. 4:1, 8 to undermine the assumption of an eschatological view in the Pastorals running counter to the Pauline view typified by use of the word παρουσία. Such reasoning belongs to the realm of fancy and has nothing to do with science.

More important appear to be the word lists that P. N. Harrison advances as evidence against the genuineness of the Pastorals.[4] He concedes that the absence of one, a half-dozen, or even a dozen Pauline words is not necessarily significant. Yet he views the persistent absence of just such a quantity of Pauline vocabulary to constitute a decisive objection to the genuineness of the Pastorals.

Let us examine these lists in detail. Of the 2645 words that occur in Paul, eighty-eight (3.33%) are isolated in the first list as appearing in none of the three pastoral letters. In the second list, 112 (4.23%) are isolated in the same way. It would have been just as easy to compile lists of lacking occurrences of the same magnitude for every other Pauline epistle.

In the first list, "Pauline Words absent in the Pastorals" (see List 5, p. 94), the words cited are by no means words that occur in each of the other ten Pauline letters. Their distribution is very uneven. One of the words is found in only three letters, while eight occur in no more than four letters (see List 5.1 below). Forty-one words are encountered in only five of Paul's letters (see List 5.2 below). This means they are found in just half of his epistles besides the Pastorals.

Only nineteen of these eighty-eight words (21.59%) are found in six epistles (see List 5.3 below). Those occurring in seven drop to ten, those in eight to six, those in nine to no more than four (just 4.54%; List 5.4, 5.5, and 5.6). None of the words whatsoever occurs in all ten letters. Not one of the eighty-eight words listed is attested in all of those Pauline epistles regarded as genuine. Seventy-eight words

(88.64% of those on the list) are absent from at least three Pauline letters outside of the Pastorals. The quantitative distribution of the eighty-eight words is likewise negligible. Fifty words (56.82% of the list) crop up fewer than thirteen times, which means that they could not possibly occur in all thirteen letters in the first place. A high percentage of the words occur only once even in the longer epistles. Statistically speaking, what right do we have to expect to find a word in the short epistle to Titus when that same word occurs only once in Romans, an epistle ten times as long?

The lack of eighty-eight "Pauline" words in the Pastorals would be significant only if Paul used them in all of his other ten letters. For that to be possible, each of these words would have to occur at least ten times. Otherwise, their appearance in all ten letters would obviously be impossible. (A word that occurs fewer than ten times in Paul cannot appear in all ten of the letters that Harrison regards as Pauline.)

Now it must be noted that Harrison concedes that the lack of as many as a dozen Pauline words in a single writing would tell us nothing. Taking that into account, we conclude that according to Harrison each of Paul's ten writings must have at least seventy-six of these eighty-eight words ($88 - 12 = 76$). In that case we could expect 760 occurrences (10×76). Nevertheless, this would be sufficient only in the event that there was proportional distribution among the letters. In point of fact, the eighty-eight words are missing from the Pauline letters as follows: Romans lacks thirteen and 1 Corinthians lacks twelve of them, 2 Corinthians twenty-two, Galatians thirty-two, Ephesians thirty-eight, Philippians forty-three, Colossians thirty-five, 1 Thessalonians forty-four, 2 Thessalonians fifty-nine, Philemon seventy-nine. Thus only Romans and 1 Corinthians fulfill Harrison's condition. And it must be remembered that these eighty-eight words were selected precisely because they are not found in the Pastorals!

Of the particles that Harrison mentions as absent from the Pastorals (see List 6, pp. 96–97), they are absent in the Pauline letters as follows: Romans lacks fifty-four of them, 1 Corinthians forty-three, 2 Corinthians fifty-nine, Galatians sixty-nine, Ephesians ninety, Philippians eighty-two, Colossians ninety-four, 1 Thessalonians eighty-four, and 2 Thessalonians and Philemon each 100!

Out of the New Testament's theoretical 880 uses of the 88 core Pauline words (see table on this page) in the ten epistles accepted as Pauline, 238 (27.05% of 880) are single occurrences.

Non-usage or deficiencies of the listed words can be observed in all Pauline writings. In the nature of the case this is more apt to take place in the shorter letters than in the longer ones. Non-occurrences or deficiencies of the listed words total 377, or 42.84% of 880.

The number of Harrison's 88 words actually present in all Pauline letters amounts to 503 (57.16% of the theoretical 880). Of these, however, only 265 occur more than once. That is 52.68% of the actual 503, or 30.11% of the theoretical 880. Two hundred thirty-eight occurrences of the 503 are singles. That is 47.32% of the 503 words, or 27.05% of the 880. If a word occurs only once in other Pauline epistles, its absence in the Pastorals is no criterion of inauthenticity.

To represent this schematically:

Pauline words listed by Harrison	Words listed as absent from individual epistles	Words of the 880 actually present in all Pauline letters
880 theoretical occurrences	377 occurrences (42.84% of 880)	503 occurrences (57.16% of 880)

Singles: 238	Occurring more than once: 265
27.05% of 880	30.11% of 880
47.32% of 503	52.68% of 503

Only ten of the words are found in more than seven epistles; that is 11.36% of Harrison's list and 1.88% of the 532 words that occur in more than one Pauline epistle as well as elsewhere in the New Testament. That is damning for the chief argument against the genuineness of the Pastorals that Harrison seeks to draw from this data—namely, the improbability that the author just a few years later would no longer use these eighty-eight words in the production of three epistles. The distribution of the 1229 occurrences which Harrison notes (in his list of 88 words lacking in the Pastorals; see List 5, p. 94) across the pages of the ten accepted Pauline epistles results in a favorable average, but that is cold comfort for his theory. The words are quite unevenly distributed, with most of them found in only a few of the ten epistles. That spells death for the argument.

Harrison would pose a more serious objection to the genuineness of the Pastorals if he could sustain his argument that 112 particles, prepositions, and pronouns found in the ten accepted Pauline letters are lacking in the three pastorals (see List 6, p. 96).[5]

Where Harrison is cited, the impression often arises that these 112 words are all found in the ten accepted letters without exception. But as soon as one looks at his actual charts (in a book not easy to find!), this impression is proven false. As Harrison states, "Of the 112 Pauline particles, &c. . . . Rom. has 58, 1 Cor. 69, 2 Cor. 53, Gal. 43, Eph. 22, Phil. 29, Col. 18, 1 Thess. 27, 2 Thess. 12, and even Philem. in its page and a quarter has 12."[6]

What this means is that even Romans, the longest of the epistles, contains only 51.79% of these 112 words, just over half. The highest percentage is 61.61% (1 Corinthians) and the lowest 10.71% (both 2 Thessalonians and Philemon). It is true that 10% is more than the 0% in all three pastorals. But it must not be forgotten that the list was compiled in the first place on the basis of words absent from the Pastorals. The seventy-seven Pauline particles, etc., that *are* found in the Pastorals are excluded at the outset. That is 40.74% of the total of 189 Pauline particles, etc., of which Harris is aware. The positive overlap here between the Pastorals and the other Pauline writings is by no means insignificant.

A closer look at Harrison's list of 112 particles, prepositions, and pronouns reveals the following. Thirty-six of these words (32.14% of the total) occur only once in Paul and can therefore obviously not be expected to show up in the Pastorals anyway. In contrast, of the seventy-seven particles, etc., that Harrison leaves off the list, all occur at the very least twice: once in the Pastorals and once in one of the other Pauline letters. It would be no more than fair and objective to observe that the seventy-seven particles, etc., which the Pastorals contain simply counterbalance the seventy-eight that they do not.

None of the 112 particles, etc., is present in all ten Pauline letters.

Only one (0.89%) is found in nine epistles, four (3.57%) in eight, and six (5.36%) in seven as well as another six in six (again, see List 6 below). Ninety-six (85.71%) occur in five of the ten epistles or less. Of these, as already noted, 36 (32.14%) occur in only one epistle, and 60 (53.57%) in two to five epistles. There is a difference between the quantities that Harrison primes us to expect and the numbers we actually encounter:

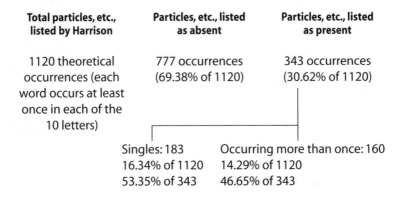

Total particles, etc., listed by Harrison	Particles, etc., listed as absent	Particles, etc., listed as present
1120 theoretical occurrences (each word occurs at least once in each of the 10 letters)	777 occurrences (69.38% of 1120)	343 occurrences (30.62% of 1120)

Singles: 183	Occurring more than once: 160
16.34% of 1120	14.29% of 1120
53.35% of 343	46.65% of 343

We see that the particles, etc., listed as absent amount to more than two-thirds of the 1120 occurrences necessary to validate the argument. Of the actual occurrences, 53.35% occur only once. Only twenty-five words occur often enough for there to be enough words, at least theoretically, to suffice for all thirteen letters. That is 22.32%. Practically, however, this figure is too high, because it still assumes an even distribution of occurrences that is generally not to be found at all.

The imposing list of 112 particles, etc., amounts therefore to deceptive advertising. In addition, Harrison measures with two different scales:[7]

1. The seventy-seven Pauline particles, pronouns, and prepositions that are also found in the Pastorals are simply not presented as a list. This makes a comparison impossible and provides no way to determine how many of the words of this list are found in one,

two, or three of the Pastorals, respectively, nor in how many of the other ten Pauline letters these words occur.

2. Harrison plays down the importance of these seventy-seven words by noting that they all appear in the apostolic fathers and apologists. But there is no counterbalancing figure telling how many of the 112 words that are listed can also be found in these sources. There is also no proof provided that these words were not yet in use at the time of authorship of the ten accepted Pauline letters. The reader is simply manipulated with suggestive allusions.

3. It is objected that "the great majority" occur "in practically every book of the N.T."

    a. There are no concrete references to show how great the majority is.

    b. "In practically every book" is a vague statement that cannot be tested, since the list of the seventy-seven particles, etc., is missing.

    c. To the extent that these particles, etc., also occur elsewhere in the New Testament, it is illicit to object regarding them that they are found in the apostolic fathers and apologists. The two arguments are at odds with each other.

4. Strangely, Harrison in a negative argument notes that 36 of the 77 particles that occur in all the Pastorals are all found in Romans; 35 in 1 and 2 Corinthians, Ephesians, Philippians, and Galatians; 33 in Colossians; 31 in 2 Thessalonians; and 30 in 1 Thessalonians and Philemon. Surely this high correspondence with the so-called genuine Pauline letters speaks clearly for the genuineness of the Pastorals. In addition, here Harrison minimizes his third argument mentioned above: the "great majority" melts down to between 36 and 30 out of 77 (46.75%–38.96%), which is not even a "majority," much less "great." Then with sleight of hand, a second argu-

ment is fabricated out of the same state of affairs: a word that is found in every book of the New Testament must, of course, a priori occur also in the Pastoral Epistles!

5. A series of individual statements are brought together to make a negative argument. But these statements by no means point in the negative direction Harrison assumes.

   a. "Of the remaining 41, 7 occur in only one Pauline letter."

   To put in plainly, they are found in the three pastorals and in one additional Pauline letter. To compare: of the list of 112, 36 occurred in only one Pauline letter (32.14%), whereas here we are dealing with 7 of 77 (9.09%)! Moreover, they occur, in addition to this one Pauline letter, in one to three of the Pastorals, which actually means in two to four epistles.

   b. "17 [occur] in only one of the Pastorals."

   In the list of 112, Harrison is not bothered that only 8 of the 27 words in 1 Thessalonians are also found in 2 Thessalonians. Even of the 69 words in 1 Corinthians, 23 are lacking in 2 Corinthians. Conversely, of the 53 words in 2 Corinthians on Harrison's list of 112, 9 are lacking in 1 Corinthians. Only 6 of the 22 listed words from Ephesians are identical to words found in Colossians. Unless one is content to apply a double standard, Harrison's argument here is without force.

   c. "10 [occur] only once in the Pastorals."

   That is 30 single occurrences out of the 231 particles, etc., listed as present, or 12.99%. By way of comparison, the number of single occurrences in Galatians is 18 of 43, or 41.86%; their number in the two Thessalonian letters is 23 of 39, or 58.97%! Not all that Harrison advances as argument turns out to be usable!

Harrison's arguments do not withstand scrutiny. He fails to show that the seventy-six Pauline particles, etc., that occur in the Pastorals are no counterweight to the 112 that do not occur. Regarding the question of the genuineness of the Pastorals, we can forget Harrison's lists, just like all the rest that have been constructed to dispute their genuineness.

B. Word occurrence in the Pauline letters—the presupposition for objective statistical argumentation in questions of genuineness

We turn now to the question of how things stand with Paul's word usage in general (see bar graphs under "Pauline Epistles," p. 99 below).

We count thirteen Pauline letters. If one sorts them according to their length, 1 Timothy stands in seventh place, 2 Timothy in tenth place, and Titus in twelfth place. We should be quite clear about the fact that these three epistles are exceedingly short. The following comparative material underscores this.

The Pastorals in comparison to Romans:

Total words in Romans: 7099	Vocabulary of Romans: 1066 different words
Total words in 1 Timothy: 1589 = 22.38%	Vocabulary of 1 Timothy: 538 = 50.47%
Total words in 2 Timothy: 1237 = 17.42%	Vocabulary of 2 Timothy: 457 = 42.87%
Total words in Titus: 664 = 9.35%	Vocabulary of Titus: 305 = 28.61%

The Pastorals in comparison to the Pauline letters *in toto:*

Total words in Paul: 32,352	Vocabulary of Paul: 2645
Total words in 1 Timothy: 1589 = 4.91%	Vocabulary of 1 Timothy: 535 = 20.34%
Total words in 2 Timothy: 1237 = 3.82%	Vocabulary of 2 Timothy: 455 = 17.28%
Total words in Titus: 664 = 2.05%	Vocabulary of Titus: 305 = 11.53%

On the basis of the numerical proportions shown above, it is only to be expected that a considerable percentage of the Pauline vocabulary would be missing from the Pastorals. That has nothing to do with the question of genuineness. So far no theologian has proposed declaring Philemon inauthentic due to its lack of Pauline vocabulary. This fact alone clearly shows that the argument from lack of Pauline vocabulary is not the basis but only a pretense for disputing the genuineness of the Pastorals.

As we saw in the preceding section, Pauline vocabulary lists compiled to distinguish Paul's other letters from the Pastorals do not necessarily prove what is claimed for them, either qualitatively or quantitatively.

The actual Pauline vocabulary—that is, New Testament words found only in Paul—are even less capable of yielding an index for the question of authenticity. For this vocabulary's occurrence is too limited for us to expect to find any one of these words in all thirteen Pauline letters (see List 7 below, p. 98, columns 4, 6, 8).

Of the Pauline vocabulary 1135 words occur in the Pauline corpus only once. These Pauline "singles" (used by Paul just once) encompass 42.91% of the Pauline vocabulary (List 7, column 3). Five hundred ninety-eight (52.69%) of these "singles" are New Testament hapax legomena; they comprise 22.61% of the Pauline vocabulary (List 7, column 4). The rest of Paul's "singles" are found in other places in the New Testament but occur only one time in Paul. They could be called Pauline hapax legomena. They make up 537 words, or 20.30%, of the Pauline vocabulary (List 7, column 5).

In each of the Pauline letters there is a considerable presence of words that Paul uses but once. These consist of New Testament hapax legomena, of Pauline hapax legomena, and of "singles" that are used only once in any given Pauline letter but found several times in both the New Testament and in the Pauline corpus generally. The percentage of words used but once in an epistle varies in the individual letters, but we may place it roughly between 45.5% and 73.5%. In general it can be said that the shorter an epistle is, the greater the number of singular words it will contain (List 7, column 3).

It has so far escaped notice, I believe, that in addition to the New Testament hapax legomena there are words that occur repeatedly but only in one of the New Testament books. They could be called "*mia-graphē* legomena" (occurring once [Greek *mia*] in one writing [Greek *graphē*] among several). Paul has ninety-two of them, occurring as follows: Romans seventeen; 1 Corinthians twenty-one; 2 Corinthians twenty-seven; Galatians and Ephesians, five each; 2 Timothy three; Philippians and 2 Thessalonians two each; Colossians and 1 Thessalonians, one each; 1 Timothy nine; and Titus and Philemon each has zero (see List 7, column 6). Of these 92 words, 16 occur three times, 4 four times, 1 five times, and 1 six times. All the rest occur twice.

The high usage of "singles," hapax words, and *mia-graphē* legomena in the Pauline epistles means that the vocabulary in individual epistles is not uniform. Each letter contains words that are lacking in all the others. Each letter lacks words that are well known from other letters and that are regarded as typically Pauline (see List 2 below). One cannot rightly expect to find words distributed everywhere when 42.91% of those words occur only once. Words that are restricted to only one writing must be absent from twelve of the thirteen others. This finding shows the absurdity of attempts to prove the inauthenticity of a Pauline letter by referring to the absence of Pauline vocabulary or the occurrence of "non-Pauline" words. Just as a witch trial leads inexorably to convictions once the proceedings get underway, so the verdict of "inauthentic" hovers over an epistle as soon as it falls under suspicion; other epistles escape judgment only because it is decided in advance to exempt them from such skepticism.

But as soon as the attempt is made to proceed scientifically, investigating the entire corpus of epistles according to the same criteria, it turns out that the Pastoral Letters are not basically different from the others. There is a difference insofar as they happen to be brief compositions, but in this respect they comport with other short epistles in the New Testament: the percentage of the occurrence of singular words is higher. If one pulls the statistical trick of making three short epistles into one of medium length, the inevitable result is a distortion, because the distinctives of a short epistle are multiplied by three in the resulting fabrication, which can no longer be considered a short epistle (see List 7, column 4 below).

The high frequency of New Testament hapax legomena in the Pastorals (see List 7, column 4 below) is admittedly a striking phenomenon, but it is not to be viewed in isolation. If we make a general comparison between the percentage of New Testament hapax legomena as a portion of the vocabulary of each individual Pauline epistle, we see that the results range from 3.17% to 13.13%. The average lies at 8.15%, with five epistles having a lower percentage and eight having a higher. No standard value exists that could be regarded as the standard for genuineness. As soon as one begins to work objectively, i.e., scientifically in the true sense, objections against the genuineness of the Pastorals dissipate like fog under bright sun.

It should not be forgotten that there is a second group of multiply-attested words in Paul ("poly-Paulines"; words occurring only in Paul, but in more than one of his writings). Do they perhaps give evidence for the question of genuineness (see List 7, column 8)? This group encompasses 167 words, only 6.34% of Paul's vocabulary: 79 occur twice, i.e., once in each of two different epistles: 41 occur three times, distributed among two or three epistles; 18 words occur four times; 8 occur five times in varying combinations; 8 words occur six times; 4 occur seven times; 3 occur eight times; 2 occur nine times; 1 solitary word occurs ten times; and another solitary word thirteen times. But none of these multiply-attested words is more or less evenly distributed throughout the Pauline corpus. To take an example, the last-named word, found thirteen times and thus the only word that could in theory be found in every Pauline letter, occurs 9 times in 2 Corinthians, twice in Galatians, once in 1 Timothy, and once in 2 Timothy.

The Pastorals contain a good number of these "poly-Paulines." Even if the total number of occurrences is corrected by subtracting the sum of those words that occur only in the Pastorals, the outcome is not drastically different. To remain objective this correction must of course also be performed on the other groups of letters. For comparison we refer to those letters that are closest to the individual Pastoral Letters in the number of words they contain:

There are 167 "poly-Paulines," 63 of which are in the Pastorals = 37.72%
Only in the Pastorals: 19
In the Pastorals and other Pauline letters: 44 = 26.35%

Uncorrected	**Corrected**
in 1 Timothy: 45 = 26.95%	27 = 16.07%
in Colossians: 33 = 19.76%	22 = 13.17%
in 2 Timothy: 25 = 15.12%	15 = 8.98%
in 1 Thessalonians: 17 = 19.18%	14 = 8.38%
in Titus: 24 = 14.37%	14 = 8.38%
in 2 Thessalonians: 11 = 6.59%	8 = 4.79%

Even the clearly Pauline multiply-attested words, therefore, are unsuited for grounding arguments against the genuineness of individual Pauline letters. Their occurrence is too meager (6.31%) and their distribution too irregular for this. What is more, the high percentage of them present in the Pastorals makes them witnesses for rather than against their genuineness. When the deceptive packaging is torn off and the numbers are laid out openly, the arguments for declaring Paul's writings inauthentic are seen for what they are. Truth wins the day.

What goes for Paul's epistles can also be said of the New Testament in general. The vocabulary yields no arguments for declaring certain writings to be inauthentic—whether we speak of entire writings or for individual sections of them. It is true that the hapax legomena have been seized on eagerly; but that move is ruled out when we recognize that 35.61% of the New Testament's words are hapax legomena. In addition, the phenomenon of "singles" is so much a part of all New Testament writings that we must reject the whole mode of argumentation based on allegedly genuine words that are lacking, or allegedly non-genuine words that are present. Such argumentation would permit a scholar to declare inauthentic whatever writing, or section of a writing, that he wished, on equally justified (or rather unjustified) grounds. That would apply to Romans as well as to the Pastorals, to 1 Corinthians 13 as well as to the allegedly spurious ending of Mark. This procedure could have enjoyed favor for so long only because proponents of historical-critical theology were content not to fulfill even the minimal requirements for scientific work, which would have called for the percentage relationships in general to be investigated, or at least for a counter-comparison to be undertaken.

Endnotes

1. Udo Schnelle, *The History and Theology of the New Testament Writings*, trans. M. E. Boring (Minneapolis: Fortress, 1998), 330.
2. Ibid., 330–31.
3. Ibid., 331.
4. P. N. Harrison, *The Problem of the Pastoral Epistles* (London: Oxford University Press, 1921), 31f., 36f.

5. Ibid., 36f.
6. Ibid., 35.
7. Ibid., 38.

List 1: Characteristic terms for the theology of the Pastoral Epistles (according to Udo Schnelle)

	Occurrences according to Morgenthaler	Paulines	Rom	1 Cor	2 Cor	Gal	Eph	Phil	Col	1 Thess	2 Thess	1 Tim	2 Tim	Titus	Phlm
ἀγάπη	75	9	14	9	3	10	4	5	5	3	5	4	1	3
ἁγνός	5	-	-	2	-	-	1	-	-	-	1	-	1	-
αἰών	38	6	8	3	3	7	2	1	-	-	4	3	1	-
ἀλήθεια	47	8	2	8	3	6	1	2	-	3	6	6	2	-
διδασκαλία	19	2	-	-	-	1	-	1	-	-	8	3	4	-
διδάσκειν	15	2	2	-	1	1	-	3	-	1	3	1	1	-
δικαιοσύνη	57	33	1	7	4	3	4	-	-	-	1	3	1	-
δόξα	77	16	12	19	1	8	6	4	3	2	3	2	1	-
εἰρήνη	43	10	4	2	3	8	8	2	3	3	1	2	1	1
ἐπίγνωσις	15	3	-	-	-	2	1	4	-	-	1	2	1	1
ἐπιφάνεια	6	-	-	-	-	-	-	-	-	1	1	3	1	-
εὐσέβεια	10	-	-	-	-	-	-	-	-	-	8	1	1	-
καθαρός	8	1	-	-	-	-	-	-	-	-	2	2	3	-
κακός	26	15	3	1	-	-	1	1	2	-	1	1	1	-
καλός	40	5	6	2	2	-	-	-	1	-	16	3	5	-
λόγος	84	7	17	9	2	4	4	7	9	5	8	7	5	-
μανθάνειν	16	1	3	-	1	1	2	1	-	-	3	3	1	-
μῦθος	4	-	-	-	-	-	-	-	-	-	2	1	1	-
πίστις	142	40	7	7	22	8	5	5	8	5	19	8	6	2
πνεῦμα	146	34	40	17	18	14	5	2	5	3	3	3	1	1
συνείδησις	20	3	8	3	-	-	-	-	-	-	4	1	1	-
σώζειν	29	8	9	1	-	2	-	-	1	1	4	2	1	-
σωτήρ	12	-	-	-	-	1	1	-	-	-	3	1	6	-
ὑγιαίνειν	8	-	-	-	-	-	-	-	-	-	2	2	4	-

List 2: Theological terms lacking in the Pastoral Epistles (according to Udo Schnelle)

	Paulines	Rom	1 Cor	2 Cor	Gal	Eph	Phil	Col	1 Thess	2 Thess	1 Tim	2 Tim	Titus	Phlm
δικαιοσύνη θεοῦ	9	8	-	1	-	-	-	-	-	-	-	-	-	-
ἐλευθερία	7	1	1	1	4	-	-	-	-	-	-	-	-	-
σάρξ	24	13	1	1	7	-	-	1	-	-	1	-	-	-
(in contr. to πνεῦμα)														
σταυρός	10	-	2	-	3	1	2	2	2	-	-	-	-	-
σῶμα χριστοῦ	18	1	3	-	-	8	1	5	-	-	-	-	-	-
υἱός θεοῦ	17	7	2	1	4	1	2	2	-	-	-	-	-	-

List 3: Distribution of characteristic Pauline words lacking in the Pastoral Epistles

	ἀποθνῄσκειν	εἴτε	ἕκαστος	καυχᾶσθαι	οὔτε	σύν	σῶμα	ὥστε
Overall	42	63	42	35	33	37	91	39
Romans (7094 words)	23	4	5	5	10	4	13	5
1 Corinthians (6807 words	7	27	22	6	13	7	46	14
2 Corinthians (4448 words)	5	14	2	20	-	5	10	7
Ephesians (2425 words)	-	2	5	1	-	2	9	-
Galatians (2220 words)	2	-	2	2	5	4	1	5
Philippians (1624 words)	1	6	2	1	-	4	3	3
1 Timothy (1586 words)	-	-	-	-	-	-	-	-
Colossians (1577 words	2	6	1	-	-	7	8	-
1 Thessalonians (1472 words)	2	2	2	-	5	4	1	3
2 Timothy (1235 words)	-	-	-	-	-	-	-	-
2 Thessalonians (824 words)	-	2	1	-	-	-	-	2
Titus (663 words)	-	-	-	-	-	-	-	-

List 4: Word groups characteristic of Paul, absent in the Pastorals

	ἀποκαλύπτειν ἀποκάλυψις	ἐνεργεῖν ἐνέργεια ἐνέργημα ἐνεργής	καυχᾶσθαι καύχημα καύχησις	περισσεύειν περίσσευμα περισσός περισσῶς περισσοτέρος	ὑπακούειν ὑπακοή	φρονεῖν (φρόνημα) φρόνησις φρόνιμος φρονίμως
Rom	3, 3	1, -, -, -	5, 1, 2	3, -, 1, -, -	4, 7	9, 4, -, 2
1 Cor	3, 3	2, -, 2, 1	6, 3, 1	3, -, -, 4, -	-, -	1, -, -, 2
2 Cor	-, 2	2, -, -, -	20, 3, 6	10, 2, 1, 2, 6	-, 3	1, -, -, 1
Eph	1, 2	4, 3, -, -	1, -, -	1, -, -, -, -	2, -	-, -, 1, -
Gal	2, 2	4, -, -, -	2, 1, -	-, -, -, -, 1	-, -	1, -, -, -
Phil	1, -	2, 1, -, -	1, 2, -	5, -, -, -, 1	1, -	10, -, -, -
1 Tim	—	—	—	—	—	—
Col	-, -	1, 2, -, -	-, -, -	1, -, -, -, -	2, -	1, -, -, -
1 Thess	-, -	1, -, -, -	-, -, 1	3, -, -, -, 1	-, -	-, -, -, -
2 Tim	—	—	—	—	—	—
2 Thess	3, 1	1, 2, -, -	-, -, -	-, -, -, -, -	2, -	-, -, -, -
Titus	—	—	—	—	—	—
Phlm	-, -	-, -, -, -	-, -, -	-, -, -, -, -	-, 1	-, -, -, -

List 5: Pauline words absent in the Pastorals (according to Harrison)

1. In the New Testament only in four Pauline Epistles

ἀγαθωσύνη, ἄπειμι, ἁπλότης, εἰκῇ, εἴπερ, ἐνέργεια, κενόω, ὑπερβολή.

2. In other NT writings and five Pauline Epistles	Rom	1 Cor	2 Cor	Gal	Eph	Phil	Col	1 Thess	2 Thess	Phlm	Total
ἀδικέω	-	2	3	1	-	-	1	-	-	1	8
αἷμα	3	4	-	1	3	-	1	-	-	-	12
ἀκροβυστία	10	2	-	3	1	-	2	-	-	-	18
ἄλλος	-	23	4	2	-	1	-	1	-	-	31
ἀνάγκη	1	3	3	-	-	-	-	1	-	1	9
ἀξίως	1	-	-	-	1	1	1	1	-	-	5
ἀσθενής	1	9	1	1	-	-	-	1	-	-	13
δεξιός	1	-	1	1	1	-	1	-	-	-	5
διαθήκη	2	1	2	3	1	-	-	-	-	-	9
δοξάζω	5	2	2	1	-	-	-	-	1	-	11
ἐλεύθερος	2	6	-	6	1	-	1	-	-	-	16
ἐξέρχομαι	1	2	3	-	-	1	-	1	-	-	8
ἐξουθενέω	2	3	1	1	-	-	-	1	-	-	8
ἔπαινος	2	1	1	-	3	2	-	-	-	-	9
ἐρῶ	13	3	2	1	-	1	-	-	-	-	20
εὐλογία	2	1	3	1	1	-	-	-	-	-	8
ζῆλος	2	1	5	1	-	1	-	-	-	-	10
θυμός	1	-	1	1	1	-	1	-	-	-	5
καταλαμβάνω	1	1	-	-	1	3	-	1	-	-	7
καταρτίζω	1	1	1	1	-	-	-	1	-	-	5
κατεργάζομαι	11	1	6	-	1	1	-	-	-	-	20
καύχημα	1	3	3	1	-	2	-	-	-	-	10
κόπος	-	2	4	1	-	-	-	3	1	-	11
μέρος	3	7	4	-	2	-	1	-	-	-	17
νήπιος	1	6	-	2	1	-	-	1	-	-	11
νουθετέω	1	1	-	-	-	-	2	2	1	-	7
παλαιός	1	2	1	-	1	-	1	-	-	-	6
παράπτωμα	9	-	1	1	3	-	2	-	-	-	16
παρουσία	-	2	3	-	-	2	-	4	3	-	14
πλεονάζω	3	-	2	-	-	1	-	1	1	-	8
πλεονεξία	1	-	1	-	2	-	1	1	-	-	6
πλήρωμα	4	1	-	1	4	-	2	-	-	-	12
πνευματικός	3	13	-	1	3	-	2	-	-	-	22
σοφία	1	17	1	-	3	-	6	-	-	-	28
σταυρός	-	2	-	3	1	2	2	-	-	-	10
τέλειος	1	3	-	-	1	1	2	-	-	-	8
τρέχω	1	3	-	2	-	1	-	-	1	-	8
ὑπακούω	4	-	-	-	2	1	2	-	2	-	11
ὑπάρχω	1	5	2	2	-	2	-	-	-	-	12
ὑστέρημα	-	1	4	-	-	1	1	1	-	-	8
φοβέομαι	3	-	2	2	1	-	1	-	-	-	9

List 5: Pauline words absent in the Pastorals (according to Harrison) continued

	Rom	1 Cor	2 Cor	Gal	Eph	Phil	Col	1 Thess	2 Thess	Phlm	Total
3. In six Epistles											
ἀκαθαρσία	2	1	-	1	2	-	1	2	-	-	9
ἀποκαλύπτω	3	3	-	2	1	1	-	-	3	-	13
ἀποκάλυψις	3	3	2	2	2	-	-	-	1	-	13
ἐπιστολή	1	2	8	-	-	-	1	1	4	-	17
εὐαγγελίζομαι	3	6	2	6	2	-	-	1	-	-	20
ἐχθρός	3	2	-	1	-	1	1	-	1	-	9
κατέχω	2	3	1	-	-	-	-	1	2	1	10
καυχάομαι	5	5	17	2	1	1	-	-	-	-	31
κοινωνία	1	3	4	1	-	3	-	-	-	1	13
μέσος	-	2	1	-	-	1	1	1	1	-	7
ὀφείλω	3	5	2	-	1	-	-	-	2	1	14
παραλαμβάνω	-	3	-	2	-	1	2	2	1	-	11
πορνεία	-	4	1	1	1	-	1	1	-	-	9
πρόσωπον	-	2	12	3	-	-	1	3	1	-	22
σκότος	2	1	2	-	3	-	1	2	-	-	11
στήκω	1	1	-	1	-	2	-	1	1	-	7
φρονέω	8	1	1	1	-	10	1	-	-	-	22
χαίρω	3	3	8	-	-	8	2	2	-	-	26
ὥρα	1	2	1	1	-	-	-	1	-	1	7
4. In seven Epistles											
ἀποθνήσκω	22	7	5	2	-	1	2	2	-	-	41
βλέπω	6	7	7	1	1	3	3	-	-	-	28
γνωρίζω	3	2	1	1	6	2	3	-	-	-	18
ἐνδύω	2	4	1	1	3	-	2	1	-	-	14
εὐδοκέω	2	2	2	1	-	-	1	2	1	-	11
κενός	-	4	1	1	1	2	1	2	-	-	12
περισσεύω	3	3	10	-	1	5	1	3	-	-	26
πράσσω	10	2	2	1	1	1	-	1	-	-	18
συνεργός	3	1	2	-	-	2	1	1	-	2	12
ψυχή	4	1	2	-	1	2	1	2	-	-	13
5. In eight Epistles											
δέχομαι	-	1	5	1	1	1	1	2	1	-	13
ἐργάζομαι	4	4	1	1	1	-	1	2	4	-	18
θλίψις	5	1	9	-	1	2	1	3	2	-	24
σῶμα	13	43	9	1	9	3	8	1	-	-	87
υἱός	12	2	4	13	4	-	2	3	1	-	41
χαρίζομαι	1	1	5	1	2	2	3	-	-	1	16
6. In nine Epistles											
ἐνεργέω	1	2	2	4	4	1	1	1	1	-	17
εὐχαριστέω	6	6	1	-	2	1	3	3	2	1	25
οὐρανός	2	2	3	1	4	1	5	2	1	-	21
περιπατέω	4	2	5	1	8	2	4	4	2	-	32
Overall	244	283	206	96	102	83	89	74	42	10	1229

List 6: Pauline particles, prepositions, pronouns, etc., that do not occur in the Pastorals (according to Harrison)

In one Epistle

1. Otherwise absent from the NT

Rom. ἤτοι; 1 Cor. διόπερ (2), μήτι γε, νή, ὡσπερεί; 2 Cor. ἡνίκα (2), ὑπερλίαν (2)

2. In other NT writings

Rom. ἀπέναντι, δεῦρο, μεταξύ, πού, ὡσεί; 1 Cor. δή, ἐπάνω, ὅλως (3), οὐδέποτε, ποίνυν; 2 Cor. ἔσωθεν, μήτι (2), ὑπεράνω (2), ἀμφότεροι (3); Phil. ἐξαυτῆς, καίπερ; 1 Thess. τοιγαροῦν; Col. ὑπεναντίος

	Rom	1 Cor	2 Cor	Gal	Eph	Phil	Col	1 Thess	2 Thess	Phlm	In Paul
In one Epistle	7	9	6	5	4	2	1	1	0	0	35
Includ. repetitions	7	12	11	5	8	2	1	1	0	0	47
In two Epistles											
ὑπερεκπερισσοῦ	-	-	-	-	1	-	-	2	-	-	3
τάχα	1	-	-	-	-	-	-	-	-	1	2
δίς	-	-	-	-	-	1	-	1	-	-	2
ἕνεκεν	2	-	4	-	-	-	-	-	-	-	6
ἐπειδή	-	4	-	-	-	1	-	-	-	-	5
ἐφάπαξ	1	1	-	-	-	-	-	-	-	-	2
ἡλίκος	-	-	-	1	-	-	1	-	-	-	2
καθό	1	-	2	-	-	-	-	-	-	-	3
κἄν	-	5	1	-	-	-	-	-	-	-	6
κατέναντι	1	-	2	-	-	-	-	-	-	-	3
κατενώπιον	-	-	-	-	1	-	1	-	-	-	2
μενοῦνγε	2	-	-	-	-	1	-	-	-	-	3
ὁμοίως	1	3	-	-	-	-	-	-	-	-	4
ὅμως	-	1	-	1	-	-	-	-	-	-	2
σύ	1	-	3	-	-	-	-	-	-	-	4
οὐθείς	-	1	1	-	-	-	-	-	-	-	2
οὔπω	-	2	-	-	-	1	-	-	-	-	3
πάντως	1	4	-	-	-	-	-	-	-	-	5
ποῖος	1	1	-	-	-	-	-	-	-	-	2
σός	-	2	-	-	-	-	-	-	-	1	3
τοσοῦτος	-	1	-	1	-	-	-	-	-	-	2
τοὐνάντιον	-	-	1	1	-	-	-	-	-	-	2
ὧδε	-	1	-	-	-	-	1	-	-	-	2
In three Epistles											
ἄνω	-	-	-	1	-	1	2	-	-	-	4
ἅπαξ	-	-	1	-	-	1	-	1	-	-	3
ἔνι (= ἔνεστι)	-	1	-	3	-	-	1	-	-	-	5
ἐπεί	3	5	2	-	-	-	-	-	-	-	10
ἔπειτα	-	7	-	3	-	-	-	1	-	-	11
ἕως (prep.)	2	5	3	-	-	-	-	-	-	-	10
ὁποῖος	-	1	-	1	-	-	-	1	-	-	3
ὅπου	1	1	-	-	-	-	1	-	-	-	3
ὄφελον	-	1	1	1	-	-	-	-	-	-	3
πλήν	-	1	-	-	1	3	-	-	-	-	5
πόσος	2	-	1	-	-	-	-	-	-	1	4
ποῦ	1	8	-	1	-	-	-	-	-	-	10

List 6: continued

	Rom	1 Cor	2 Cor	Gal	Eph	Phil	Col	1 Thess	2 Thess	Phlm	In Paul
In four Epistles											
καθάπερ	6	2	4	-	-	-	-	4	-	-	16
οὐ μή	1	1	-	2	-	-	-	2	-	-	6
ναί	1	-	6	-	-	1	-	-	-	1	9
ὁ μέν ... ὁ δέ	-	1	-	1	1	1	-	-	-	-	4
οὖ	3	1	1	-	-	-	1	-	-	-	6
οὔτε	10	15	-	5	-	-	-	5	-	-	35
οὐχί	3	13	1	-	-	-	-	1	-	-	18
παρά (w. acc.)	7	3	2	2	-	-	-	-	-	-	14
ὑμέτερος	1	2	1	1	-	-	-	-	-	-	5
εἰχῇ	1	1	-	2	-	-	1	-	-	-	5
εἴπερ	3	2	1	-	-	-	-	-	1	-	7
μήπως	-	2	5	2	-	-	-	1	-	-	10
In five Epistles											
ἀντί	2	-	-	-	-	1	-	-	-	-	3
αὐτὸς ὁ	1	3	-	-	-	-	-	-	-	-	4
ἄχρι	-	1	-	1	-	-	-	-	-	-	2
οὐκέτι	1	-	3	-	-	-	-	-	-	-	4
πάλιν	-	1	1	-	-	-	-	-	-	-	2
τε	-	2	-	-	-	1	-	-	-	-	3
ὥσπερ	1	4	-	-	-	-	-	-	-	-	5
In six Epistles											
ἄν	7	8	5	3	-	1	1	-	-	-	25
ὁ αὐτός	6	17	9	-	1	8	-	1	-	-	42
ἐμαυτοῦ	1	6	4	1	-	1	-	-	-	1	14
νυνὶ δέ	7	4	2	-	1	-	2	-	-	2	18
ὅπως	3	1	2	1	-	-	-	-	1	1	9
ὑπέρ (w. acc.)	-	2	3	1	2	1	-	-	-	2	11
In seven Epistles											
ἄρα	11	5	3	5	1	-	-	1	1	-	27
γε	3	3	2	1	2	1	1	-	-	-	13
ἔτι	5	4	1	3	-	1	-	-	1	1	16
κἀγώ	2	10	9	2	1	2	-	1	-	-	27
τότε	1	6	1	3	-	-	1	1	1	-	14
ὥστε	5	14	7	5	-	3	-	3	2	-	39
In eight Epistles											
διό	6	2	9	1	5	1	-	2	-	1	27
εἴτε	4	27	14	-	2	6	6	2	2	-	63
ἐμός	2	9	3	2	-	2	1	-	1	3	23
σύν	4	7	6	4	2	4	7	4	-	-	38
In nine Epistles											
ἕκαστος	5	22	2	2	5	2	1	2	1	-	42
Total	58	69	53	43	22	29	18	27	12	12	112
Includ. repetitions	187	288	163	89	38	54	31	51	15	16	932
In 5 or more epist., Includ. repetitions	116	165	100	50	25	39	20	22	13	12	562

List 7: The word structure of the Pauline Epistles

Epistle	1 Wd. Ct.	2 Vocabulary	3 Singles	4 HapaxNT	5 HapaxPl
Rom	7099	1066	578 = 54.22%	115 = 10.79%	116 = 10.88%
1 Cor	6816	960	445 = 46.35	82 = 8.54	96 = 10.00
2 Cor	4456	788	400 = 50.76	68 = 8.63	63 = 7.99
Eph	2428	529	311 = 58.79	35 = 6.62	39 = 7.37
Gal	2223	526	301 = 57.22	30 = 5.70	45 = 8.55
Phil	1624	444	277 = 62.39	40 = 9.01	31 = 6.98
1 Tim	1589	538	343 = 63.75	66 = 12.27	46 = 8.55
Col	1584	432	267 = 61.80	37 = 8.56	24 = 5.55
1 Thess	1478	363	205 = 56.47	18 = 4.96	13 = 3.58
2 Tim	1237	457	310 = 67.83	60 = 13.13	37 = 8.10
2 Thess	826	252	152 = 60.32	8 = 3.17	10 = 3.97
Titus	664	305	219 = 71.80	32 = 10.49	14 = 4.59
Phlm	328	139	85 = 61.15	7 = 5.04	3 = 2.16
Total	32,352	2645	1135 = 42.91%	598 = 22.61%	537 = 20.30%

Epistle	6 MiaNT	7 MiaPl	8 PolyPl	9 MonoPl
Rom	17 = 1.59%	4 = 2.25%	66 = 6.21%	198 = 18.57%
1 Cor	21 = 2.19	32 = 3.33	64 = 6.65	167 = 17.40
2 Cor	27 = 3.43	18 = 2.28	60 = 7.60	155 = 19.67
Eph	5 = .94	2 = .38	36 = 6.83	76 = 14.37
Gal	5 = .95	8 = 1.71	23 = 4.41	58 = 11.03
Phil	2 = .45	18 = 4.05	18 = 4.04	60 = 13.51
1 Tim	9 = 1.67	8 = 1.49	45 = 8.41	120 = 22.30
Col	1 = .23	2 = .46	32 = 7.51	70 = 16.20
1 Thess	1 = .27	1 = .28	17 = 4.70	36 = 9.92
2 Tim	2 = .44	1 = .22	25 = 5.49	87 = 19.04
2 Thess	2 = .79	1 = .40	11 = 4.45	21 = 8.33
Titus	-	3 = .98	24 = 8.05	56 = 18.36
Phlm	-	-	12 = 8.82	19 = 13.67
Total	92 = 3.48%	101 = 3.82%	167 = 6.34%	857 = 32.40%

Pauline Epistles (see page 86 above)

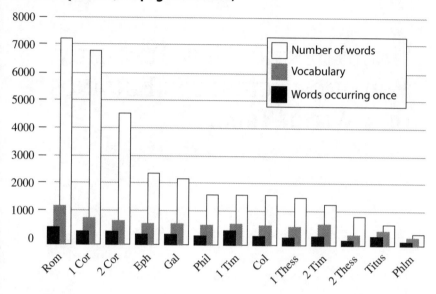

## Chapter Four

"INAUTHENTIC" NEW TESTAMENT WRITINGS: SCIENTIFIC FINDINGS OR A WITCH TRIAL?

A STANDARD GERMAN New Testament introduction, Udo Schnelle's *Einleitung in das Neue Testament* (1994), typifies historical-critical theology. It states:

> Of the 27 books of the New Testament only Paul's authentic letters were penned by the person named in the title. Revelation and the latter two Johannine epistles mention their original authors (Rev. 1:1, 4, 9; 2 John 1; 3 John 1), but in contrast to Paul's authentic letters it is unclear just who stands behind the seer "John" of Revelation and "the elder" of 2 and 3 John. Seven New Testament writings were authored anonymously, the authors' names being added in the titles at a secondary level in the course of tradition (Matthew, Mark, Luke, Acts, John, Hebrews, 1 John). The other New Testament writings must be termed pseudepigraphic—that is, they were published under names that are historically inaccurate.[1]

This summary of what is almost universally agreed on in historical-critical theology even made its way into the newsmagazine *Der Spiegel* (23 [1996]: 64) thanks to widespread interest in questions of New Testament introduction stirred up by Gerd Lüdemann, who contended that much of what the New Testament contains actually does not belong there at all.

So then, ten New Testament writings are simply pseudepigraphic, each wrongly bearing a given title that was usurped by means of a lie. Among these are six letters that we know as Pauline epistles: Ephesians, Colossians, 2 Thessalonians, and the three pastoral letters. In addition are four general (catholic) letters: James, 1 and 2 Peter, and Jude. Liberal theology of a previous era declared such writings to be "inauthentic" and distinguished them from those that are "authentic." Below I will use these terms for practical reasons, since they are more concise than *pseudepigraphic*.

Historical-critical theology passes on to us its declarations of "inauthentic" as the result of scientific investigation. Doesn't this mean that science has spoken; the matter is settled; we must abide by this result whether we like it or not? Absolutely not. True, there is a consensus in this matter within historical-critical theology. But it is by no means the case that we are dealing here with the transparent and definitive results of research. For a long time evangelical theologians have marshaled at least one counterargument to every historical-critical argument.[2] But as a rule, these counterarguments are ignored by the historical-critical camp. What historical-critical theology passes along as fact is by no means the objective outcome won by means of investigation freed of presuppositions. It is rather merely the presentation of its own position with no regard for dissenting statements.

It makes little sense to perfect evangelical counterarguments to the historical-critical hypotheses when they are being ignored. Instead, the need is to mount a general assault on declarations of inauthenticity—a good offense is the best defense—and to put the critics' mode and various types of argumentation to the test. The various types of their arguments will be scrutinized and in that context the individual arguments assessed. The following areas call for investigation:

A. Linguistic argumentation
  1. Hapax legomena as evidence for inauthenticity
  2. Word lists of typical terms whose occurrence speaks against authenticity

3. Word lists of typical terms whose absence speaks against authenticity
4. Lists of stylistic distinctives whose absence or presence speaks against authenticity
B. Literary dependence
C. Historical placement
D. Theological classification
E. Description of phenomena with expressions that can be neither objectified nor quantified
F. Results

A. Linguistic argumentation

1. Hapax legomena as evidence for inauthenticity

Words that occur only once in the New Testament (hapax legomena) play a large role in the question of authenticity in historical-critical theology. So does the frequent occurrence of distinctive words in an individual document. In Udo Schnelle's *Einleitung*, for example, these furnish the first and most weighty argument for ascribing pseudonymity to Colossians, Ephesians, and the three pastoral letters.

Strangely, hapaxes in the other writings that are likewise held to be pseudepigraphic are not even mentioned. That is understandable in the case of 2 Thessalonians, for the percentage of hapaxes in this epistle is small and would not make an impressive argument. With respect to James, Jude, and the Petrine epistles, hapaxes have obviously drawn little attention because sufficient other effective and long-standing arguments are available to dispute their genuineness. In the context of the New Testament writings that are regarded as authentic, the term *hapax legomena* does not occur in Schnelle and other historical-critical New Testament introductions, since in these cases no argument is required to dispute their genuineness.

Let us then summarize: only in the case of those New Testament writings that have fallen under suspicion of being inauthentic is the question of occurrence of hapax legomena broached, and even then only when other arguments against authenticity do not receive preference. Is such a process objective? Can it be called scientific? Is it not rather like a witch trial, in which a characteristic of the suspect (say, red hair) is declared to be evidence of occult involvement, while other people having the same characteristic escape implication, simply because no one has suspected them of witchcraft?

Only in the case of those New Testament writings suspected of being inauthentic is the *number* of their hapax legomena chalked up as evidence against genuineness. What goes unmentioned is how high the percentage of hapaxes in other New Testament books is. Is such a procedure objective, and does it deserve to be called scientific? Doesn't it rather resemble a witch trial in which one automatically deduces, based on the production of butter produced by those accused, that they must have used witch's potion—without ever clarifying the normal range of output in butter production and which factors affect it?

Scientific procedure would be to establish the number of hapax legomena for all New Testament writings and to work out their percentage of occurrence within the vocabulary of each writing in turn. The results would be compiled in a list in which the writings were ordered according to how high the percentage of occurrence turned out to be. Since historical-critical theology regards the quantity of hapax legomena as evidence against genuineness, the list should be laid out so as to begin with the writings with the lowest percentage of hapaxes. Only on the basis of such a list would it be possible to determine whether the occurrence of hapaxes so clearly distinguishes the so-called pseudepigraphical writings from those regarded as authentic that it is rightly regarded as evidence against authenticity.

Since to my knowledge this task has never been undertaken I have done it myself. With the aid of Morgenthaler's *Statistik des Neutestamentlichen Wortschatzes,*[3] I have set forth the number of hapax legomena in the individual New Testament writings as well as their percentage of each book's total vocabulary. Because New Testament introductions in their numerical figures often do not limit "hapax legomena" to its strict definition of only those words that occur one time in the New Testament—they often add in words that occur multiple times, though only in one particular New Testament book—I include such words, too. (These words should actually be called *mia-graphē* legomena, words occurring in only one New Testament writing, as opposed to hapax legomena, words occurring but once in any New Testament writing at all; see pp. 87–88.) For practical reasons both classes of words count as hapax legomena in the list below. Since Morgenthaler makes no new entries to the vocabulary of the New Testament writings in his supplement to the third and fourth editions, I have calculated this myself using corrected numbers and figured the percentages of hapax legomena accordingly.

Hapax legomena in the New Testament	
1. 1–3 John	3.31% of the vocabulary
2. 2 Thessalonians	3.97% of the vocabulary
3. Philemon	5.04% of the vocabulary
4. 1 Thessalonians	5.23% of the vocabulary
5. Jude	5.73% of the vocabulary
6. Mark	6.39% of the vocabulary
7. Galatians	6.65% of the vocabulary
8. Ephesians	7.36% of the vocabulary
9. Matthew	8.52% of the vocabulary
10. Colossians	8.80% of the vocabulary
11. Philippians	9.46% of the vocabulary
12. John	9.69% of the vocabulary
13. 1 Peter	10.28% of the vocabulary
14. James	10.36% of the vocabulary
15. Titus	10.49% of the vocabulary
16. 1 Corinthians	10.73% of the vocabulary
17. 2 Corinthians	12.05% of the vocabulary
18. Revelation	12.23% of the vocabulary
19. Romans	12.38% of the vocabulary
20. 2 Timothy	13.57% of the vocabulary
21. 1 Timothy	13.94% of the vocabulary
22. Hebrews	14.16% of the vocabulary
23. 2 Peter	14.21% of the vocabulary
24. Luke	14.45% of the vocabulary
25. Acts	26.55% of the vocabulary

If we take into account the hapaxes in all the New Testament writings—an obvious enough requirement for work wishing to be regarded as scientific—then it becomes evident that it is absurd to use their occurrence as a criterion for authenticity. Anyone reluctant to admit this ought to be at least consistent enough to acknowledge the first sixteen writings in the list above as authentic, and to start the list of inauthentic writings with the quantitative jump that takes place at entry 17, the only strikingly sudden leap in the whole list apart from the very last entry. The result, however, would then look quite different from what one normally reads in the historical-critical introductions—2 Thessalonians, Ephesians, Colossians, 1 Peter, James, as well as Titus would belong among the authentic books, while Romans and 2 Corinthians would have to be declared inauthentic!

Nothing is changed here by an additional argument used variously to buttress arguments based on hapax legomena. This argument asserts that only a portion of the hapaxes occur in the LXX. In keeping with the procedure already seen above, this phenomenon is only given weight in the case of those writings suspected of being inauthentic. But it is present in all New Testament writings. Of the 596 hapax legomena in Paul's letters (not including the *mia-graphē* legomena), 270 are absent from the LXX: that is 45.15%. This additional argument falls to the ground anyway when the main argument proves untenable (as we have seen above it does). It would therefore be superfluous to cite the evidence for hapax frequency in the NT vis-à-vis the LXX for the entire range of New Testament books.

Occasionally it does dawn on Schnelle—in connection with Colossians, for instance—that "the indisputably genuine Pauline letters also exhibit numerous hapax legomena."[4] But that does not prevent him from using the frequent occurrence of hapax legomena as a main argument in declaring other New Testament writings to be inauthentic.

The investigation above makes clear that historical-critical theology's use of (frequent) occurrence of hapax legomena as evidence in questions of genuineness is due solely to ignorance, inconsistency, and lack of scientific rigor. We should stop being impressed by the claim that its disputing of the genuineness of New Testament writings is based on scientific results.

2. Word lists of typical terms whose occurrence speaks against authenticity

The sort of word lists which I have in mind are adduced by, for example, Udo Schnelle for certain New Testament writings declared to be inauthentic (pseudepigraphic).

Regarding Colossians Schnelle states, "In addition, Colossians contains 28 words attested elsewhere in the New Testament but not in the indisputably genuine Pauline letters."[5] Since he does not furnish the list, it cannot be checked. But basically the reply must be that 537 words (20.30%) of the Pauline vocabulary can be found elsewhere in the New Testament yet occur only once in the Pauline letters. In a vocabulary of 432 words (the number of lexemes used in Colossians), 28 amounts to just 6.4%—hardly a striking finding. The correct number of Pauline hapax (see previous chapter), however, comes to only 24, or 5.55%. In Romans the percentage of Pauline hapax legomena is 10.88%; in Philippians, 6.98%. The list of 28 words in Colossians is no evidence against authenticity. It can only be regarded as a criterion for authenticity if one swallows it uncritically; it does not stand up to careful scrutiny.

For Ephesians, eleven expressions are listed as proof of deutero-Pauline authorship. These are turns of phrase "which do not appear in the proto-Pauline writings but which mark the theology of Ephesians."[6] For a list of these expressions, see List 1 on p. 161 below.

Since Paul did not compile his letters from a stock of constantly repeated stereotypical expressions, singular utterances can also be found in each of the letters recognized as authentic, especially in such brief compass in comparison with the total vocabulary of Ephesians (529 words). If we look more carefully at the terms that constitute these utterances, it turns out that all of them (except for one hapax) occur from 2 to 548 times in the other Pauline letters!

Word lists are also marshaled against the genuineness of 2 Thessalonians: "Typical ideas, words, and expressions point to a more developed situation in doctrine and forms of Christian life than is seen in 1 Thessalonians and all the other undisputed Pauline letters."[7]

Far-reaching inferences are drawn from an epistle that consists of 826 words and has a vocabulary of 252 words!

Schnelle notes, "That there are seventeen expressions in 2 Thessalonians that occur nowhere else in the New Testament is very revealing."[8] The occurrence of singular turns of phrase is no proof of pseudepigraphy. Such phraseology is to be expected in every New Testament writing, because every one contains hapax legomena and *mia-graphē* legomena. Their presence in 2 Thessalonians is actually fairly minimal, altogether 3.97%, while Romans has such words to the tune of 12.38% of its total vocabulary. The eight hapax legomena of 2 Thessalonians together with the double occurrence of two *mia-graphē* legomena already account for thirteen of the seventeen turns of phrase. Further, all distinctive content requires distinctive formulations; it is therefore ill-advised to deduce epochal differences from the four remaining phrases—or even all seventeen. Before drawing such far-reaching conclusions, the occurrence of singular phrases in the whole New Testament needs to be studied.

"The manner of expression of 2 Thessalonians" is, according to Schnelle, marked by "42 words and phrases . . . that are used twice or more."[9]

The vocabulary of 2 Thessalonians contains 100 words that occur multiple times. Sixty-two of them are found between 100 and 19,734 times in the New Testament and therefore shed little light on 2 Thessalonians in particular. Of the 38 words that occur fewer than 100 times in the New Testament, 12 are attested between 20 and 63 times in Paul; accordingly, they are general Pauline vocabulary and not characteristic of 2 Thessalonians alone. Two of the remaining 26 are *mia-graphē* legomena; one occurs in Paul only in 2 Thessalonians; and one occurs, outside of 2 Thessalonians, only in a disputed Pauline letter. Twenty-two of the 26 words also appear in the so-called "genuine" Pauline letters: 2 in five of them, 5 in four, 4 in three, 8 in two, and 2 in one. Even if they do mark "the manner of expression of 2 Thessalonians," as Schnelle has it, they are not proof of "a . . . more developed situation than . . . all the other undisputed Pauline letters."[10] To make this argument one could at most adduce the 17 phrases mentioned above—presupposing that they would stand up to scrutiny and that they really only occur in 2 Thessalonians. Even then, however, a whole lot may not be proved. Second Thessalonians contains 47 verses.

Assuming that each verse contains an average of 3 phrases—a number that is probably too low—then the epistle would have 141 phrases. Dividing 17 by 141 yields 12.02%. This percentage would have meaning only if it were previously established that the percentage of singular phrases in the "genuine" Pauline letters is substantially lower.

I have already explored lists of words found in the Pastoral Letters in the previous chapter. Of Schnelle's list of twenty-four "terms characteristic of the theology of the pastoral letters," there remain after closer scrutiny no more than seven that occur only in the Pastorals exclusively or primarily. That furnishes no evidence in the question of genuineness, since every Pauline letter contains singular terms.

Regarding 1 Peter, Schnelle gathers "central terms and ideas of Pauline theology" that determine "even the theology of 1 Peter."[11] These may be found in List 2, p. 161 below. Apart from the ἐν Χριστῷ ("in Christ") formula, these number no more than five, 0.92% of a vocabulary of 545 words, an amount that is negligible and proves nothing. Two of them can hardly be described as central Pauline concepts, since one occurs but 7 times scattered across four Pauline letters, and the other 13 times in four "genuine" and three "inauthentic" Pauline letters. All five individual words are represented in the LXX, four of them with 2–6 columns devoted to them in Morgenthaler's compilations. All occur elsewhere in the New Testament corpus—2 in three writings, 1 in six, and 2 in ten. Their use in 1 Peter does not, therefore, necessarily stem from Pauline influence.

A word list used as evidence for inauthenticity is also made available for 2 Peter. (See List 3 on p. 161 below.) "The obvious use of the religio-philosophical terms of Hellenism is striking."[12] Here again one finds a mini-list of 8 words, barely 2% of a 401 word vocabulary, which has *no* value statistically anyway. Such a list suffices for historical-critical theology to confidently lay down the verdict that the author of the letter was not the apostle Peter but "an educated Hellenistic (Jewish) Christian" of the second century A.D.!

Yet as soon as the alleged "religio-philosophical terms of Hellenism" are checked word by word, it turns out that all occur in the LXX, albeit two are only in the Apocrypha. Even the phrase consisting of two terms (θεία δύναμις, "divine power") is attested there.

Apart from the hapax legomenon ἐπόπτης (eyewitness) and the partial concept θεία (divine), the terms are all present in Paul. What is more, they occur in one to six additional New Testament writings, not including 2 Peter. The list Schnelle gives is therefore absolutely unworkable as a basis for demonstrating that the author of 2 Peter cannot have been Peter but could only have been a Hellenistic Christian of the second century.

If one is not prematurely swayed by unfounded claims but rather puts adduced material to the test, it turns out that none of the word lists of typical terms whose occurrence is supposed to speak against the authenticity of New Testament writings succeeds in fulfilling its function. None of them stands up to careful scrutiny; most are mini-lists without statistical significance.

3. Word lists of typical terms whose absence speaks against authenticity

These lists are not so common as those mentioned in the previous section. Essentially they restrict themselves to the Pastoral Letters and Colossians.

I have already dealt with these sorts of lists dealing with the Pastoral Epistles in the preceding chapter, where I determined that none of them can be taken seriously as evidence against the genuineness of these letters.

Schnelle adduces a list containing central Pauline concepts that are not found in Colossians.[13] (See List 4 on p. 162 below.) These are only thirteen in number. One is not told how high the total number of "central Pauline concepts" is nor how many of them are actually present in Colossians. So the only way to assess the list is with respect to the vocabulary of Colossians, and in comparison to the epistle's 432 words, the words listed amount to only 3.01%, a quantity of no significance. Of these thirteen Pauline theological concepts, which were chosen according to the criterion that they are not present in Colossians, twelve are absent from Philemon. Using some other selection of concepts— e.g., if the words χάρις (grace), ἔργον (work), or οἰκονομία (management) had been included in the selection of concepts—one would have arrived at far more than 13 central Pauline ideas lacking in Philemon, whose genuineness no one doubts. Ten of the words do not occur in 1 Thessalonians, a number which could easily be brought up to 13 with another selection of concepts. Yet 1 Thessalonians has never fallen under suspicion of being a pseudepigraph. The lack of some quantity of central Pauline concepts is, then, not the compelling *basis* that necessitates seeing Colossians as pseudepigraphic. It is rather a far-fetched *argument* used to declare a writing to be inauthentic when acceptance of that letter, for whatever reasons, is not an option.

4. Lists of stylistic distinctives whose absence or presence speaks against authenticity

Regarding the Pastoral Epistles, noteworthy are Harrison's lists of "Pauline Particles, Prepositions, Pronouns etc." I already examined these in the previous chapter. The result was that out of a minimal list of core Pauline words—assuming one occurrence of each word in each letter for the sake of argument—only 30.62% are present. This means that Harrison's long list is highly misleading. It is unsuited to count as evidence against the authenticity of the Pastoral Epistles.

Things are no better when it comes to the alleged "frequently encountered Pauline connectives and inferential particles" lacking in Colossians.[14] (See List 5 on p. 162 below.) These come to six and four respectively, for a total of ten words or expressions in all, 2.35% of the vocabulary of Colossians. Of these ten, only one is found in all the Pauline letters except for Colossians, and only one more in all of Paul's letters held to be genuine. Two are lacking in one of the genuine Pauline letters, 1 in two, 3 in three, and 2 in four of these seven letters. To put it another way, while Romans lacks none of the expressions, 1 Corinthians lacks three, 2 Corinthians two, Galatians and 1 Thessalonians three, Philippians four, and Philemon six of this list of ten!

In addition, the list is drawn up arbitrarily, purely according to the viewpoint that the particles listed are lacking in Colossians. If the allegedly scientific historical-critical theology worked in a truly scientific manner, the use of particles in the Pauline letters generally would first have been determined, and then in this framework the usage in Colossians assessed.

In order to redo at least partially the rudimentary spadework that historical-critical theology has muffed, I use Harrison's list of particles, prepositions, pronouns, etc., that are absent from the Pastorals. I wish I had a complete list including the seventy-seven that are present, but such a list is not accessible to me.

If the absence of particles, etc., counts as proof against authenticity, as Schnelle asserts with respect to Colossians, then as already pointed out everyone who wishes to work with scientific rigor should first produce and state objectively the number of lacking particles for each individual Pauline letter, calculating these as a percentage of total vocabulary in that letter. Those Pauline letters in which the fewest are lacking (again, calculated as a percentage of total vocabulary in that letter) would accordingly have to be the most authentic. If one assesses the Pauline letters by this criterion, it turns out that 1 Corinthians, Romans, 2 Corinthians, and Galatians occupy the first four slots, as one would expect. (See List 6 on p. 163 below.) But in such a list Ephesians would be more genuine than Philippians, and 1 Timothy and Colossians more genuine than 1 Thessalonians. Not only 2 Thessalonians—which by the way stands just behind 1 Thessalonians in this reckoning—but also Titus and 2 Timothy would be genuine by a much greater margin than Philemon, accepted on all hands as authentic! This shows what absurd outcomes result when this sort of arbitrary stylistic analysis is subjected to careful scrutiny. As long as one picks out criteria in subjective fashion, each as necessary to prove the argument, one ends up with suggestive claims subject to misuse. As soon as the stylistic distinctives are objectively grasped, however, and scientifically investigated, they no longer furnish an argument in questions of authenticity.

To seize on accidental characteristics is not scientific procedure. It is true that Colossians contains not even one interrogative sentence, but in the whole of Philippians there is only one question mark.

"Like Colossians, Ephesians shows a preference for inordinately long sentences (cf. Eph. 1:3–14) and the piling up of synonymous words (cf. Eph. 1:19; 6:10)."[15] Once more the observation of characteristics in a letter suspected of being inauthentic is made into an argument too hastily, without asking whether that characteristic actually occurs only in that writing.

If one proceeded in a scientific fashion, one would first establish objectively the sentence length in the deutero-Paulines and then in the proto-Paulines and how the frequencies are distributed. Just a cursory comparison using a few casually selected excerpts shows that sentence lengths similar to those of Colossians and Ephesians also occur in the Pauline letters held to be authentic:

Ephesians			**Romans**		
1:3–5	=	66 words	2:5–8	=	55 words
1:7–10	=	66 words	2:9–11	=	38 words
1:11–12	=	30 words	2:12–13	=	29 words
1:13–14	=	40 words	2:14–16	=	60 words

Cf. however also Rom. 3:22b–26 = 74 words; Rom. 4:4–8 = 62 words; 1 Cor. 15:3–8 = 70 words.

When the allegedly scientific results of historical-critical theology are tested, they turn out to be unfounded claims that have been made into an argument for whatever issue is at hand. That is no scientific procedure; it is rather how a witch trial is conducted.

Whether in the case of Eph. 1:19 and 6:10 we are truly dealing with the piling up of words that actually have the same meaning (as alleged in Schnelle's quote above) is a matter that would first have to be shown lexically. Just a cursory check of casually chosen passages like Rom. 2:4 and 2:7–10; 11:29; or 11:33–36 shows that similar piling up also occurs in the proto-Paulines. Such passages could be multiplied. Scientific procedure would be to put forward in its entirety the occurrence of such formulations in all Pauline letters and only then, within that context, to take stock of possible striking features in individual Pauline letters—if there are any. In historical-critical theology, however, striking features are sought—in a priori fashion—only in certain letters, and for that reason are found only there. Then, for any reasons whatsoever, they are declared to be inauthentic. A double standard is applied, and only in this way are the desired results achieved. If we investigated all New Testament writings using the same criteria, as one would expect in scientific work, then there would be no arguments left to declare these writings inauthentic.

B. Literary dependence

This section must run somewhat longer than the previous one, because in it I must bring to bear my own investigations to a much larger extent. Please forgive the lack of symmetry in length.

It is necessary to place the investigation of literary dependence on a solid methodological foundation. This foundation has been worked out in my book *Gibt es ein synoptisches Problem?* and applied in the first chapter of the present book in a study of Q. But this foundation is not yet commonly accepted, and in connection with the question of pseudepigraphs is used here for the first time.

With the help of the claim of literary dependence, historical-critical theology has declared some New Testament letters to be inauthentic. They are characterized as pseudepigraphs, writings whose titles (which give their authors' alleged names) are a lie and have no right to be called letters of Paul or Peter, of Jude or James. God's Word, the Word of Truth, is charged with falsehood.

1. The Epistle to the Ephesians

The fourth of five reasons given by Schnelle why Ephesians is declared inauthentic runs, "Ephesians obviously used Colossians as its literary source."[16] Schnelle continues:

> This is verified by the numerous agreements between both letters.
> 1) Points of contact in macrostructure . . .
> 2) Points of contact in language and theme . . .
> 3) Agreements in shorter turns of phrase . . .
> 4) Agreements in terminology when there is intellectual difference. . . .[17]

Do these sorts of arguments show literary dependence? Let us look at each of Schnelle's points individually.

With respect to the first argument, Schnelle cites "the partitioning into two sections, a doctrinal and a paranetic," along with "agreements" "right down to prescript and postscript." That is no argument for literary dependence but simply indicates that Ephesians, like Colossians, is shaped according to the same schema as all the Pauline letters—a schema that corresponds to the formula of ancient private letters, as Roller showed decades ago (which Schnelle is aware of; see pp. 53–58 of his *Einleitung*; English edition pp. 35–40).

When in the postscript of both letters Tychichus is named as the courier who is to explain more fully Paul's situation to both the Ephesians and the Colossians, this is no evidence for literary dependence. It rather shows the historical state of affairs: both letters were relayed to Asia Minor via the same messenger. From this may be inferred that they were composed at the same time and in the same situation, which explains a number of similarities both in content and construction as well as in mode of formulation. Anyone who has ever been in the position of sending letters to various addressees at the same time, such as messages from the mission field, is familiar with this phenomenon: the second letter is not copied from the first, yet the second contains (more or less) the same thing, whatever lies on the writer's heart just at that time. Stereotypical formulations are not apt to be absent, and the same turns of phrase recur, although there are naturally also differences in the letters, appropriate to the particular recipients. The same phenomenon occurs with postcards sent while on vacation. That should be borne in mind in assessing the following argument by Schnelle: "The structure of Eph. 5:19–6:9 / Col. 3:16–4:1 is striking: following the similar directions for worship (Eph. 5:19f. / Col. 3:16f.) are the respective household codes."[18]

Comparable construction of sections falls short of being proof of literary dependence. It is rather no more than the presupposition for being able to show identical words in parallel verses, which is the actual proof for it—assuming that their frequency falls significantly outside the levels of the ordinary. The number of these identical words, however, amounts to no more than 59—which is 16.16% of the 365 words in the Ephesians section and 35.33% of the 167 words in the Colossians section. That is very far from being evidence of literary dependence. In addition, along with the similarities the differences must also be noted; these are considerable, even in the paragraphs which contain the greatest number of identical words: Eph. 6:5–8/ Col. 3:22–4:1 have 24 identical words. That is 40.68% of the 59 words of the Ephesians section, 43.64% of the 55 words in the Colossians section. But the 60 differences run to 101.70% in Ephesians and 109.09% in Colossians. This sort of numeric data does not prove literary dependence.

With respect to Schnelle's second argument ("points of contact in language and theme"), the nine parallel passages adduced are actually only eight, for Eph. 3:3–5 is contained in 3:1–13, and Col. 1:26 in 1:23–28. Of these eight, four cannot really count as parallels, because they stand in entirely different places in the letters being compared. In one case Schnelle goes so far as to claim two verses as parallels which are found in two different chapters and separated from each other by eleven verses. Below I give, however, the number of the identical words in these eight passages and the total number of words they contain—whether they are parallel or not.

Eph. 1:6f. / Col. 1:13f.:	8	identical words, Ephesians 31/ Colossians 27 words
Eph. 1:10 / Col. 1:20:	10	identical words, Ephesians 23/ Colossians 27 words
Eph. 1:13 / Col. 1:5:	0	identical words, Ephesians 25/ Colossians 18 words
Eph. 1:15f. / Col. 1:3f.:	12	identical words, Ephesians 31/ Colossians 29 words
Eph. 1:20 / Col. 2:12; 3:1:	5	identical words, Ephesians 17/ Colossians 38 words
Eph. 2:1–6 / Col. 2:12f.:	9	identical words, Ephesians 103/ Colossians 42 words[19]
Eph. 3:1–13 / Col. 1:23–28:	11	identical words, Ephesians 202/ Colossians 140 words
Eph. 4:22–24 / Col. 3:9f.:	5	identical words, Ephesians 38/ Colossians 25 words

We see, then, that 60 identical words are found, out of 470 words in Ephesians and 346 words in Colossians, or 12.77% and 17.34%, respectively. This negligible number of identical words cannot bear the burden of proof for literary dependence. And this is to say nothing of the numerous differences between the passages, which would cast even more doubt on literary dependence.

"It is also worthy of notice that in the ethical section comparable virtues . . . and vices appear."[20] The virtues listed in Eph. 4:2f. are introduced with the words "live a life worthy of the calling you have received." In Col. 3:12, however, we read, "Therefore, as God's chosen people, holy and dearly loved, clothe yourselves. . . ." In Ephesians the verses containing the virtues, 4:2f. and 4:32, are separated by twenty-seven verses; in Col. 3:12–14 the virtues are all listed together. That does not suggest literary dependence. The eight virtues cited in Ephesians stand in contrast with six in Colossians, and only two in each are completely identical. Two more are the same in terms of the main concept, but they are not identical in syntactic particulars. Such numeric proportions are not evidence of literary dependence.

Things are no better with respect to the catalogs of vices. Schnelle's assignment of Col. 3:1 as parallel to Eph. 4:19 must be an error; he probably means Col. 3:5. The connection is again varied. Ephesians 4:19 says, "[The Gentiles] have given themselves over to sensuality," while Col. 3:5 runs, "Put to death, therefore, whatever belongs to your earthly nature." Ephesians 4:31 stands in the context of the admonition of 4:30: "And do not grieve the Holy Spirit"; Col. 3:8 says, "But now you must rid yourselves of all such things." Due to the different introductions, these verses may have a few words with the same linguistic roots, but none of the words is identical. In addition, the sequence in which things are expressed is only partially the same in both passages. One will seek in vain here proof of literary dependence.

Regarding Schnelle's third argument above (agreements in smaller turns of phrase), close scrutiny once again produces meager results. The context in which ἀμώμους κατενώπιον αὐτοῦ ("blameless before him") appears (Eph. 1:4) is different from the context in Col. 1:22; incidentally, ἀμώμους (blameless) is also found in Phil. 2:15. Πλοῦτος τῆς δόξης (riches of glory) is found not only in Ephesians and Colossians but also in Rom. 9:23. Πλοῦτος (riches) is found some 15 times in the canonical Pauline corpus, δόξα (glory) no fewer than 77 times. "The formulations with 'the powers'" of which Schnelle tries to make much also prove little. Only three of the five concepts in Eph. 1:21 and of the four in Col. 1:16 share the same root; none is identical, nor does the sequence in which they are mentioned match. The sentences in which they occur are not parallel from the standpoint of content. The theme of circumcision does not make Eph. 2:11 and Col. 2:11 parallel verses, for they are materially quite different, and their one shared identical word doesn't change that fact. Innumerable treatises can be written on the same theme, but that does not make them literarily dependent on each other.

Regarding Schnelle's final argument (agreements in terminology with intellectual differences), this does not speak for but against literary dependence. It is not normal for someone using a writing as a source not to take up the ideas that he finds there as they are given but to impart to them a different sense. The author of an original writing, on the other hand, can exploit the spectrum of meaning of a word and use it—corresponding to his communicative intention—variously in different writings. He can also connect a formal concept with different expressions.

None of the four reasons brought forward for assuming Ephesians' literary dependence on Colossians stand up to scrutiny. Historical-critical theology therefore sees itself obligated once again to summon up a bit of fantasy in order to bring the findings in line with the hypothesis: "The author of Ephesians did not use Colossians schematically. He rather took up only those ideas that were of use to him given his concerns."[21] As long as no proof of literary dependence is adduced, as long as it is by no means demonstrated *that* the writer of Ephesians had a copy of Colossians before him as he wrote, it is a futile enterprise to speculate *how* he could have used it. The use of a source such as Schnelle envisions may appear plausible to a modern theologian but does not do justice to the historical situation. In any case frivolous fantasy cannot replace the still-lacking proof for the literary dependence of Ephesians on Colossians. And it only partially conceals the nakedness of the argumentation advanced. There is really no way you can call this procedure scientific.

2. Second Thessalonians

Regarding 2 Thessalonians Schnelle states,

> The literary dependence of 2 Thess. on 1 Thess. is and remains a chief argument for the pseudepigraphic character of 2 Thess.[22]

> First Thess. served as the literary basis for 2 Thess. This can be seen both from the parallels in construction of the two letters as well as in the repeated agreements in wording.[23]

The claimed agreements in construction are essentially the same as the basic layout of the Pauline letters: prescript; proem (preface), which in keeping with convention contains the thanksgiving; a first, theological and a second, paranetic main section; and the epistolary closing.

Inconsistently, Schnelle lets the designation "first expression of thanks" follow the term "prescript" instead of the proem (preface). He alleges parallels as follows.

- "First expression of thanks":
  1 Th 1:2f. with 2 Th 1:3: 41/26 words, 5 of them identical—as an expression of thanks formally parallel
  1 Th 1:6f. with 2 Th 1:4: 32/27 words, 3 of them identical (2 of these καί ["and"])—as basis of the expression of thanks formally parallel. But 1 Th 1:5 is suppressed.
  1 Th 1:2, 3, 4 with 2 Th 1:11: In order to produce a parallel with 2 Th 2:11, the same verses—this time in the form of pieces of a puzzle—are used again. Even then with 50/25 words, only 2 are identical, of which one was already counted in the first pair of comparisons. The verses 2 Th 1:5–10 are suppressed!
  Such a procedure cannot be termed scientific. No proof for literary dependence can be arrived at using this sort of manipulation.

- "Second expression of thanks":
  As for 1 Thess. 2:13 / 2 Thess. 2:13, this may be said: formally these parallels are worthy of attention. But the content is dissimilar: the basis

for thanks is different in each passage. In addition there are only two identical words out of 34 and 27 words in each passage, respectively, and the number of differences between the two comes to 57. What is more, the value of the formal parallels is lessened in that there are three expressions of thanks in 1 Thessalonians in contrast to the two in 2 Thessalonians—a third is found in 1 Thess. 3:9. The alleged agreement in construction is considerably jeopardized by this.

- "Transition to paranesis":
Also in 1 Thess. 3:11, 13 / 2 Thess. 2:16, 17, the agreement in construction leaves much to be desired. The paranesis does follow immediately after 1 Thess. 3:11, but it does not appear until five verses after 2 Thess. 2:16–17. It is therefore incorrect to designate the passage as "transition to paranesis." In terms of content, the allegedly parallel passages do not agree anyway, not even if one follows Schnelle in disregarding 1 Thess. 3:12. Much less can there be any talk here of correspondence in actual wording.

- "Request and admonition":
1 Thess. 4:1 / 2 Thess. 3:1
1 Thess. 4:1 / 2 Thess. 3:6
1 Thess. 4:10–12 / 2 Thess. 3:10–12

What a peculiar "agreement in construction" it is when 1 Thess. 4:1 must be used twice as a parallel, even though it has not the least bit in common with 2 Thess. 3:1 and agrees with 2 Thess. 3:6 only insofar as that in one case Paul admonishes, while in the other he makes a request. But this means the content is different!

What a peculiar "agreement in construction" it is when in 1 Thess. 4, verses 2–9 and in 2 Thess. 3, verses 2–5 and 7–9 must be suppressed, so that at least by this means an impression of some degree of parallelism may be created.

- "Disorderly persons in the congregation":
Regarding 1 Thess. 5:14 / 2 Thess. 3:6, 7, 11, the admonition to "warn those who are idle" is rightly seen as somewhat parallel to the

command "to keep away from every brother who is idle," although the content of the verses is not identical and the command is stronger than the admonition. Yet an "agreement in construction" is not present, since 2 Thess. 3:6 was already made use of in the preceding paragraph. The same goes for 2 Thess. 3:11, which is likewise contained in 2 Thess. 3:10–12 (see preceding paragraph). In spite of not being expressly cited, 2 Thess. 3:7 may not be cut out of 3:6–12 arbitrarily. Second Thess. 3:6–12 would then have belonged under the heading "Disorderly persons in the congregation," just like 1 Thess. 4:10–12. But then the paragraph "Request and admonition" would have become invalid and the alleged "agreements in construction" even more meager. In order to avoid this impression, the sleight-of-hand is used of cashing in on the same verse twice. That is not scientific!

Regarding remaining possible instances of agreement in construction, there is no need to explain them as "happenstances." They are rather the result of the formula common to the Pauline letters, which lies at the base of both epistles. They also result from the thematic commonality due to the continued presence of a problem in the congregation. The occurrence of more than one thanksgiving in both letters is more a coincidental phenomenon than a formal similarity in construction. In any case the entirety of the Pauline letters would first have to be investigated to see if none of them contains a second expression of thanks outside the proem (preface). Only then might it be possible to draw a conclusion from this fact in the Thessalonian epistles.

As a second proof of the literary dependence of 2 Thessalonians on 1 Thessalonians, agreements in wording are cited: "As examples, three central text complexes should demonstrate the relation of dependence."[24] However, the only text complexes one finds is the one promised in Schnelle's headings, under which one finds only individual verses. They are picked out like raisins from a cake because they contain formulations with the same wording. Schnelle doesn't bother with even a surface investigation of the literal agreement in both letters, which would be the sole adequate proof for literary dependence. Instead he contents himself with insinuating that the three text-complexes have exemplarily demonstrated literary dependence, and that therefore the same dependence is found in other texts, which is by no means the case. But that's how scientific "scientific" theology is. Even the verses he provides furnish no evidences for literary dependence.

First Thess. 1:1 / 2 Thess. 1:1, 2: The word count in the verses is 19 and 28, respectively, and the number of identical words comes to 18. This is noteworthy. Yet these verses are no evidence of literary dependence. The fact that the author and recipients as well as the co-senders are the same in both passages could all be due to historical rather than literary factors. Παῦλος (Paul) without apposition is also found in Phil. 1:1; τῇ ἐκκλησίᾳ (the church) likewise in 1 Cor. 1:2 and 2 Cor. 1:1, just as the plural ταῖς ἐκκλησίαις in Gal. 1:2. It is not necessary to trace these agreements back to the literary dependence of 2 Thess. on 1 Thess. The agreement in the formula ἐν θεῷ πατρὶ καὶ κυρίῳ Ἰησοῦ Χριστῷ ("through God the Father and the Lord Jesus Christ") is striking, but it depends on a disputable text-critical decision. In ℵ, A, (D), and 𝔐, it begins in 1 Thess. 1:1 not with ἐν but with ἀπό, which (because of the change in case) does away with the identity between six of the seven words. The text read in Nestle-Aland[27] is found, in addition to B, only in three manuscripts of the 9th or 10th century! The last four common words, χάρις ὑμῖν καὶ εἰρήνη ("grace and peace be with you"), stand in just the same form in Rom. 1:7; 1 Cor. 1:3; 2 Cor. 1:2; Gal. 1:3; Eph. 1:2; Phil. 1:2; Col. 1:2; and Philem. 1:3. They should be regarded as belonging to the common stock of Pauline material.

First Thess. 3:11 / 2 Thess. 2:16 contain 18 and 25 words, respectively. Eleven of them are identical, but they receive different placement, and the number of differences comes to 21. The same (though differently placed) words of an ordinary Pauline designation for God in these verses with differing content are no proof of literary dependence.

First Thess. 5:23 / 2 Thess. 3:16 contain 30 and 20 words, respectively, of which 5 are identical. The number of differences comes to 40. Expressed in percentage, 16.67% and 25% of the words in each passage are identical, while the percentage difference comes to 133.33% and 200%! The formula ὁ θεὸς τῆς εἰρήνης ("the God of peace") is found also in Rom. 15:33; 16:20; 2 Cor. 13:11 (expanded);

and Phil. 4:9. Ὁ κύριος τῆς εἰρήνης ("the Lord of peace"), however, is found only in 2 Thess. 3:16. In the common formulation of six words, the chief idea is not identical, and in addition this customary Pauline expression occurs in sentences with contrasting content. This is surely no evidence of literary dependence.

First Thess. 5:28 / 2 Thess. 3:18 contain 9 and 10 words, respectively, of which seven are identical. Since this formula occurs again in almost all Pauline letters, the occurrence in 1 and 2 Thess. is no proof of literary dependence.

Neither the agreements in construction nor the agreements in wording are sound evidences for the literary dependence of 2 Thess. on 1 Thess. This weakness is not hidden by ascribing to the author of 2 Thess. "selective acceptance of individual themes." As long as no comprehensive comparison shows the literary dependence of 2 Thess. on 1 Thess., and as long as even the comparison of handpicked "parallel verses" also do not make the point, it is a futile game to vent opinions on how 2 Thess. used 1 Thess.

The data in 2 Thess. can be thoroughly explained without the acceptance of literary dependence:

- The common formulations are found elsewhere in the linguistic usage of the same author.
- The same epistolary formula used by the author here as well as elsewhere leads to similar expressions.
- Continuance of the same intention in writing in the second letter to the same congregation leads to expressions with similar content, which can result in identical formulations.
- Continuance of the same states of affairs in the congregation leads to expressions with similar content, which can result in identical formulations and more besides.

3. Second Peter

With the help of the idea of literary dependence, the genuineness of 2 Peter is also disputed. Schnelle states, "Second Peter claims to be the testament of the apostle Peter. What speaks against the historicity of his authorship is chiefly three observations."[25] The first, and probably also the most important is: "Second Peter incorporates Jude almost completely. . . . Such a procedure rules out the apostle Peter on material and chronological grounds."[26]

"Second Peter incorporates Jude almost completely." That is asserted as fact; but is it really? What can be objectively established is correctly relayed by Schnelle: "Close points of contact exist between 2 Peter and Jude."[27] Nevertheless, he then renders the premature verdict, "Obviously Jude was integrated almost completely into 2 Peter."[28] With the lofty assertion "obviously" the reader is manipulated; it is insinuated that what Schnelle says requires no proof. But what he says contains several unsupported claims:

1. Jude is older than 2 Peter. No proof of this is given; in fact, Schnelle had earlier stated, "Second Peter's provenance and time of writing is nothing more than guesswork."[29] Yet this notion is made the basis for the subsequent claim that Peter could not have written 2 Peter on chronological grounds!

2. Jude is integrated into 2 Peter. That is not self-evident; the opposite conclusion is likewise possible.

3. The integration as such—namely, that literary dependence is a given—is an unproven claim. For just saying there are "close points of contact" falls short of being proof of the statement.

From this statement, formulated as a grounded claim and containing several unproven assertions, Schnelle arrives at "the studied use of Jude by 2 Peter . . . as a literary-critical hypothesis."[30] What a solid foundation such a historical-critical hypothesis has: An assertion suffices that must be based on three additional, easily shaken assertions, the whole thing serving as foundation for the momentous decision that 2 Peter is literarily dependent on Jude and can therefore only be regarded as pseudepigraphic.

But what about the "close points of contact" between Jude and 2 Peter? What is the nature of the list of parallels Schnelle offers, and what inferences can be drawn from it?

1. The parallels are plucked out of both Jude and 2 Peter quite arbitrarily:

> The paragraph begins in Jude not with verse 2 but verse 3; it also does not end with verse 18 but with verse 19. The break after 2 Peter 2:18 tears apart a single sentence which does not conclude until 2:19. A gap of five verses exists between 2:18 and 3:2! Even more adventurously, 1:12 is given as a parallel between 2:3 and 2:4. The contacts between Jude 2 and 2 Peter 1:2 exist because these verses belong to their respective prescripts and therefore quite naturally contain similarities in both form and content.

2. Arbitrary exclusion of verses:

> Verses 3, 5b, 14, and 15 are left out of the section comprising Jude 2–18.
> Verses 5, 7–9, 14, and 16 are left out of the section comprising 2 Peter 2:1–18.

3. Arbitrary assignment of verses from other chapters: 2 Peter 1:2 and 1:12; 3:2 and 3:3.

4. Double use of verses: Jude 12 is assigned two parallels, both 2 Peter 2:13 and 2:17.

5. Assignment of several verses to one parallel verses: 2 Peter 2:1–3 to Jude 4; 2 Peter 2: 6, 10a to Jude 7.

6. Arbitrary rearrangement of verses: 2 Peter 2:13 is placed after 2:15.

Only with the help of these manifold manipulations can the parallels between 2 Peter and Jude be constructed. But the result is not satisfactory. In spite of points of contact at the level of content and occasionally also at the linguistic level, almost none of the verses claimed as parallels actually are. For in addition to differences in content and language, they do not occur in the same order.

Even if one sets those objections aside and focuses on the identical words in these verses, the result is meager: In the parallel sections, cobbled together with so much effort, the parallel verses contain only 53 identical words. That is 18.15% of the 292 words in the Jude excerpt and 19.56% of the 271 words in the 2 Peter excerpt. Even if the manipulated text is accepted, the result is no evidence for literary dependence.

This "literary-critical hypothesis" is dependent on a welter of supplementary hypotheses that must explain why the data look different than the hypothesis would cause one to expect, why Jude's formulations are not actually found in 2 Peter. A number of activities are ascribed to the author of 2 Peter: He "tightens up the material," "inserts it corresponding to the situation," "does not . . . take up," "does not . . . make use of," "leaves . . . out, because. . . ."[31]

How does one know that the author did all this? Has he left statements somewhere to this effect? By no means. That the author performed these activities, even permitting insight into his motivations, is pure fantasy, fiction and not facts! The facts, the text of Jude and the text of 2 Peter, speak against the literary-critical hypothesis. In order to bring the hypothesis at least somewhat into conformity with the facts, it is claimed that the material in 2 Peter that is different from Jude was altered by the author of 2 Peter. Instead of perceiving that the hypothesis is unworkable on the basis of the evidence and yielding the floor to views that do the evidence more justice, our vision is clouded by the invention of statements. Thinking up for oneself how things could have been once upon a time is not an art but child's play. If at the end the results of such fantasy games are still regarded as facts, that has absolutely nothing to do with science. Proof of literary dependence is not yet produced by referring to similarities in content, nor by the presence of a few similar formulations—not even if these contain a few words sharing common roots. Literary dependence can only be demonstrated on the basis of a high percentage of identical words in parallel verses.

C. Historical placement

1. The Epistle to the Ephesians

> The list of offices in Eph. 4:11f. refers to a congregational struc-
> ture that stands in stark contrast to that familiar to Paul.[32]

The slight differences between Eph. 4:11 and 1 Cor. 12:28 are said to prove this point. In Ephesians evangelists and pastors are mentioned, in addition to apostles, prophets, and teachers, and the concept *teacher* shifts from third to fifth place. True, evangelists are not mentioned by Paul elsewhere, but that is hardly a new development, for Philip was already designated by that title (Acts 21:8). Pastors (literally "shepherds," ποιμένας), are found only here in Paul, but their absence elsewhere does not justify the conclusion that this function cannot have existed at the time of Paul.

> Ephesians lacks charismatic offices, e.g., miracle workers, healers,
> and speaking in tongues. Ephesians presupposes official offices. . . .[33]

"Charismatic offices" is an oxymoron: spiritual gifts were not offices. The connection between offices and grace gifts is furnished in 1 Cor. 12 by the context: there are different grace gifts (1 Cor. 12:4), and the members of Christ's body have various functions in the body (12:27–30). It is absurd to posit a different understanding of the church offices just because spiritual gifts are not mentioned in Ephesians. If an author mentions spiritual gifts together with offices in one case, that does not justify the assumption that he always does so. No one would do the same thing with the other Pauline letters in which they are also not mentioned, such as 2 Corinthians, Galatians, Philippians, and Philemon. Such unequal handling is not a scientific procedure but that of a witch trial: the laws are rigged for the person who is to be condemned.

> Ephesians 1:15; 3:2 [give rise to] the impression that apostle and
> congregation did not know each other.[34]

It is true that 1:15 could be written to a congregation that did not know the letter writer personally, but that does not necessarily have to be the case. He could just as easily be referring to a recent report about the faith of a congregation that he knows from earlier association. Ephesians 3:2 is not evidence that the author of the letter did not know the congregation; εἴ γε no more introduces a question here than it does in 2 Cor. 5:3 or Gal. 4:3. In addition, it is announced to the Ephesians in 6:21 that Tychicus will pass along to them information about the apostle's personal circumstances.

> Moreover, the entire document conveys a very impersonal impression; thus, e.g., Ephesians contains no personal greetings to members of the congregation.[35]

That the document makes an impersonal impression is a subjective statement that cannot be verified. It is not proven by the absence of a personal greeting to members of the congregation; this does distinguish Ephesians from Romans and 2 Timothy but not from the other Pauline letters. If that were a proof of inauthenticity, then both the Corinthian letters along with Galatians and Philippians would have to be declared inauthentic!

> Finally, the stated destination . . . cannot be regarded as original.[36]

That the name "Ephesians" is lacking in a few very ancient manuscripts (p[46], ℵ*, B*) is offset to a considerable extent by that fact that it is found in others (ℵ, A, B[2], among others). Not only that: there is the testimony of the church fathers, which predates the oldest of the manuscripts just cited. The omission of the recipients is not necessarily to be traced to the fact that the scribe of p[46] did not find it in the copy he used; it is just as possible that he was uncertain because this letter was called by Marcion the Epistle to the Laodiceans, and so he wanted to leave the question of the recipients' name open for the time being. The omission was perhaps never corrected and could then have found followers in other manuscripts. Of course that is only speculation, but it shows that the conclusion, based on the manuscript evidence, that the stated destination is inauthentic, is not unalterable. The attempt to use historical placement as a means of stigmatizing Ephesians as pseudepigraphic must be regarded as wrong-headed. There can be no talk here of a "scientific result."

2. The Pastoral Epistles

> The situation presupposed in the [Pastoral] Letters cannot be squared with either the testimony of Acts or that of the proto-Pauline epistles.[37]

If Schnelle had given due attention to Jakob van Bruggen's *Die geschichtliche Einordnung der Pastoralbriefe*, published already back in 1981, he could have known better than that.[38] I have here neither the space nor the desire to repeat van Bruggen's arguments but instead move on to Schnelle's next section.

> In the Pastorals are mirrored the problems of the third Christian generation. The ecclesiastical conception is further advanced than in Paul. The organizational structure is no longer that of the house church but of the local or village congregation, set up according to the model of the ancient household (cf. 1 Tim. 3:15; 2 Tim. 2:20f.; Titus 1:7).[39]

"No longer a house congregation but a local congregation." That is an assertion; will it stand up to careful scrutiny? House congregation can mean two things: either the congregation is composed only of the members of one household, or the congregation holds its meetings in a private home. In the latter case there need have existed no dichotomy between house congregation and local congregation, for the ancient household of a well-heeled citizen could likely hold more than one hundred persons in its atrium. However that may be, a difference from the time of Paul—the time of the first generation—is not detectable. Even then there was already the house congregation in the second sense, as 1 Cor. 11:20–22 makes clear: they were obviously not coming together in their own homes, for reference is made to the fact that they have their own houses where they can eat and drink before they assemble together. In addition, in those early years there was the possibility of gathering in a rented building (Acts 19:9). Distinguishing between house congregation and local congregation cannot be used as evidence for determining the time when the Pastorals were written. The verses that Schnelle cites do not work in serving his purpose. In 1 Tim. 3:15, the house of God is not a building but the fellowship of the living God, which is characterized as the pillar and foundation of the truth. Second Timothy 2:20 does not name an assembly point, neither a local congregation nor a house church; indeed, it does not even mention a house. The writer refers to the master of a house and to the devices that are in it, i.e., his own possessions. There is nothing here about congregational structure. The same goes for Titus 1:7, where the writer simply states qualifications for a bishop (ἐπίσκοπος).

> Bishops, presbyters, and deacons are placed into their offices permanently through the laying on of hands of other ecclesiastical authorities, and they have the right to financial support (cf. 1 Tim. 1:18; 3:1–7, 8–13; 4:14; 5:17–22; 2 Tim. 1:6; 2:1f.; Titus 1:5–9).[40]

The laying on of hands for installation into an office is not an indicator of the third Christian generation; it already took place in the earliest congregation (cf. Acts 6:6; 13:3). Moreover, 1 Tim. 4:14 and 2 Tim. 1:6 do not speak of installation into office via laying on of hands but of the passing on of a spiritual gift. Which spiritual gift he has in mind is not stated. The gift abides in Timothy; he should not neglect it; he should remember to kindle it. These are statements that cannot be correlated with an office. In 1 Tim. 1:18, the present tense of παρατίθημι (entrust, pass along) rules out a reference back to an initiation into office that took place in former times. Paul was familiar with the right for financial support of those serving the congregations, although he made no use of this himself by his own decision (cf. 1 Cor. 9:14f.).

> The charismatic-functional congregational structure of Paul (cf. 1 Cor. 12:4–11, 28f.; Rom. 12:3–8) is replaced by a system of office holders. As leading persons they have public interests, and they

must conduct themselves accordingly (cf. 1 Tim. 3:7, 10; 5:8, 14; 6:11ff.; Titus 2:5, 8).[41]

There is no hint of any difference between a Pauline "functionally charismatic congregational structure" and a "system of office bearers" found in the Pastoral Epistles. When in both epistles Timothy is summoned not to neglect the grace gift that is in him (1 Tim. 4:14), but rather to kindle it (2 Tim. 1:6), that is quite in keeping with 1 Cor. 12:4–11, 28ff.; Rom. 12:3–8 and not in opposition to those passages! 1 Tim. 3:1–7, 8–13 as well as Titus 1:6–9 give no information about the congregation's organizational structure. They reveal only what the necessary qualifications are for someone to serve as overseer or deacon. Nothing is mentioned that Paul would not have expected as well from anyone whom he utilized in one of the congregations he founded. That goes also for the admonition to Timothy in 1 Tim. 6:11ff. First Timothy 5:8 speaks not of officeholders but of believers in general and particularly of young widows. Titus 2:5, 8 comprise respectively the conclusion of admonition to wives and to the young men. A "system of office bearers" is not discernible in this.

A threefold hierarchical gradation (ἐπίσκοποι, πρεσβύτεροι, διάκονοι) is not to be found in the Pastorals. In no passage are these three groups found together. In 1 Tim. 3:1–13, only overseers and deacons are mentioned. This juxtaposition is not a new development cropping up in the Pastorals for the first time; it is already found in Phil. 1:1. What is said in 1 Tim. 5:17–21 about the elders must relate to the same group described as overseers in 3:1–7. Otherwise we would have the curious situation that the elders should receive income and protection of their honor but the overseers should not.

Accordingly, the texts cited furnish no evidence that the Pastorals reflect a congregational structure that did not appear until the third Christian generation.

> Of foundational significance is the apostolic tradition of belief that appears as "sound doctrine" (cf. 1 Tim. 1:10). Office bearers confess allegiance to it at their installation in the presence of witnesses (cf. 1 Tim. 6:12f.; also 4:6).[42]

According to the context in which the term "sound doctrine" occurs in 1 Tim. 1:10, it is not a "tradition of belief," not a collection of doctrinal formulas that are traditionally passed along. It is rather the right understanding of the relation between law and gospel as opposed to that which the false teachers claim.

The good testimony before many witnesses (1 Tim. 6:12f.) has nothing to do with the installation of an office bearer, for installation is not the occasion of laying hold of eternal life. Rather, the reference here may be to baptism, in which indeed the belief of the heart is confessed with the mouth (cf. here Rom. 10:10, which expressly states, "With the mouth one confesses unto salvation").

First Timothy 4:6 speaks neither of installation into office nor of confession before many witnesses, and it certainly does not refer to the tradition of apostolic belief. This verse deals with how the office is to be conducted.

> Disputes with Judaism are no longer of importance; the deliberations are rather centered on the position of the Christian congregation within a non-Christian environment.[43]

Even if it were true that disputes with Judaism are not significant in the Pastorals, this would not permit assigning these letters to another epoch by means of the unjustified alteration of "not" to "no longer." In all fairness all one could infer is one piece of information about the congregation's situation at that present time. Schnelle's claim presupposes that in apostolic times *every* Gentile Christian congregation was in *constant* disputation with Judaism, and that in this era it was not possible to write a letter to a congregation or individual without going into this problem. Such an absurd notion is necessary if one is determined at all costs to ascribe the Pastorals to the third Christian generation.

One might note in passing that 1 Tim. 1:5–11 implies that the false teaching opposed there had a Jewish cast, for the false teachers make the claim to be *nomodidaskaloi* (teachers of the law).

> Christians must respect the government authorities and live quietly in piety and uprightness (cf. 1 Tim. 2:2).[44]

The verse cited calls for intercession for government leaders and makes clear that upon this depends the possibility of leading a peaceful and quiet life. It is no indicator of postapostolic times for Christians to be summoned to respect authorities; Paul had already made that obligatory in Rom. 13:1–7.

Now that I have sifted Schnelle's claims one by one, it is clear how groundless the judgment is that the Pastorals mirror "the problems of the third Christian generation." Not one of the numerous hypotheses adduced to support this judgment stands up to careful testing.

3. The Epistle of James

Primarily on the basis of historical placement, James the brother of Jesus is ruled out as the author of the Epistle of James. Although Schnelle must admit that there is some evidence for James being the author, he arrives at the conclusion:

> Yet weighty reasons speak against the Lord's brother being author of the Epistle of James. Central themes of a strict Jewish Christian theology, like circumcision, Sabbath, Israel, purity laws, and the temple play no role in the epistle. James is among the few New Testament writings in which neither Israel nor the Jews are expressly mentioned. The use made of Old Testament figures . . . and even references to the law . . . are kept very general and would be in place anywhere within earliest Christianity . . . the problem of Gentile vs. Jewish Christianity does not [appear] in James.[45]

This is a provocative assertion that does not stand up to scrutiny.
- The foundational convictions of the author are as a rule not the theme of an epistle. The theme is rather what the author sees as deficient in the readership, be it in terms of knowledge, understanding, or practice. Apart from some special cause no basis existed, even for a Jewish Christian writer, to fill his letter with the central themes of Jewish Christian theology.
- The Old Testament figures that appear in the New Testament are as a rule not the object with respect to whom something singular is passed along; it is rather presupposed that they are well known,

and they are adduced to support the argumentation in a particular respect.

- The incident at Antioch, in which indeed James himself was not a participant, lay in the past when the epistle was composed. In the meantime the apostolic council in Jerusalem had arrived at clarity in the question of Jewish and Gentile Christians.
- The word *Israel* is lacking not only in James but also in Colossians, 1 Thessalonians, 2 Thessalonians, 1 Timothy, 2 Timothy, Titus, Philemon, 1 Peter, 2 Peter, 1 John, 2 John, 3 John, and Jude. That comes to thirteen of the twenty-seven New Testament writings, which is not "few" but almost half of them (48.15%).
- The word Ἰουδαῖος is missing not only from James but also from Ephesians, Philippians, 2 Thessalonians, 1 Timothy, 2 Timothy, Titus, Philemon, Hebrews, 1 Peter, 2 Peter, 1 John, 2 John, 3 John, and Jude. That is fourteen of twenty-seven, or 51.85 percent, of the New Testament books. Is it right to call that number "few"?
- That James in his letter does not highlight himself as the Lord's brother or one of the three pillars is a sign of his modesty and no proof that he did not write this epistle.

Instead of producing proof for the assertion that the well-known Lord's brother of this name cannot be the author of the Epistle of James, historical-critical theology *invented* a brother of the Lord, James, who is regarded as not possibly being the author: *an incurable, narrow-minded Judaist, for whom there could be no other themes than circumcision, Sabbath, purity laws, and the temple, along with the conflict between Jewish and Gentile Christians. The words* Israel *or* Judah *fell constantly from his lips, and he conveyed "special" messages about Old Testament figures and the law* (historical-critical theology does not clarify here what distinguishes the "special" from that which is "very general and would be in place anywhere within earliest Christianity").

There are no biblical supports for such a James. He is neither the James of Acts nor the James of the epistle. He is not even identical with the image that emerges from Paul's references to his Judaistic opponents. Beyond this, what right does anyone have to associate James with those references, when Acts yields a completely different picture?

After historical-critical theology manufactured its own picture of the Lord's brother James—without consideration of the historical givens—it states that this picture, which shows him to be an incurable Judaist, does not correspond to the reality of the Epistle of James. Instead of correcting this false picture, it concludes that the Epistle of James cannot have been written by the Lord's brother of this name. That's how scientific "scientific theology" is!

4. First Peter

Schnelle writes:

> Decisive for our determination of the recipients' situation is the interpretation of the conflict situation presupposed in the exhortations about suffering. . . . Does it have to do with local repressions, or must we assume that more widespread operations against Christians were already underway? . . . A few passages in 1 Peter cannot be explained adequately as a reaction to social tensions. According to 1 Pet. 4:15f., Christians were condemned by courts . . . as murderers, thieves, or evildoers solely because they were Christians. A purifying fire is falling upon the Christians (cf. 1 Pet. 4:12); they should resist the devil, who prowls around the entire world inflicting the same suffering on all Christians (1 Pet. 5:8f.). Here the persecution clearly has a different perspective and quality; it involves more than local repressions. This points to the latter years of Domitian's reign.[46]

Three passages, each one or two verses in length, pieced together from two chapters, are claimed to bear the burden of proof for the historical placement of 1 Peter in the reign of Domitian. This excludes the apostle Peter as author. What is inferred from these verses does not at all agree with their clear, indubitable sense; it is rather read into them by means of a dubious interpretation:

- First Peter 4:15f. by no means contains a statement that Christians are being "condemned in courts as murderers, thieves, or evildoers." We read μὴ γάρ τις ὑμῶν πασχέτω ὡς ("For let none of you suffer as. . . ."). This passage is dealing with the reason for suffering: whether as a criminal deserving punishment or as a Christian who is "maligned in the name of Christ." The flow of thought is similar to that in 3:12–14. There too, those who suffer for the sake of righteousness are juxtaposed with those who (suffer because they) do evil (cf. 3:17). First Peter 4:15 does not say that being a Christian is "already punishable crime," and 4:14 speaks of being "maligned for Christ's sake," not of incarceration and martyrdom.

- First Peter 4:12 refers to "fire among *you*," not to a purifying fire that falls upon "the Christians" in their entirety. The verse offers no support for a general persecution of Christians.

- First Peter 5:8f. cannot bear the burden of proof placed upon it, either. The verses are not found in the context of 4:12–19, which deal with persecution; they rather follow the summons to cast all cares upon the Lord. It does not say there that the devil "prowls around the entire world inflicting the same suffering on all Christians." The addressees are called on to resist the devil, firm in faith, in the knowledge that the same sufferings—in the context, the attacks of Satan, the exact nature of which is not specified— are also befalling their brotherhood in the world. These sufferings are the attacks of Satan, according to the context, and their exact nature is not specified. The call in verse 7, to cast *all* care upon the Lord, forbids narrowing it down to persecution alone.

Accordingly, it is not necessary to date 1 Peter to the time of Domitian. It could have been written in Nero's time, during which, in addition to persecution in Rome kindled by the emperor, there could have been local persecutions elsewhere. The emperor's strategy of making Christians scapegoats could have found echoes in the provinces. The fact that extra-biblical sources are lacking to substantiate this is no reason to dismiss as lies the biblical sources we have. It must be taken into account that we cannot furnish documentary proof for

'hat took place in the Roman provinces. Historical
⸺ᴀᴋs in favor of the emperor's attitude toward Christians
⸺ıown in the provinces and having a ripple effect there on how
⸺ɪristians were treated.

5. Second Peter

"In 2 Pet. 3:4, the author betrays," according to Schnelle, "the fictional authorship that he himself created: the fathers have already passed away, so that now doubts about the parousia are springing up. Peter himself is one of these (deceased) fathers!"[47]

Has 2 Peter thus unveiled its own pseudepigraphical status? Absolutely not; rather, Schnelle has blown his own cover with argumentation that maintains as self-evident that which is not self-evident at all.

- Nowhere in the New Testament do the apostles bear the title "fathers."
- Second Peter 3:4 cannot be used to show that the deceased generation of "fathers" includes the apostles, only that those believers who belonged to that generation are dead. Since 3:3 comes before the statement of the mockers, it is not justified to relate the generation of the fathers to the apostles mentioned there. For these apostles are paired conceptually with the prophets and are not to be separated from them arbitrarily.
- Paul has already spoken in 1 Cor. 15:19, 29 and 1 Thess. 4:13–14 concerning believers who have passed away. According to the law of probability, these deceased ones would have been primarily those who were already older when they became believers and so did not belong to the younger but the "father" generation within the early church.

Nothing is to be said in favor of a "collection of Pauline letters presupposed in 2 Pet. 3:15f."[48] From these verses can be inferred that Peter knows of a series of Pauline epistles, among them a few in which Paul speaks "of these things." It does not say that he knew all of Paul's letters, nor that they lay before him in collected form. Like others we have seen, this argument of biblical criticism against the authenticity of 2 Peter is so much wind.

6. The Epistle of Jude

Against Jude's authorship are the following arguments: a) Why does he not directly designate himself to be Jesus' brother?[49]

The answer is obvious: he is mindful that Jesus is not only the son of Joseph and Mary but God's Son.

b) The term ἀδελφός [brother] has several meanings; in the New Testament it is often used in the sense of *coworker.*[50]

Where that is the case, ὁ ἀδελφός (the brother) stands in apposition to the named coworker and not in a genitival connection to the name of the person whose coworker he is. The usage in Jude 1 is precise; Schnelle's argument is far-fetched.

c) The concept of tradition in Jude 3 and 20, the dispute between orthodoxy and heresy, and the topos of the onset of false doctrines in the end times (cf. 1 Tim. 4:1–3; 2 Tim. 4:3f.; 1 John 2:18; 4:1–3; Didache 16:3) refer to the postapostolic era.[51]

The concept of tradition occurs repeatedly in Paul. To name just two passages: in 1 Cor. 11:2, Paul lauds the Corinthians "for holding to the traditions, just as I passed them on to you." In 15:2 he writes to them, "For I passed along to you first of all that which I also received." Disputation with false teachers takes place in practically all Pauline letters; to the extent that sound doctrine is set over against false, one can speak here precisely of the dispute between orthodoxy and heresy.

Whether the topos of the onset of false teachers in the end times refers to the postapostolic era stands or falls with a presupposition not explicitly stated here. It is this: that the epistles to Timothy as well as the Johannine letters and—the here unnamed—2 Thessalonians first arose at this time and that 2 Peter too was not written by the apostle. Declaring this list of writings as inauthentic is supposed to support the declaration of Jude as inauthentic—which is circular reasoning. Therefore this argument against the genuineness of the letter of Jude has no weight.

> d) With Jude 17f. the author locates himself in the late era of early Christianity, as looking back on the epoch of the apostles and the founding of the faith.[52]

When Jude states that the apostles have already foretold the onset of mockers (with respect to the return of Christ), he is not locating himself in another epoch. The fulfillment of such a prophecy does not assume the passing from the scene of the one who made it. But even if Jude was supposedly written after the death of Peter and Paul— which cannot be inferred from Jude 17f.—the document still does not belong in the postapostolic era. Mark 6:3 names Jude as the third brother of Jesus, after James and Joses, and sisters too are mentioned. Jude is accordingly some years younger than Jesus and can easily have outlived Peter and Paul, since they died as martyrs and not of natural causes. The death of Peter and Paul was not the end of the apostolic time. James the son of Zebedee did suffer martyrdom earlier than they did, but we have no knowledge of the dying off of the rest of the apostolate prior to this point in time.

None of the arguments brought forth by Schnelle against an authorship by the Lord's brother turns out to be convincing. His historical placement of Jude's letter is untenable.

D. Theological classification

With reference to a few Pauline letters—Ephesians, Colossians, 2 Thessalonians, and the three pastorals—"material-theological" differences are taken up as evidence of pseudonymity. Against this practice speak the following fundamental objections:

1. Various theological *contents* are no proof of various authors. It is normal for an author to treat different matters in various writings, and all the more in the case of shorter treatises, none of which can contain the richness of his thoughts. The Pauline letters, however, are— in spite of their weighty content—to be viewed as shorter writings.

The longest, Romans, comprises thirty-one pages in Nestle-Aland[27], the average length of a theological article. Galatians fills barely eleven pages, the normal length of a lecture. Philemon comes to two pages, very brief indeed. Of these pages in Nestle-Aland, about ten to twenty percent are filled with the critical apparatus. When a theme is broached in such short writings, we are not to suppose that Paul in that passage wrote everything he knew about the theme.

No one would propose the idea of inferring different authors for Romans and 2 Corinthians, or for Galatians and Philippians, based on the differences in content between them. To restrict that procedure to those writings singled out as pseudepigraphic, however, cannot be called scientific!

2. It is normal for an author to pass along new thoughts in a new book. Only persons with weak mental resources, or who are committed to the dissemination of a particular message, write the same thing decade after decade with little variation.

3. The material-theological breadth of one author can vary from writing to writing. It depends on the writing's extent of coverage, its temporal proximity or distance, and its recipients and their circumstances at the time. In view of these multiple factors that influence the material-theological formation of occasional writings, which epistles are, it is practically impossible to derive indicators regarding the authorship question from material-theological differences. Only in the case of unambiguous and highly pertinent discrepancies that have been worked out carefully in view of all an author's known writings would that be thinkable. I have not encountered that sort of painstaking care, however, in studying Schnelle's *Einleitung in das Neue Testament.*

4. The occurrence in so-called pseudepigraphical writings of formulations which are lacking in those letters held to be genuine, or the absence of formulations in the "pseudepigrapha" which can be documented as thematic in the "authentic writings," is no proof of different authors. Even if stereotypical formulations occur, no author always uses just the same words in speaking his mind on the same theme. That is readily recognizable from study of the seven Pauline letters whose genuineness is not disputed.

One cannot conclude that there are different authors on the basis of formulations that are one sentence—or half a sentence—in length and occur in one of the "genuine" letters but are lacking in some letter suspected of being inauthentic. Still less can the occurrence of an expression carrying a similar meaning—possibly even in a similar formulation—be explained away as pseudepigraphical imitation. That is not scientific method but circular reasoning: the pseudepigraphical character of the writing is already presupposed, even though that is precisely what is supposed to be proven. That is how witch trials are conducted: everything brought forward as evidence, even those charges that contradict, are utilized without exception against the accused. Unfortunately Schnelle's work often reflects this tendency.

If those writings whose genuineness was never doubted were subjected to the same procedure, they could not pass muster, either.

1. The Epistle to the Ephesians

The theology of Ephesians reveals significant differences from the proto-Paulines, and on the other hand substantial agreement with Colossians.[53]

The agreement with Colossians is readily explained by the fact that both were obviously written at the same time: both were carried to these congregations by Tychicus, who was to bring them up to date on Paul's circumstances (Eph. 6:21f.; Col. 4:7–9). It is a natural phenomenon for someone with heart and head full of freshly arrived-at insights to write more or less the same thing to different recipients. This results in both stereotypical formulations and considerable divergences in expression, since a process takes place in which the new insights are coupled with familiar ideas.

In its Christology, the idea of the cosmic lordship of Christ dominates.[54]

But the passages cited have proto-Pauline parallels: for Eph. 1:20, see Rom. 8:34; for Eph. 1:22a, see 1 Cor. 15:25–28. Admittedly, there is no parallel to Eph 1:23, although the term πλήρωμα (fullness) occurs repeatedly in the "genuine" Pauline letters. A singular expression, however, says nothing about pseudonymity. The proto-Paulines, too, contain singular expressions.

> As in Paul the church has its origin in the cross of Christ. . . . At the same time however, the Pauline conception of the church as the body of Christ in Paul is transformed in Ephesians, through the mediation of Colossians, into the spatial-static idea of Christ, the head, and the church, his body.[55]

"Spatial-static"—with this assertion aspersions are cast on Ephesians. How is it static if the writer speaks of the body and its head, but presumably dynamic if he speaks of another aspect of the same figure using the body and its members? The relation of the head to the body is everything but static: It "fills all in all," which therefore includes also the body (1:23). The body is built up (4:12); it is held together by the "joints of ministry" (4:15f.) and enjoys organic growth. As head of the fellowship, the body, Christ is Savior (5:23), and the believers are members of one body (5:30). Nothing "static" is to be seen here, much less "spatial."

> In keeping with the world view of Ephesians, an eschatology dominates that is mainly fixed on the present (cf. Eph. 2:5, 6, 8, 19; 3:12).[56]

None of the verses cited speaks of eschatology; they deal rather with the salvation Jesus Christ has attained for us. In the proto-Paulines too, this is not reserved for the eschatological future. I confess that I do not know of a parallel to Eph. 2:5, but 2:6 is paralleled in Phil. 3:20, Eph. 2:8 in Rom. 5:1 and 8:24a. Ephesians 2:19 may be compared with Phil. 3:20; to have "citizenship in heaven" corresponds with being "members of God's household." Ephesians 3:12 has a parallel in Rom. 5:2 that corresponds very precisely. Schnelle makes an assertion that is not supported by the Scripture passages given.

> The doctrine of justification sounds forth only in completely unpolemical tones within the framework of the statements on baptism (cf. Eph. 2:5, 8–10).[57]

The verses cited say nothing of baptism; they speak only of salvation by grace, not by works. The pair of opposites *works-grace* is dealt with unpolemically in 1 Thessalonians, too: in fact, it is entirely absent there. It is true that in Philippians there is an exchange regarding circumcision, but the opposites *faith-works* are lacking here, too. Objections are lodged about epistles suspected of being inauthentic, while "genuine" letters having the same characteristics are not incriminated. This is the procedure in witch trials; it is not scientific work.

2. The Epistle to the Colossians

Theological classification plays a primary role in the question of the genuineness of the Colossian epistle: "The linguistic and stylistic peculiarities alone cannot demonstrate the deutero-Pauline authorship of Colossians. These peculiarities first come to light when they are connected with the material-theological distinctives of the letter."[58]

> 1. Christology: The significance of the saving work of Jesus Christ for the entire cosmos stands at the center of the Colossian letter.[59]

The falsity of this assertion becomes readily clear when we investigate the use of the term κόσμος (world) in Colossians: none of the four κόσμος passages speaks of Christ's saving work for the cosmos. Colossians 1:6 deals with the proclamation of the gospel in the entire world. In 2:8 and 2:20, the elements of the world are mentioned, elements to which the Colossians have died, so that they should no longer conduct themselves as still living in the world.

What is really written in Colossians does not distinguish itself all that much. Schnelle himself must admit, "The cosmic Christology of Colossians . . . can link up with statements in the proto-Paulines."[60] But then by means of hairsplitting a contradiction is construed where none exists:

> 2. Eschatology: . . . already in its basic starting point cosmologically oriented.[61]

Schnelle adds in a footnote that "spatial paired opposites clearly dominate in Colossians: e.g., 'hidden-revealed,' 'below-above.'"[62] If *hidden* and *revealed* must be pressed into service as "spatial paired opposites," this only shows the questionable nature of construing an opposite between Colossians and the proto-Paulines by the assertion of a "cosmologically" oriented eschatology. That "the powers belong to the realm of what is below" is expressed also in Phil. 2:10; that "Christians should conduct themselves in view of the things above" is reflected likewise in Phil. 3:14. There is not the slightest justification for claiming that according to Colossians, the "new existence of Christians" is "demonstrable in an inner-worldly way." The "eschatological reserve" is also not lacking in Colossians, for life "is hidden with Christ in God" and will first be manifest when Christ is revealed. In view of Col. 3:3f., to assert a present-oriented eschatology in Colossians in contrast to the proto-Paulines is a shameless denial of the truth; Schnelle pulls it off only by means of some hairsplitting. But it is not only Colossians that knows of "Hope as the substance of salvation that is objectively present in the age to come"; this is also attested numerous times in the other Pauline letters (Rom. 8:24f.; 1 Thess. 4:13f.; 5:8). As a result, unbelievers can be characterized as persons who have no hope.

> 3. Ecclesiology: The σῶμα Χριστοῦ ("body of Christ") idea forms the center of the ecclesiology of Colossians. . . . In Colossians a cosmological significance is ascribed to it. The church is the sphere of salvation empowered and ruled by Jesus Christ (cf. Col. 1:18, 24; 2:17, 19; 3:15).[63]

The passages cited say nothing of a "sphere of salvation." According to 1:18 Christ is the head of the body, which is the church; 1:24 speaks of the suffering of the apostle, through which he supplements what remains unfinished in Christ's affliction for his body. Colossians 2:17 does not speak at all of the body of Christ but of the human body. Also in 2:19, where Paul writes about the ligaments and joints of the body, which grows from the head by the growth God supplies, there is nothing said of a "sphere of salvation." That the head is in heaven and the body on earth does not make the ecclesiology of Colossians more cosmological than it is in other Pauline letters in which the ἐκκλησία is not depicted as the body of Christ. The essential meaning is the same: Christ sits at God's right hand, while the church still finds itself on this earth.

Historical-critical theology does not hesitate to advance the assertions it makes as facts and to cite as proof-texts passages that do not square with the assertions. It survives because only seldom does someone take the trouble to check out its statements. Such a procedure is not scientific.

> Colossians does not develop the Pauline conception but seizes on ideas current in Hellenistic Judaism (cf. 5, 3, 8): the idea of a divine reality reigning over the expanse of the All. . . . Christ created the All, reconciled it, and as the head of the body he presently exercises his lordship in it.[64]

Nowhere do we read that Christ created "the All" and reconciled it; this term is not found in Colossians. Tὰ πάντα does not occur as a stand-alone substantive; πάντα is appositional to τὰ . . . ἐν τοῖς οὐρανοῖς καὶ ἐπὶ τῆς γῆς ("the things . . . in heaven and on earth"). That *Christ* created all things, and that all things have their being in him, could not be learned from Hellenistic Judaism; it is rather in 2 Cor. 6:18 that the Lord is called παντοκράτωρ (Almighty). That it pleased "all the fullness" "to reconcile to himself τὰ πάντα" (Col. 1:20) is also not found in Hellenistic Judaism, though it has a parallel in 2 Cor. 5:19: "God was reconciling the world to himself in Christ." The similarities of Colossians with the proto-Paulines are therefore far greater than with Hellenistic Judaism.

> 4. The function of the apostle: Whereas Paul proclaimed the gospel of Jesus Christ, the central message of Colossians appears to be τὸ μυστήριον τοῦ Χριστοῦ or θεοῦ ["mystery/secret of Christ" or "of God"] (cf. Col. 1:26, 27; 2:2; 4:3).[65]

Once again an artificial dichotomy is construed between Colossians and the other Pauline epistles. That is done by means of assumptions that do not stand up to scrutiny. Μυστήριον τοῦ Χριστοῦ or θεοῦ occurs only in two of the four passages cited as a term in the context. In one of the two, 4:3, is it materially identical with the gospel. In 2:2, by contrast, Christ himself is the mystery. There can be no talk, therefore, of a newly coined term. To declare a formulation as the central concept of the epistle when it occurs only twice in Colossians, and contains different nuances each time, is absurd. But historical-critical theology does not hesitate to resort to such absurdities when it wishes to declare, at any price, a New Testament writing to be inauthentic.

Μυστήριον is a formal term and carries various meanings in Paul. Romans 11:25 and 16:25 are very similar to Col. 1:26f. First Corinthians 2:1 and 2:7 share similarities with Col. 4:3. First Corinthians 13:2; 14:2; and 15:51 show how variously the word's meaning can be pressed, which corresponds to the linguistic usage observed in Colossians.

As we saw, the content of the mystery of Christ, not only in Colossians but also elsewhere in Paul, can be identical with the gospel. There is no contrast. It is true that the formulation "gospel of Jesus Christ" does not occur in Colossians, but elsewhere in Paul, too, it occurs without "of Jesus," and by no means as frequently as would be expected when such a contrast has to be assumed. Among the 60 occurrences of the word *gospel* in Paul, of which two occur in Colossians, only ten of them are in connection with τοῦ Χριστοῦ (of Christ). From this standpoint too, the artificially construed dichotomy does not hold water.

> ... therefore the person and the suffering of the apostle are also the content of the mystery (cf. Col. 1:24, 29).[66]

In neither of the verses cited is the word *mystery* found, nor is it spoken of materially. In 1:26–27, where "mystery" does occur, there is no talk of "the person and suffering of the apostle." The mystery is "Christ among you, the hope of glory." Colossians 1:28 and 1:29 do not take up again the term *mystery*.

> The gospel is defined not only based on its content, Jesus Christ,
> but essentially through the proclamation of the apostle.[67]

From Col. 2:5 Schnelle draws the (skewed) inference that the person of the apostle is no longer separable from the content of the gospel. He devotes not a single word to the exact parallel in 1 Cor. 5:3. From Col. 2:6 he deduces that the church "should now proclaim Christ as the apostle proclaimed him." But the verse says nothing about proclamation; it speaks rather of *walking* in Christ. Still less does one read in 2:8 "that every other proclamation" is to be regarded as the "doctrine of men." It is not "another proclamation" by which the Colossians are not to be misled but by *"philosophy* and empty deception, according to the tradition of men, according to the elements of the world and not in keeping with Christ."

Without regard for the truth, without due care regarding that which is written, fatuous assertions are advanced and urged on the reader as facts. These alleged facts, in turn, make it impossible to accept Colossians as a Pauline writing.

> 5. The concept of faith: If Paul characterizes πίστις [faith, trust] as
> the gift of a new relationship with God and new self-understanding, the author of Colossians uses πίστις in Col. 1:23; 2:5, 7 in connection with terms of holding fast. Expressions connoting remaining, persevering, and being grounded suggest that πίστις in Colossians signifies standing firm in the tradition.[68]

This observation holds true for 3 of the 5 occurrences of the term. One of the incriminated expressions is a hapax legomenon, another occurs only in Ephesians and Colossians. But it is premature to posit another concept of faith on the basis of these three formulations. And in addition a false alternative is posed. It is not Paul who speaks of "new self-understanding" but Bultmann; yet he would never have anachronistically transposed this idea back into Paul. Outside of Colossians Paul also uses πίστις "in connection with terms of holding fast" (e.g., Rom. 11:20; 1 Cor. 16:13; 2 Cor. 1:24). Ἑδραῖοι (steadfast) in 1 Cor. 15:58—though without being connected to πίστις—is used in the same sense as in Col. 1:23. The object of being grounded in Col. 1:23 is not tradition, also not "the gospel that you heard," but "*the hope* of the gospel." Colossians 2:5 does not say "the firmness of your faith in the tradition" but "the firmness of faith *in Christ*." In Col 2:7, being rooted and built up and confirmed in faith are qualifications of *walking* in Christ Jesus. The point of contact is not tradition but a person. What πίστις in Colossians connotes is recognized not in concepts alone, but in the concepts seen within the context in which they are used. And the connotation is not holding fast to the tradition but devotion to Jesus, both in the hope of the gospel and in practical living.

The positing of another concept of faith is, then, just as untenable as the other assertions used to place the genuineness of Colossians in question. None of them stands up to testing.

> 6. Pneumatology: Striking is the receding of pneumatology in Colossians; πνεῦμα [spirit] appears only in Col. 1:8; 2:5.[69]

True, in Philippians and 1 Thessalonians, works of comparable length to Colossians, the term occurs five times. But if that sort of a difference is held to be proof of genuineness, then one should declare 2 Corinthians as inauthentic all the more, for the term is found there only seventeen times, while in 1 Corinthians it occurs forty times. Or is Ephesians more authentic than Philippians and 1 Thessalonians because πνεῦμα occurs there fourteen times, almost three times as frequently? As soon as this kind of argumentation is used, not only on the epistles incriminated as inauthentic, but also on the epistles as a whole (an evenhanded approach that should be self-evident in a scientific work), it becomes clear that historical-critical theology does not hesitate to go to foolish lengths. The witch trial runs its course; what was once suspected of inauthenticity cannot substantiate its genuineness.

Pneumatology "in Colossians . . . is merely a secondary theme." Is the situation essentially any different in 1 Thessalonians? True, the term occurs there five times, but the Holy Spirit is mentioned only appositionally in 2 occurrences of πνεῦμα in the proem (preface). The third occurrence, in 4:8, is found in a dependent clause in which the object is the Holy Spirit. Also in 5:19 he is the object; here the theme is not the Holy Spirit but rather the response to him. First Thessalonians 5:23 speaks of the spirit of the Thessalonians, not of the Holy Spirit.

If the presupposition is without weight, then the warrants showing why pneumatology in Colossians is but a secondary theme are mere speculation. The point need not be belabored.

The material-theological distinctives of Colossians, which along with the linguistic, stylistic features form a second argument against the Pauline authorship of Colossians, have evaporated in the course of our investigation. Nothing remains that compels us to doubt the genuineness of the Colossian epistle.

3. Second Thessalonians

> A fundamental difference exists between the eschatological instructions of 1 Thess. 4:13–18; 5:1–11; and 2 Thess. 2:1–12; 1: 5–10. The eschatology of 1 Thessalonians is marked by expectation of the imminent parousia, which until Philippians comprises the material center of all [Pauline] eschatological statements (cf. Phil. 4:5b).[70]

We cannot go into the question of Paul's expectation of Christ's imminent return here. Philippians 4:5b is in any case a poor supporting passage for the view: the context of the words "the Lord is near" says nothing about the parousia. Neither the gentleness of which the passage speaks, nor the admonition to be anxious about nothing, is made dependent on the imminent arrival of the Lord. Since ἐγγύς (near) is here applied to the Lord, without a word being said about his return, the word can be understood spatially as well as temporally; it can refer just as much to the presence of the Lord among his people as to his imminent return. In three of the other four passages where ἐγγύς occurs in Paul (Rom. 10:8; Eph. 2:13, 17), it is not possible to interpret what he says as referring to temporal nearness. We read nothing in 1 Thessalonians of expectation of an imminent parousia. First Thessalonians 4:13–18 does not deal with the imminent return of the Lord; it rather makes clear why there is hope for those who have died in Christ. The passage in 5:1–3 reminds the Thessalonians that no one can know the exact time, because the day of the Lord comes like a thief in the night, like sudden destruction. But as they maintain alertness, they will not be taken by surprise.

> In 2 Thess. 2:2 the author turns against the slogan ἐνέστηκεν ἡ ἡμέρα τοῦ κυρίου [the day of the Lord is here] and then proceeds to outline a time schedule of final events. This schedule cannot be squared with the depiction of final events in 1 Thessalonians.[71]

Second Thessalonians 2:1 presupposes a situation that did not yet exist when 1 Thess. 5:1–3 was composed. The writer was at that time able to assume that his readers themselves know very well "the times and the seasons." In the meantime they have let themselves be shaken by bogus prophecies (2 Thess. 2:2: "through a spirit"), words, or letters purporting to be from Paul. The differences between 1 and 2 Thessalonians do not come about because of a different theology but due to an altered situation. The author does not outline a "schedule of final events"; he rather reminds them of what he had already passed on to them orally (1 Thess. 2:5), because it has already been written by the prophets.

Not the whole course of end events is conveyed, just the particular insight that first apostasy must come and the man of lawlessness be revealed. Like 1 Thessalonians, 2 Thessalonians deals with a partial aspect of eschatology. The former deals with the question of how things stand with those who have already died at the parousia. The latter speaks of the great falling away and of things that pertain to the coming of the man of lawlessness. Contrasting details are not contradictions. If 2 Thess. 2 actually contained a complete eschatological timetable in which all points were plotted out, then resurrection and rapture would not be missing. The σὺν Χριστῷ εἶναι (being with Christ) as "goal of the eschatological event" has its place where the union of believers with Christ is spoken of, however, and not in connection with the man of lawlessness. Not unless we found irreconcilable statements regarding one and the same point could we speak of different theologies. But that is not the case in the two Thessalonian epistles.

4. The Pastoral Epistles

The Pastorals diverge considerably from the theology found in the proto-Paulines. Missing are terms like. . . .[72]

We have already investigated the six "missing terms"[73] and determined that they are missing not only from the Pastorals but also from 1 Thessalonians and Philemon. Only one of the six is found in the other five "proto-Paulines," two are lacking in one of them, two are lacking in two, and one is lacking in three. When a theological concept occurs only in Romans and once in 1 Corinthians, or when another is lacking in Romans and 2 Corinthians, it is completely arbitrary to declare the Pastorals to be inauthentic because they lack these concepts.

Διδασκαλία (teaching) becomes a central word. Of its 21 occurrences in the New Testament, 15 of them are in the Pastorals alone.[74]

That has no bearing on the question of genuineness. Every epistle has a central word. Romans contains 33 of the 57 Pauline occurrences of δικαιοσύνη (righteousness); 1 Corinthians has 10 of the 13 Pauline occurrences of βαπτίζειν (to baptize) and 15 of Paul's 24 uses of πνευματικός (spiritual), just to cite a few examples.

Faith assumes the shape of right belief in contrast to heresy.[75]

That is true of only four of the six proof texts cited, which comprise only 18.18 percent of the thirty-three occurrences of πίστις in the Pastorals anyway.

Faith can be listed in a series with other virtues like a good conscience . . . discretion, love and sanctification . . . purity . . . righteousness, godliness, patience, gentleness. . . .[76]

But a good conscience is not a virtue! Faith and love also occur together in the "proto-Paulines" numerous times, as in 1 Cor. 13:13

and 1 Thess. 3:6. A complete listing of "love, joy, peace, patience, kindness, goodness, faithfulness, gentleness, and self-control" is found in Gal. 5:22f., although the word πίστις is lacking. Yet this is not a list of "virtues" but of the "fruit of the Spirit." Besides, the term ἀρετή (virtue) does not occur in the Pastorals, either, but is found in Paul only at Phil. 4:8.

> Christ's parousia becomes his "epiphany" in the Pastorals; it occurs at a foreordained time (cf. 1 Tim. 6:14; 2 Tim. 4:1, 8; Titus 2:13).[77]

Of the fourteen occurrences of the word *parousia* in Paul, six have no relation to the return of Jesus. The term occurs with an eschatological connotation once in 1 Corinthians and seven times altogether in 1 and 2 Thessalonians. So little does *epiphany* stand in contradistinction to *parousia* in Paul that in 2 Thess. 2:8 both words can be used together. First Tim. 6:14f. furnishes at most support for a foreordained time, though "foreordained" is not found there, simply καιροῖς ἰδίοις (proper time). That gives no ground for inferring that the parousia has shifted into an indeterminate future—it is the object of a living expectation in 2 Tim. 4:8 and Titus 2:13! Moreover, it is a questionable undertaking to assert a distinctive eschatology on the basis of a single passage.

> The view of women in the Pastorals is marked by a summons to submission, in contrast to the Pauline letters, which present a model in which participation is a given.[78]

Once again we encounter a false alternative. Only from Rom. 16 can anything about shared ministry be inferred, while submission is referred to in 1 Cor. 11:3ff. and 14:34, to say nothing of Eph. 5:22f.

The attempt to call in question the authenticity of the Pastorals by referring to theological differences is wrongheaded. It would be giving the "arguments" too much credit to say that they grasp at straws; straw is more substantial than these arguments turn out to be.

E. Description of phenomena with expressions that can be neither objectified nor quantified

1. The Epistle to the Ephesians

We have already covered this in earlier sections, in connection with the historical placement and theological classification of the epistle.

2. The Epistle to the Colossians

The linguistic, stylistic, and material peculiarities of Colossians leave no alternative but to conclude that not Paul but one of his students was the author of the letter.[79]

With this apodictic assertion the reader is manipulated. Earlier Schnelle had still admitted that "the peculiarities of language and style alone" cannot "demonstrate the deutero-Pauline authorship of Colossians."[80] Accordingly, the peculiarities do not exclude the possibility that Paul can be the author of Colossians. The burden of proof therefore lies solely on the "material-theological peculiarities." But we have already seen that they are unable to bear this load.

Schnelle acknowledges agreement with the macrostructure of the "proto-Paulines," along with proximity to Philippians as a prison letter, and not least "familiarity with Pauline theology." Yet everything that is clear proof for Pauline authorship is declared to be a "device of pseudepigraphy," which is in turn sanctified by its purpose of "legitimizing and furthering the position of the author in opposition to false teaching."

There can be no talk here of scientific marshaling of proof, which carefully weighs strengths and weaknesses. At any price the suspicion, once raised, must lead to a guilty verdict. Everything that speaks for the accused is twisted against him.

3. Second Thessalonians

While 1 Thess. 5:1 expressly rejects calculations in view of the parousia, 2 Thess. 2:1–12 contains an eschatological timetable that not only permits observations and calculations but demands them (cf. v. 5!).[81]

This sentence is a prime example of the manipulation of the reader that is common in historical-critical theology (though in my opinion not always with the skill and slipperiness found here in Schnelle): First Thessalonians 5:1 says nothing about express rejection of calculations; it merely says, "Now, brothers, about times and dates we do not need to write to you." Verse 2 gives the reason: "For you know very well that the day of the Lord will come like a thief in the night." It is therefore established that the day of the Lord is not calculable. Second Thessalonians 2:5 says simply, "Don't you remember that when I was with you I used to tell you these things?" That is a question, clearly identified as such with a question mark even in Nestle-Aland[27]. It is not a summons to calculation, any more than what the Thessalonians are supposed to remember (cf. 2 Thess. 2:3f.) is such a summons. The day of the Lord does not become calculable, and his coming "like a thief in the night" is not excluded, merely because Paul says that certain events must precede it, which can be gathered from Holy Scripture itself (cf., among other passages, Daniel 11, esp. v. 36). There are only two events that temporally precede the day of the Lord: the great apostasy and the coming of the man of lawlessness, about whom more is said in appositional statements. The time span between the two, and between them and the day of the Lord, is not given. In contrast, the point in time at which a train arrives at various stations is what characterizes a timetable. Second Thessalonians 2:1–12 does not, therefore, contain an "eschatological timetable," since even many of the final events that are expected, such as the resurrection and the rapture, are not even mentioned.

As soon as the truth content of biblical criticism's heady, apodictic assertions is investigated, it turns out that they are speculative allegations made with little regard for the truth.

4. The Pastoral Epistles

The 'churchiness' of the concept of faith in the Pastorals is seen finally in the theme of being brought up in the faith. Timothy is reminded of the unfeigned faith of his mother and grandmother (cf. 2 Tim. 1:5).[82]

The following is insinuated to the reader: the concept of faith in the Pastorals is "churchy" (*kirchlich*)—whatever that means—and this supposedly distinguishes it from the proto-Paulines. Evidence for the postulated churchiness supposedly lies in being brought up in the faith. Yet 2 Tim. 1:5 does not speak of being brought up in the faith. It merely states that the unfeigned faith in Timothy, which Paul remembers, already dwelled in his mother and grandmother. Paul doesn't say how Timothy arrived at the same unfeigned faith. It is an assumption that it occurred through the way he was brought up. Even if that was how it happened, it still doesn't prove that such an upbringing was unthinkable for Paul and irreconcilable with his concept of faith.

> The author of the Pastorals . . . cites words of poetry (cf. Titus 1:12) and makes use of philosophical terms (cf. 1 Tim. 6:6, αὐτάρκεια [contentment]); he was probably an educated Hellenistic (Jewish) Christian who lived in a city of the province of Asia Minor and had in mind the congregations of his locale.[83]

Once again the reader is skillfully manipulated. The use of poetry and philosophical terms is no proof that "the author of the Pastorals" was "an unknown member of the Pauline school." Paul was also capable of those kinds of citations, as the quote from Menander in 1 Cor. 15:33 shows. By the way, the word referred to in 1 Tim. 6:6 (αὐτάρκεια) is likewise found in 2 Cor. 9:8!

5. The Epistle of James

Suggestive speculation can also be detected in the description of data regarding James's epistle: "It remains . . . striking that the author does not introduce himself as the Lord's brother and does not claim for himself . . . the title of honor στῦλος [Pillar]."[84]

Why should someone who has authority insist on it? Lack of such insistence does not speak against James's authorship: it is rather precisely a person who usurped James's name who would have valued the recognition gained by titles.

By placing himself in James 3:1–2 into the large group of early Christian teachers (cf. Acts 13:1; 1 Cor. 12:28), he dispenses with the special authority that fell to him by virtue of being the Lord's brother and one of the three 'pillars' of the early church.[85]

The exercise of a function that one shares with others is not dispensing with a special position. Someone in upper-level management could carry out teaching duties just as much as a primary school teacher. If he then mentions, perhaps at a parent-teacher conference, that he too is a teacher, and passes on advice to the elementary school teacher, that would not mean that he dispensed with his position as a member of management.

In addition, James 3:1ff. presupposes an assault on the teaching office and a related crisis, which in turn does not correspond to the exclusive position of the Lord's brother in the history of early Christianity.[86]

This is again a prime example of subtle persuasion. The admonition "let not many of you become teachers" in 3:1 is not based on an overstock of teachers but on the heavy responsibility that teachers bear. Nothing whatsoever is said of a crisis caused by such an overstock. James 3:1f. stands in connection with the warning against sins of the tongue, not in an analysis of the situation in early Christianity. Even if these false conclusions were given credence, the erroneous conclusion drawn from them would still be glaringly visible: The exclusive position of the Lord's brother James is not based on his function as teacher but as leader, and this would not have been endangered through an oversupply of teachers. What Schnelle infers from the verses, therefore, is not what they contain; he rather reads into them what he requires to deny the epistle's authorship to the brother of the Lord. In historical-critical theology there is no hesitation in cobbling together arguments that completely lack force. Any means will do if it fulfills the desired goal.

If the Lord's brother James is supposed to be the author of the writing, it is in addition astonishing that in James 5:10f. Job and not Jesus is cited as an example of willingness to suffer.[87]

As a German rhyme goes, "Und dann beweist er messerscharf, dass nicht sein kann, was nicht sein darf." Roughly rendered: "And then he proved, quick as a wink, that nothing can exist unless it's what we think." It is absurd to conclude in this way what an author can and cannot have written. Such judgments remain mired in subjectivity, unless anachronisms or other objectifiable evidence can be detected. But that is not the case here.

6. First Peter

According to Schnelle, "ancient church tradition presupposes that Peter had a very limited mastery of the Greek language."[88]

That cannot be inferred from the characterization of Mark as Peter's interpreter. For it may not have been into Greek but into Latin that Mark translated. In fact this is far more likely, since his work as translator is attested for Peter's stay in Rome, and there is no evidence that Mark accompanied Peter all the other places he traveled.

> In 1 Pet. 1:1 the author styles himself ἀπόστολος (apostle), in 5:1 however, συμπρεσβύτερος (fellow elder). A member of the Twelve, an apostle and earliest witness of the resurrection of Jesus Christ, could hardly have resorted to this title, which arises late in early Christian ecclesiology.[89]

It is asserted that πρεσβύτερος is a later title, but there is no proof. True, the word does not occur in the proto-Paulines, but that doesn't mean that the function did not exist at the time his letters were written. According to Acts 14:23, Paul and Barnabas appointed elders in every congregation. Even those who are not willing to grant Acts credibility as historically reliable should at least refrain from proclaiming with such assurance their conclusions based on *argumentum e silentio*.

A further "misgiving" "regarding Petrine authorship" is given: "The author of 1 Peter cites the Old Testament mostly from the LXX."[90]

It is normal for a missionary to use a Bible translation that is already well established on the mission field. To produce one's own translation would not only be an unnecessary expenditure of energy: the result would probably be far inferior to what was already available. This objection to the authenticity of 1 Peter is foolish.

F. Results

Linguistic, literary, theological, and historical arguments are deployed against the genuineness of ten New Testament writings in order to declare them to be pseudepigraphical. This means that their claim is without justification—better, it is a lie—that they have as authors the persons named in the New Testament.

Testing of the argumentation used in the question of authenticity has led us to conclude that the scientific nature of this procedure must be called in question. If the objections that are raised against genuineness are not naively accepted, but rather subjected to tests of their validity, then it becomes clear that they fail the test. Whatever form the objections take, they are as a rule too flimsy to stand up under scrutiny.

In legal proceedings the prevailing principle is *in dubio pro reo*. As long as guilt can be called into question, the charge cannot be sustained. Things are different in historical-critical theology: As long as there is still even a thread-thin argument fetched from whatever musty quarter against the genuineness of a New Testament writing, the charge of pseudepigraphical is made. And that is not all: immediately a verdict is proclaimed that admits of no further correction. In "scientific" historical-critical determination of questions of New Testament introduction, not a single case is known in which a biblical writing, suspected previously of pseudonymity, has emerged from the trial with an acquittal. Once suspected, forever condemned. Scientific results should be revisable; the way things proceed in questions of authenticity is however not a scientific process but the procedure of a witch trial.

Endnotes

1. Udo Schnelle, *Einleitung in das Neue Testament* (UTB 1830; Göttingen: Vandenhoeck & Ruprecht, 1994), 323f. Translations of

Schnelle in this chapter are by Robert Yarbrough unless otherwise noted. Schnelle's work has now appeared in English: *The History and Theology of the New Testament Writings*, trans. M. E. Boring (Minneapolis: Fortress, 1998); a translation of this quotation is found in the English translation (ET), pp. 276–77. References in endnotes below will include the page numbers of both German and English editions.

2. Here see Donald Guthrie, *New Testament Introduction*, 8th ed. (Downers Grove: InterVarsity, 1996); D. A. Carson, Douglas J. Moo, and Leon Morris, *An Introduction to the New Testament*, 4th ed. (Leicester: Apollos, 1994); Erich Mauerhofer, *Einleitung in die Schriften des Neuen Testaments*, 2 vols. (Neuhausen: Hänssler, 1995).

3. R. Morgenthaler, *Statistik des Neutestamentlichen Wortschatzes*. 4th ed. (Zürich: Gotthelf, 1992). Although the supplementary volume of this edition lists the vocabulary of each individual Johannine letter, missing is the information about their hapax legomena. Therefore I follow Morgenthaler in treating the Johannine epistles as a unity. In vocabulary statistics cited in this section I accept Morgenthaler's numbers and do not attempt my own calculations.

4. Schnelle, *Einleitung,* 331; ET, 283.

5. Ibid., 330; ET, 283.

6. Ibid., 349; ET, 300.

7. Ibid., 367; ET (quoted above), 317. Schnelle is citing W. Trilling.

8. Ibid. (Here Schnelle is not citing Trilling.)

9. Ibid.

10. See note 7 above.

11. Schnelle, *Einleitung,* 468f.; ET, 410f.

12. Ibid., 485 n. 183; ET, 426 n. 183.

13. Ibid., 330f.; ET, 283.

14. Ibid., 331; ET, 284.

15. Ibid., 349; ET, 300f.

16. Ibid., 350; ET, 301.

17. Ibid., 356f.; ET, 307f.

18. Ibid., 356; ET, 307.

19. Seven identical words twice.

20. Schnelle, *Einleitung,* 357; ET, 307.

21. Ibid.; ET, 308.

22. Ibid., 366; ET, 316.
23. Ibid., 371; ET, 320.
24. Ibid., 372; ET, 321.
25. Ibid., 485; ET, 425.
26. Ibid.
27. Ibid., 488; ET, 428.
28. Ibid., 489; ET, 429.
29. Ibid., 486; ET, 426.
30. Ibid., 489; ET, 429.
31. Ibid.
32. Ibid., 350; ET, 301.
33. Ibid.
34. Ibid., 351; ET, 302.
35. Ibid.
36. Ibid.
37. Ibid., 379; ET, 328f.
38. TVG 305 (Wuppertal: Brockhaus).
39. Schnelle, *Einleitung,* 380; ET, 329f.
40. Ibid.; ET, 330.
41. Ibid., 381; ET, 330.
42. Ibid., 380f.; ET, 330.
43. Ibid., 381; ET, 330.
44. Ibid.
45. Ibid., 440; ET, 385f.
46. Ibid., 461f; ET, 404f.
47. Ibid., 485; ET, 425f.
48. Ibid., 486; ET, 426.
49. Ibid., 476; ET, 417.
50. Ibid.
51. Ibid.
52. Ibid.
53. Ibid., 350; ET, 301.
54. Ibid.
55. Ibid., 350–51; ET, 302.
56. Ibid., 351.
57. Ibid.

58. Ibid., 331; ET, 284.
59. Ibid.
60. Ibid., 332.
61. Ibid.; ET, 285.
62. Ibid., n. 25.
63. Ibid., 333; ET, 285f.
64. Ibid.; ET, 286.
65. Ibid., 334; ET, 286.
66. Ibid.
67. Ibid.
68. Ibid.
69. Ibid.; ET, 287.
70. Ibid., 366; ET, 316.
71. Ibid.
72. Ibid., 381; ET, 330f.
73. See previous chapter.
74. Schnelle, *Einleitung,* 381; ET, 331.
75. Ibid., 382; ET, 331.
76. Ibid.
77. Ibid.
78. Ibid.
79. Ibid., 334f.; ET, 287.
80. Ibid., 331; ET, 284.
81. Ibid., 366f.; ET, 317.
82. Ibid., 382; ET, 331.
83. Ibid.; ET, 332.
84. Ibid., 441; ET, 386.
85. Ibid.
86. Ibid.
87. Ibid.
88. Ibid., 457; ET, 400.
89. Ibid.
90. Ibid.

List 1: "Expressions absent from the proto-Pauline writings but which mark the theology of Ephesians" (according to Schnelle)

1. εὐλογία πνευματική
2. καταβολὴ κόσμου
3. ἄφεσις τῶν παραπτώματων
4. μυστήριον τοῦ θελήματος αὐτοῦ
5. ὁ λόγος τῆς ἀληθείας
6. ὁ πατὴρ τῆς δόξης

7. αἰὼν τοῦ κόσμου τούτου
8. ἡ πρόφεσις τῶν αἰώνων
9. τὸ πνεῦμα τοῦ νοός
10. μιμηταὶ τοῦ θεοῦ
11. βασιλεία τοῦ χριστοῦ καὶ τοῦ θεοῦ

List 2: "Central terms and ideas of Pauline theology found in 1 Peter" (according to Schnelle)

1. χάρις Pl 100/1 Pet 10/NT 155
2. δικαιοσύνη Pl 57/1 Pet 2/NT 91
3. ἀποκάλυψις Pl 13/1 Pet 3/NT 18

4. ἐλευθερία Pl 7/1 Pet 1/NT 11
5. καλεῖν Pl 33/1 Pet 6/NT 148
6. ἐν χριστῷ Pl 74/1 Pet 2/NT 76

List 3: "Religio-philosophical terms of Hellenism in 2 Peter" (according to Schnelle)

	LXX	NT	Paul	Other NT writings
ἐπίγνωσις	8	20	15	Heb 1; 2 Pet 4
γνῶσις	60	29	23	Lk 2; 1 Pet 1; 2 Pet 3
εὐσέβεια	57	15	10	Apg 1; 2 Pet 4
ὑπομονή	25	32	16	Lk 2; Heb 2; Ja 3; 2 Pet 2; Offb 7
ἐγκράτεια	3 (Apoc.)	4	1	Apg 1; 2 Pet 2
ἀρετή	32	5	1	1 Pet 1; 2 Pet 3
ἐπόπτης	4 (Apoc.)	1		2 Pet 1
θεία δύναμις	2 (1 Apoc.)	1		2 Pet 1

List 4: "Central Pauline concepts lacking in Colossians" (according to Schnelle)

	Paulines	Rom	1 Cor	2 Cor	Gal	Eph	Phil	Col	1 Thess	2 Thess	1 Tim	2 Tim	Titus	Phlm
ἀποκάλυψιs	13	3	3	2	2	2	-	-	-	1	-	-	-	-
δικαιοσύνη	57	33	1	7	4	3	4	-	-	-	1	3	1	-
ἐλευθερία	7	1	1	1	4	-	-	-	-	-	-	-	-	-
ἐλευθεροῦν	5	4	-	-	1	-	-	-	-	-	-	-	-	-
ἐπαγγελία	26	8	-	2	10	4	-	-	-	-	1	1	-	-
καυχᾶσθαι	35	5	6	20	2	1	1	-	-	-	-	-	-	-
καύχημα	10	1	3	3	1	-	2	-	-	-	-	-	-	-
κοινωνία	13	1	3	4	1	-	3	-	-	-	-	-	-	1
νόμος	119	72	9	-	32	1	3	-	-	-	2	-	-	-
πιστεύειν	54	21	9	2	4	2	1	-	5	4	3	1	2	-
σῴζειν	29	8	9	1	-	2	-	-	1	1	4	2	1	-
σωτηρία	18	5	-	4	-	1	3	-	2	1	-	2	-	-
δικαιόω														

List 5: "Frequently encountered Pauline connectives and inferential particles lacking in Colossians" (according to Schnelle)

	Paulines	Rom	1 Cor	2 Cor	Gal	Eph	Phil	Col	1 Thess	2 Thess	1 Tim	2 Tim	Titus	Phlm
μᾶλλον	43	8	10	8	2	3	5	-	2	-	2	1	-	2
οὐδέ	53	7	10	1	9	-	1	-	3	1	3	-	-	-
εἴ τις	37	2	13	7	2	1	5	-	-	2	6	-	1	-
εἴπερ	6	3	2	-	-	-	-	-	-	1	-	-	-	-
οὐ μόνον δέ —														
ἀλλά καί	24	10	-	5	-	1	2	-	3	1	1	2	-	-
οὐκέτι	15	7	-	2	4	1	-	-	-	-	-	-	-	1
διό	27	6	9	9	1	5	1	-	2	-	-	-	-	1
διότι	10	5	-	-	-	-	1	-	3	-	-	-	-	-
ἄρα	27	11	3	3	5	1	-	-	1	1	-	-	-	-
ἄρα οὖν	12	8	-	-	1	1	-	-	1	1	-	-	-	-

List 6: Of the 112 Particles, etc., from Harrison's list found in . . .

	"Pauline" words missing	Percent of 112 on list	Percent of Paul's vocabulary
Rom	45	40.18%	4.22%
1 Cor	32	28.57	3.33
2 Cor	52	46.43	6.60
Gal	64	57.14	12.16
Eph	81	72.32	15.31
Phil	70	62.50	15.77
Col	79	70.54	18.29
1 Thess	76	67.86	20.94
2 Thess	87	77.88	34.52
Phlm	84	75.00	60.43

## Chapter Five

THE QUANTITATIVE STRUCTURE OF THE VOCABULARY OF THE NEW TESTAMENT

AS WE HAVE SEEN, it is a senseless undertaking to draw inferences about the author of a given writing based on lists of a few dozen words when the entire stock of relevant writings has not been considered. The frequent employment of this practice in historical-critical theology does not legitimate it; it rather raises more urgently the need for a general investigation of the quantitative structure of the vocabulary of New Testament writings.

A. Absolute quantities in the entire New Testament and in individual New Testament writings

1. Singles and multies

As far as I am aware, at least in the literature of New Testament Introduction, it has not yet been noted that a considerable percentage of the vocabulary of the New Testament consists of words that occur only a single time in a given writing.

Regarding the vocabulary of the New Testament writings, it makes sense to distinguish between the words that occur only one time in a New Testament writing and those that are attested multiple times. Only when we attain an accurate overview of the structure of the vocabulary of the New Testament in general, and then individual writings in particular, is there a sure foundation for drawing conclusions regarding findings in one particular writing.

I would like to introduce the terms *singles* and *multies* as formal terms for words that occur one time and more than one time, respectively. This pair of terms should serve as overarching rubrics under which the various kinds of words that occur once and more than once can be subsumed.

The term *singles* embraces all single occurrence of words in the New Testament. As a formal term for presenting a body of data it can serve to summarize words of various sorts that occur only once. At the same time however, the term keeps in view its adversative relation to *multies*—words that occur more than once—a relation that the term *hapax legomenon* is too narrow to express.

There are several additional kinds of occurrences that can be subsumed under the general rubric of singles—but at the same time are to be clearly distinguished from each other. There are words that (1) occur once in the entire New Testament (the New Testament hapax legomena) and (2) occur once in a group of New Testament writings. In this second group we could speak of hapax legomena if we specify in which group of Scriptures the word occurs only one time—for example, a Synoptic hapax (HapaxSyn), a Johannine hapax (HapaxJ), a Pauline hapax (HapaxPl), or a catholic letters hapax (HapaxCL). In addition, we can speak of a third group of words, those occurring one time in a single writing.

The singles *of the New Testament* are identical with the New Testament hapax legomena and are to be designated only as such. The singles *of a group of New Testament writings* can be called hapaxes or singles, depending on the context. For example, if one wishes to stress that a word occurs in Paul only once, the term *hapax* can be applied. But if the intention is to distinguish from each other words that occur once or multiply, the terms *singles* and *multies* can be used.

Accordingly, the singles in a group of writings consist of the New Testament hapax legomena and the hapax legomena of that group of writings. The singles of an individual New Testament writing consist of the New Testament hapax legomena, of the hapax legomena of the group to which it belongs, and of words that occur only once in this writing—but that still also occur within or even outside its group of New Testament writings.

The term *singles* is therefore chosen as a designation that encompasses every kind of singular occurrence in every New Testament writing. The opposite term *multies* designates all multiply occurring words.

2. Hapax legomena, mia-graphē legomena, and poly-graphē legomena

The **hapax legomena** are words occurring once, either in the New Testament or in a group of New Testament writings. The New Testament hapax legomena and the hapax legomena that occur no more than once within a group must be distinguished. The former receive no additional specification—they are hapax legomena proper—or they can be called **HapaxNT** to distinguish them from **HapaxSyn**, **HapaxJ**, **HapaxPl**, or **HapaxCL**.

Words that are multiply attested (hence *multies*, see below) but only occur within a particular book of the New Testament, are to be counted among the hapax legomena and yet distinguished from them. They are words occurring in one writing and can accordingly be called *mia-graphē* **legomena**. Corresponding to subdivisions among the hapax legomena suggested above, the New Testament *mia-graphē* legomena (which can be used with or without the prefix "New Testament") can be distinguished from the *mia-graphē* legomena of a group of New Testament writings. *Mia-graphē* legomena of such groups can be designated as **MiaSyn**, **MiaJ**, **MiaPl**, or **MiaCL**.

To be distinguished from the *mia-graphē* legomena are the *poly-graphē* **legomena**. These are *multiply occurring words that occur in the New Testament only within one group of Scriptures, but in more than one of the writings within that group.* A distinction must be made between the *number of words*, which pertains to overall word count in a respective group of writings, and the *occurrence of a word* in individual writings. The sum of the latter is considerably higher than the word count, since we are dealing with words that are multiply occurring.

While hapax legomena are singles, *mia-graphē* legomena and *poly-graphē* legomena are to be reckoned as multies.

The *mia-graphē* legomena and the *poly-graphē* legomena, like the hapax legomena, belong to the special vocabulary of the individual New Testament writings. We have to picture clearly that *every one* of these writings possesses such vocabulary. The distribution is unsystematic and permits no facile inferences in questions of authenticity.[1]

3. The monos

Every group of New Testament writings contains words that occur only within this group of Scriptures. These **monos** consist of the HapaxNT, the MiaNT, and the *poly-graphē* legomena that occur in this group. The hapax legomena and *mia-graphē* legomena of the group, however, are not components of the monos.

B. The relative quantities: solos, partials, and completes—the parallel structure in the Scripture groups

In order to give an objective foundation to the question of the relation of writings within a Scripture group, it makes sense to discover how their vocabulary is distributed among the individual writings. To grasp this parallel structure, a distinctive conceptuality is needed, one not to be confused with the categories described in the previous section. Here I have coined the terms *solos, partials,* and *completes.*

The New Testament hapaxes and *mia*s, like the hapaxes and *mia*s of each respective group of New Testament writings, may occur in an individual writing of a group as **solos**; that is, they have no parallels in other writings of the group. Other words are attested in several writings of a group, but they do not occur in all of those writings; these are **partials**, because they are found in only "part" of the writings of the group. Words that occur in all the writings of a group we may call **completes**, because they are attested in the complete number of writings in the group. It is worth the effort to investigate how these relative quantities of solos, partials, and completes relate to the absolute quantities of the singles and the multies.

C. The importance of the quantitative structure for comparison of vocabulary in writings or groups of writings demonstrated by examples

1. Structural analysis of Markan vocabulary

According to the corrected numbers of Morgenthaler's *Statistik des Neutestamentlichen Wortschatzes*, in accordance with the supplement to the third and fourth edition, which is itself based on the Nestle-Aland[27] Greek New Testament, the vocabulary of Mark's gospel consists of **632 singles** and **711 multies**. The **Markan vocabulary** comes to **1343 words**, of which **47.06%** are **singles** and **52.94% multies**. Almost half of the vocabulary occurs just a single time.

It is instructive to break down the singles and multies into solos, completes, and partials. Among the partials, two groups should be distinguished: a) Markan words that are also found in Matthew, and b) Markan words that also occur in Luke.

The more complete breakdown looks like this:

Singles	Solos	Hapax Solos	Completes	Partials a	Partials b
632	159	811	251	139	83
	26.16%	12.82%	39.72%	21.99%	13.13%

Multies	Solos	Mia Solos	Completes	Partials a	Partials b
711	26	12	592	59	34
	3.66%	1.69%	83.26%	8.30%	4.78%

The number of singles solos is six times the multies solos. The number of multies completes is nearly two-and-a-half times the singles completes.

2. Quantitative investigations of the vocabulary of Paul's letters

To round out the analyses in our earlier chapter "Pauline Authorship and Vocabulary Statistics," we here submit two additional studies. The vocabulary of the Pastoral Epistles, whose Pauline authorship is widely denied, will be compared with the vocabulary of the Pauline letters whose genuineness no one questions.

Naturally, for comparative purposes the only writings that can be used are those that are of comparable scope to the Pastorals. To compare Romans with 1 Timothy, and 1 Corinthians with 2 Timothy, would lead to skewed figures from the outset. On the other hand, Philippians, 1 Thessalonians, and Philemon correspond in extent of vocabulary to 1 and 2 Timothy and Titus to a considerable degree. If we look closely, we do note differences in scope of 38, 237, and 335 words respectively. But if these are combined as a group, the difference shrinks to sixty words: the extent of the Pastorals is therefore 1.72% larger than the extent of the comparative group of Philippians, 1 Thessalonians, and Philemon.

For comparison we pick out two segments of the larger whole of Pauline vocabulary:

> a. the amount of vocabulary that occurs in Paul two to five times or one to five times;
> b. the amount of vocabulary that occurs in Paul thirteen times and more.

a. The amount of vocabulary that occurs in Paul two to five times or one to five times

I calculated the extent of the Pauline vocabulary with the aid of the Nestle-Aland[27] Greek New Testament along with the fourth edition of Morgenthaler's *Statistik*. It encompasses **2645 words**.

The biggest share of this vocabulary in Paul consists of once-occurring words, singles, which are found just once either in the New Testament or in the Pauline corpus. They consist of New Testament hapaxes and Pauline hapaxes and number 1135 words, 42.91% of the Pauline vocabulary. Hardly any less is the portion of words that are used two to five times: they encompass 1031 words, or 38.98% of

Paul's vocabulary. Of Paul's vocabulary, 2166 words, or 81.89%, occur no more often than one to five times.

Of that portion of the Pauline vocabulary with two to five occurrences (1031 words), 491 words (47.62%) are lacking in each of the six writings under study (the three pastorals as well as the three letters of the comparison group). If to each of the six writings we add those words that, in addition, are absent only in that writing, then the number of words lacking in the vocabulary under investigation is:

Philippians	1 Thess.	Philemon	1 Tim.	2 Tim.	Titus
830	828	900	740	793	819

On the average, 818 words (79.34%) are lacking in the six Pauline letters in question, the Pastorals, and the control group of accepted Pauline writings. For the Pastorals the figure is 784 (76.04%); in the comparison group, 853, or 82.74% of the vocabulary that occurs two to five times in the Pauline letters.

Let us bring into this investigation the singly occurring words—namely, the New Testament hapax legomena that occur in the Pauline letters along with the Pauline hapax, words attested multiply in the New Testament overall but only once in Paul.[2] This adds another 1135 words to the 1031 words that occur two to five times (see preceding paragraphs). The words that occur in Paul one to five times amount, then, to 2166 words, or 81.89% of his vocabulary. This raises considerably the number of Pauline words lacking in the six writings under investigation:

Philippians	1 Thess.	Philemon	1 Tim.	2 Tim.	Titus
830	828	900	740	793	819
1061	1100	1122	1021	1033	1084
1891	1928	2022	1761	1824	1903
71.49%	72.89%	76.45%	66.58%	68.96%	71.95%

In the six Pauline letters under investigation, on the average 1888 (71.38% of the Pauline vocabulary) are lacking, just of those words that occur one to five times. In view of this finding, it makes little sense to dispute the Pauline authorship of New Testament writings clearly named as Paul's by the use of lists of a few dozen words, or indeed even with lists of 80, 120, or more words.

b. The amount of vocabulary that occurs in Paul thirteen times and more

Of course one could justifiably object that we should really only give weight to a lack of Pauline words that occur so frequently that they are at least theoretically present often enough to occur once in every Pauline letter (assuming uniform distribution). But this portion of the Pauline vocabulary proves nothing for the authenticity question either. The presupposed uniform distribution is not a given, and the entire sum of words that occur in Paul thirteen times or more comes to no more than 295, or 11.20% of his vocabulary. Of these 295 words, lacking in our six writings are:

Philippians	1 Thess.	Philemon	1 Tim.	2 Tim.	Titus
98 words	114 words	202 words	119 words	129 words	173 words

This is an average of 139 words (47.12%): in the Pastorals 140, or 47.46%, and in the control group 136, or 46.10%. The difference of 1.36% has no significance. The large number of vocabulary lacking, and the even distribution of lacking words among both groups, show clearly that even the part of the Pauline vocabulary, which occurs thirteen times and more, yields no firm ground for lists of words lacking that supposedly prove inauthenticity for these writings.

Let us summarize the results of both portions of the brief investigation above: We studied 2458 words, 92.93% of the Pauline vocabulary. The number of these lacking in each book investigated is:

Philippians	1 Thess.	Philemon	1 Tim.	2 Tim.	Titus
1989 wds.	2042 wds.	2222 wds.	1880 wds.	1953 wds.	1929 wds.
71.49%	77.20%	84.01%	71.08%	73.84%	78.49%

If we wish to establish the entire scope of words lacking of the Pauline vocabulary in the two groups above, it is not necessary to carry out yet another word count, this time of the words occurring six to twelve times. It suffices rather to subtract the vocabulary of the letters already investigated from the vocabulary of Paul. The amount of vocabulary lacking comes to:

Philippians	1 Thess.	Philemon	1 Tim.	2 Tim.	Titus
2645	2645	2645	2645	2645	2645
-444	-363	-139	-538	-457	-305
2201	2282	2506	2107	2188	2340
83.21%	86.28%	94.74%	79.66%	82.72%	88.47%

The amount of words of the Pauline vocabulary lacking in the entire Pauline corpus:

The above discussion not only achieves the task we set out to do; it also gives the key for establishing the amount of Pauline vocabulary lacking in every Pauline letter: the vocabulary of the individual letter must be subtracted from the sum of the Pauline vocabulary.

The vocabulary of the Pauline letters, according to my reckoning, comes to:

Epistle	Vocabulary	Epistle	Vocabulary
Romans	1066 words	1 Thessalonians	364 words
1 Corinthians	960 words	2 Thessalonians	252 words
2 Corinthians	788 words	1 Timothy	538 words
Galatians	526 words	2 Timothy	457 words
Ephesians	529 words	Titus	305 words
Philippians	444 words	Philemon	139 words
Colossians	432 words		

The amount of Pauline vocabulary lacking in each Pauline letter comes to:

Epistle	Vocabulary	Epistle	Vocabulary
Romans	1579 words	1 Thessalonians	2321 words
1 Corinthians	1655 words	2 Thessalonians	2393 words
2 Corinthians	1857 words	1 Timothy	2107 words
Galatians	2119 words	2 Timothy	2188 words
Ephesians	2116 words	Titus	2340 words
Philippians	2201 words	Philemon	2506 words
Colossians	2213 words		

If we list the Pauline letters according to the extent of words lacking, beginning with the epistle that lacks the least, the picture that emerges is by no means unfavorable toward the so-called pseudepigraphical writings. This is shown below; the boldfaced writings are considered authentic:

Ranking of Pauline Letters in Ascending Order of Amount of Pauline Vocabulary Lacking

1. Romans	**1579 words**
2. 1 Corinthians	**1655 words**
3. 2 Corinthians	**1857 words**
4. 1 Timothy	2107 words
5. Ephesians	2116 words
6. Galatians	**2119 words**
7. 2 Timothy	2188 words
8. Philippians	**2201 words**
9. Colossians	2213 words
10. 1 Thessalonians	**2321 words**
11. Titus	2340 words
12. 2 Thessalonians	2393 words
13. Philemon	**2506 words**

When the amount of words lacking adds up to thousands, mini-lists of 6, 24, 60, or 80 words are simply ridiculous. It is a scandal for New

Testament science, which to this very day operates with such quantities. Once again it is clear that historical-critical theology is not justified in laying claim to the label of "scientific" for itself.

D. Factors that are important for the quantitative structure of the vocabulary of a writing

1. The author

A basic starting principle is that the language usage of one author is different from that of other authors of the same era. The question is only whether this specific language usage can be verified. This can be difficult if a corpus does not consist of numerous and wide-ranging books but rather of short occasional writings, like letters to various addressees.

2. The addressee

The influence of the addressee on the language use of an author is often overlooked, but this should not be neglected. The author adapts himself to the addressee, to his level of education, his linguistic breadth and depth, his conceptions, along with the standpoint that the addressee occupies in the present controversy, if this is an issue. If an author has various addressees in mind in various writings, and if he must adapt to these readers accordingly, the spectrum of what belongs to his language use will be considerably more complex. It is not so simple to determine what he can and cannot have written.

3. Theme

Every theme calls for a specific vocabulary and suggests images, forms of speech, and linguistic stereotypes. Writings with different themes cannot be assumed to be directly comparable. The inference is not warranted that an author cannot have written something because he does not use that sort of vocabulary elsewhere. Before we begin to construct hypotheses, we should first compare all the writings of the author. The vocabulary distribution of the author's writings must be investigated and its structure ascertained. Thereafter it is possible to research in a general way the interconnection of vocabulary and thematic in this author. Not until after this is done may one possibly venture to draw careful inferences about individual writings of an author on the basis of vocabulary structure.

4. Range

In comparing various writings that claim the same author, it is unfortunate that far-reaching hypotheses are constructed without registering the differences in the range and scope of the writings. A short letter has a different structure from a long treatise. As a rule the short writing has a comparatively more extensive vocabulary, but this vocabulary will consist for the most part of singles. Since it usually concentrates on one theme, and this theme was possibly not yet taken up by the author elsewhere, the probability is greater that the short letter will fall outside the framework of the normal language use of an author.

5. The author's circumstances

The author's situation plays a considerable role in occasional writings. That is true, first of all, in view of the author; we see this for example clearly in the case of Paul. When Paul, in the course of his labor as tentmaker, dictates an epistle to one of his coworkers, the demands of his work and concentration on the dictation of his letter could occasionally compete with each other. Breaches in grammatical continuity and other stylistic rough spots are the natural outcome. When he writes in a different situation, such as in the private residence of his imprisonment in Rome, then he can concentrate completely on the epistle, and it is no wonder if the result distinguishes itself by a markedly better style.

E. Summary

The investigations of the quantitative structure of New Testament vocabulary have opened up a new field of labor. This field is given structure by distinctive features, definition, and the assigning of terms that leave room for many other fruitful studies.

But it should also have become clear what care must be exercised when we undertake to draw inferences about an author from the particulars of the vocabulary of a writing. Lists thrown together with haste on the basis of subjective impressions get us nowhere. The entire range of data must be carefully brought to light if the claim to a scientific modus operandi is going to be made. We have constructed a few standards, but much work remains. If I have overlooked studies that have done this, I regret the oversight and will welcome instruction and correction.

Endnotes

1. See Lists 1–6 at the end of the previous chapter.
2. Cf. List 7, "Singles," col. 3, at end of chapter 3 above, p. 98.

## Chapter Six

EVANGELICAL AND HISTORICAL-CRITICAL THEOLOGY

A. The foundations

1. The concept of "theology" is not used univocally but equivocally

The word has a different sense in historical-critical theology than it has among evangelicals.[1] We are accustomed to speaking of Bultmann's theology, or Barth's, or Moltmann's, or Jüngel's. But which of us would speak in the same sense of Spener's theology, or Wesley's, or Moody's, or Spurgeon's? Did the latter group somehow fail to make a theological contribution? Of course not. But they did not develop **their own** theology. That is, they did not construct a theology that could be named after them, containing specific, subjective divergences from God's Word.

It is only at the cost of a considerable independent divergence from God's Word that a theologian's achievement wins renown in the current setting. The person who takes every thought captive to the obedience of Christ (2 Cor. 10:5) and loyally subordinates his thinking to God's revelation constructs no such theology. That person also no longer faces pressure to make a name for himself. For him it is enough if the Lord says to him, "Well done, thou good and faithful servant."

2. The roots of historical-critical theology

There is nothing in historical-critical theology that has not already made its appearance in philosophy.[2] Bacon (1561–1626), Hobbes (1588–1679), Descartes (1596–1650), and Hume (1711–1776) laid the foundations: inductive thought as the only source of knowledge; denial of revelation; monistic world view;[3] separation of faith and reason; doubt as the foundation of knowledge. Hobbes and Hume established a thoroughgoing criticism of miracles; Spinoza (1632–1677) also helped lay the basis for biblical criticism of both Old and New Testaments. Lessing (1729–1781) invented the synoptic problem. Kant's (1724–1804) critique of reason became the basic norm for historical-critical theology. Hegel (1770–1831) furnished the means for the process of demythologizing that Rudolf Bultmann (1884–1976) would effectively implement a century later—after the way had already been prepared by Martin Kähler (1835–1912).

Kierkegaard (1813–1855) served as the executor of Kant's philosophy in the theological realm. The "melancholy Dane" reduced faith to a leap that left rationality behind. He cemented the separation of faith and reason and laid the groundwork for theology's departure from biblical moorings. It is, therefore, not surprising that he wished late in life for a reformer with the boldness to forbid Bible reading among the common people, or that he harbored the opinion that Bible societies (groups intent on propagating the Bible and its message worldwide) had caused irreparable damage.[4] After all, the person who knows God's Word does not let himself be blown about by every wind of doctrine that philosophy kicks up.

Kierkegaard procured for biblical criticism a broad entrance into theology by writing such criticism off as benign: it could do no harm, he maintained, to a genuine faith. This view spread with disastrous effectiveness in part because Kierkegaard was a pious man who uttered many an insightful word. But it is precisely the pious among biblical critics who are most effective at winning to their cause those persons who at first—and on sound biblical grounds—oppose them. Kierkegaard's influence on Bultmann and Barth is understandable, but it is surprising that he became a kind of church father for so many evangelicals.

Heidegger (1889–1976) laid the groundwork for reducing the Christian faith to a possibility of self-understanding; he also had considerable influence on Bultmann's theology. From Karl Marx—who not only condemned the Christian faith as the opium of the people but was probably also a satanist[5]—come Marxist wolves in the guise of (Christian) sheep with their baleful ideologies: theology of hope, theology of revolution, theology of liberation.

Positivism, for which all God-talk is meaningless, and for which the word *God* itself is already dead, produced the various "God is dead" theologies. Here the connection to the Bible is no more than a nostalgic reminiscence that grounds the new theology in the emotional realm, thereby helping it sound more convincing.

The imposing oak of historical-critical theology is not rooted in God's Word but in a philosophy that is inherently hostile to God, does not recognize God's revelatory acts and words, and withholds due recognition from the One who has already appeared as "the way, the truth, and the life" (John 14:6). This philosophy, undeterred, continues its vain quest for truth.

3. Evangelical theology—what it is, and what it should be

a. It should be characteristic of evangelical theology that it is rooted in God's Word and relies on God's revelation as its source of knowledge.

The path to fidelity to Scripture passes through the narrow gate of conversion and repentance, a comprehensive turning to Jesus as Savior and Lord. Included in this is the conversion of one's thinking. This in turn brings with it the repudiation, in Jesus' name, of the influence of historical-critical theology by those who had succumbed to its wiles.

b. Along with being rooted in God's Word, a second indispensable feature of evangelical theology should be that the mind takes its bearings from God, the triune Father, Son, and Holy Spirit.

The mind is like the needle of a compass: without the presence of magnetic north, the needle would swing aimlessly, helpless to resist diversions. Only the magnetic pole enables it to serve as a reliable guide—as long as it takes its bearings from it.

Reason is a whore, Luther says. There is nothing for which logical arguments cannot be adduced. We should resist beguilement through logical arguments. Our minds are swayed by logical arguments, but such arguments are never free standing. They are always wrapped up in a complex of presuppositions. It is not just that questionable arguments exist: arguments themselves are questionable—that is, they must be traced back to their presuppositions. Insofar as they are logical, they may appear to be neutral, but they are most assuredly not.

That is why God's Word admonishes us: "Trust in the LORD with all your heart and lean not on your own understanding" (Prov. 3:5). Is this a denigration of our God-given intellectual capacity? No; it is simply a reminder of why our minds were given and what they were never designed to be: objects in which to place our total trust.

c. Evangelical theology should be alert, mindful of the hidden presence of the historical-critical theologian in even the most pious evangelical.

This hidden presence is the flesh, the sinful nature, and the question is whether we will heed the admonition of the Word of God: "Make no room for the flesh" (Gal. 5:13). It is also true for the conversion of one's thinking that the Christian life is an ongoing process of repentance. That does not mean wearisome agony but rather joyful purifying and liberating jettisoning of deadening encumbrances.

To summarize: evangelical theology should be a mighty oak, rooted in God's revelation and growing toward the guiding light of God's presence. But is this image really accurate—or is the actual situation often otherwise? Are the following factors not often in evidence, despite honest effort to avoid such pitfalls?

1. A naive, uncritical acceptance of the methods and tools of historical-critical theology, with no careful consideration of the philosophical-atheistic background that permeates and largely determines the usage of those methods and tools.

One also finds wholesale acceptance of most basic assumptions of historical-critical theology. But whoever takes up historical-critical theology's tools and fundamental assumptions, insofar as they appear acceptable or at least not dangerous, becomes enmeshed in their presuppositions, whether he is aware of it or not. He goes astray even when he then takes a stance in direct opposition to historical-critical theology.

2. Thoroughgoing acceptance of *Meinungsstatistik*, the tallying up of scholarly opinion rather than the citation of biblical truth, as a method of establishing facts and validating arguments.[6] It is dangerous even when the lists of authorities cited distinguish themselves to some extent by the inclusion of work by evangelical scholars. The truth of God's Word is not, however, dependent on the exegetical solutions that are favored by the majority.

3. There is often the attempt to give evangelical answers to historical-critical questions—within the framework established by historical-criticism. Distinctively evangelical ways of posing the questions hardly come into view.

4. Selection of non-controversial, out-of-the-way topics for personal research, such as biographical subjects or some other inoffensive matter. This tendency is quite understandable among doctoral candidates for the sake of avoiding conflict that could be deadly to receiving their degrees. But is it any less common among established persons? Is there, perhaps, at work here a strong desire to receive recognition as "scientific" or "critical" right alongside historical-critical colleagues?

5. Isn't it the case that answers to problems are not sought in God's Word, but rather—for evangelicals as for historical-critical theology—in the secondary literature, although the evangelical will show a certain preference for evangelical secondary literature?

Especially symptomatic is remoteness to the Bible. God's Word is hardly to be found in theological works, unless it happens to be the explicit object of investigation. *God's revelation is not taken seriously as a source of knowledge.* One essentially shares the understanding of Scripture common to historical-critical theology, even if one has no intention of taking up all of its results. In intellectual labor one does not live on the Holy Scriptures, because one is still wrapped up in the separation of faith and thought, a separation that historical-critical theology picked up from philosophy. One is not dependent on the Holy Spirit, the third person of the Trinity, who should lead us into all truth, according to Jesus' own words. That spiritual matters require spiritual understanding (cf. 1 Cor. 2:12–16) receives no consideration; Jesus Christ, our Savior and Lord, appears at most as the object of theology.

To a considerable degree, unfortunately, evangelical theology does not resemble a tree that—rooted in God's Word—grows independently. It resembles rather an ivy plant that, even if rooted in God's Word, ekes out a somewhat meager existence draped around the tree of historical-critical theology. It is not fully one with the tree, but it is also never fully removed from it. It occasionally distances itself from its host, but basically maintains constant close contact.

B. The implementation

1. Historical-critical theology = scientific theology? Claim and reality

a. The claim: historical-critical theology lays claim to exclusive validity in scientific theology.

In the area of theology, whatever does not conform to historical-critical conventions is not acknowledged as scientific; it accordingly remains disregarded and is suppressed. The blessing of "scientific" extends only to those who accept historical-critical premises and move within the traditional framework of the disciplines.[7]

b. Reality: the actual procedure does not measure up to the demands that one could reasonably make of a scientific approach.

The premises employed are not openly admitted, and their prejudicial character, which is by no means the result of scientific work, is suppressed. In the implementation of research these premises are treated as established verities and passed along to students as unassailable facts and foundational knowledge.[8] These premises include the following:

1. Research must proceed as if God does not exist.

   In this way God's revelation is barred from consideration at the outset, for the manifest God will not bear being pushed to the side, even provisionally, as if he were not there. Anyone who speaks like this does not realize what he is saying. As a basic principle this premise is a-theistic or, more correctly, anti-theistic. It denies God, who revealed himself and is therefore manifest. One cannot suspend belief in this God for the sake of research goals. But with this unjustified demand, historical-critical theology makes the denial of belief in the living, triune God one of its basic premises. Spurgeon rightly concluded that "the weed of modern theology is nothing other than unbelief that is too cowardly to own up to its name."[9]

2. The world view of monism, which gained ascendancy in the philosophy of the Enlightenment. This is made a foundation of theological thought and discourse.

3. Kant's critique of reason is respected like an unalterable decree of the Medes and Persians.

   I can still remember how Bultmann stated in his lectures: We must bear in mind that we live after Kant and that it is no longer permissible to think as people were allowed prior to Kant's philosophy. Even where it is not so clearly formulated as this (which is a flat contradiction of the first Barmen thesis[10]), the state of affairs that Bultmann describes is widely adhered to.

4. Every new philosophy that appears is treated as a revelation commanding respect.

Without realizing it, many follow in Hegel's train by treating the
philosophical constructs of an individual as the self-disclosure of
the absolute Spirit. These constructs are immediately generalized:
thus thinks modern man. Such generalization leads subsequently
to the propagation of these individual mental games. The foundation here is not God's Word but rather—following Hegel—the
dubious concept of truth as conceived in humanism.

5. In historical-critical theology "scientific work" is held to take
place when one sets up a hypothesis, supports it using a few arguments, and stabilizes the original hypothesis using additional
ones. In this manner card houses are erected that arrogantly call
themselves "scientific" but share with real science only the
name.[11]

In the natural sciences, a hypothesis is the foundation for research.
It is tested either through experiments or through methodologically
arrayed, wide-ranging observation. If it fails this testing, it is rejected.
In so-called "scientific" theology, however, there seems to be widespread ignorance of the fact that a hypothesis—a supposition that
something is so—is nothing more than an assertion, for which one
must, according to basic mathematical procedure, first clarify the
presupposition and adduce the proof. Instead, hypotheses that have
found acceptance are treated like scientific results and circulated as
facts. Certainly, experimental confirmation is not often possible in
the realm of the humanities; still, particularly when one claims to
do scientific work, one should feel obligated to adduce data that will
furnish at least some broad evidential coverage of one's claims. Instead of this many are content to make isolated observations in support of a hypothesis, treating contrary considerations as if they simply
did not exist.[12]

Less concern is shown for the object of research than for—largely
rhetorical—interaction with other hypotheses. "Scientific knowledge"
is seen as that which has become established in the interplay of opin-

ions and not—as one might expect—that which has withstood earnest investigation subjecting a given hypothesis to searching light.

> c. *Result: under close scrutiny, the results that form the basic scaffolding of theology's major disciplines turn out to be that which will—for whatever reasons—furnish the basis for a consensus.*

As soon as one ceases to be deterred by the consensus of established opinions and arbitrary judgments, as soon as one ceases pitting hypothesis against hypothesis, but rather begins to investigate the object of the hypotheses with scientific rigor, one finds that the—allegedly scientific—results that have become the supporting pillars of historical-critical theology are untenable. Six examples of widely held but finally untenable hypotheses are as follows:

1. The carving up of the five books of Moses into various sources (the documentary hypothesis) can be passed along to students only by ignoring the findings of the last 100 years in archeology, and by closing one's eyes to the manner in which this alleged "assured result" of research of Old Testament theology ever gained currency in the first place.[13]

2. The alleged assured results of historical-critical theology into the Exodus and the Conquest turn out to be untenable if, first of all, one makes use of the wealth of material furnished by archeological research in recent times, and second, one employs a synchronic chronology instead of trusting the fictitious Egyptian chronology of Manetho (ca. 280 B.C.). Manetho's concern in gathering his material was to win respect from the Greeks for the Egyptians. He did this in part through greatly exaggerating the length of their history.[14] The biblical Scriptures find ample confirmation through extra-biblical documents (such as the Ipuwer papyrus) and require no critical adjustment or correction.

3. The prophetic books, seen in their simultaneous and subsequent historical context, make critical reconstructions that regard as

genuine only a few verses in every chapter, seem ridiculous. The evidence that the prophets' promises were fulfilled right down to the fine details was set forth long ago.[15] It is still, however, widely disregarded.

4. Literary criticism of the New Testament including form criticism and redaction criticism turn out to be untenable, because precise investigation of the evidence in the Synoptic Gospels reveals that the alleged synoptic problem does not exist. There are no conclusive data that support theories of literary dependence among the Synoptics; that leaves the two-source theory (and all other such theories) hanging in thin air. The literary criticism of the New Testament is in this sense finished. For form criticism, which built "the history of the synoptic tradition" on the foundation of the two-source theory, has no foundation, and redaction criticism, which constructed the theology of the evangelists from the changes they allegedly made to the written sources they had before them, turns out to be groundless.[16]

5. It has long since been shown through detailed study of Gnosticism that none of the Gnostic literature known to us arose until after the onset of the Christian era. In spite of this, historical-critical theology still makes use of Gnosticism as a source and origin of essential segments of the New Testament (e.g., John 1, Phil. 2:6–11). The literary evidence renders acceptance of a pre-Christian Gnosticism impossible, but this is conveniently ignored by maintaining the existence of traditions that allegedly existed in pre-Christian times; these are said to have formed the basis for Gnostic treatises. Why argue for such pre-Christian traditions? Because there is evidence for them? No; one will search in vain for such evidence. The reason is rather apt to be that otherwise one could not chalk up the New Testament passages that speak of Jesus' preexistence to Gnosticism and thereby dismiss these passages as nonbinding.

6. Another set of allegedly pre-Christian traditions that will not stand up to scrutiny are those relied on by theories of pre-Christian Jew-

ish apocalyptic. Such theories have been widespread even though historical-critical theology itself dates nearly all the Jewish apocalyptic writings to a time when the New Testament writings had already been completed. Certain parts of the Book of Enoch were dated to the first or second century B.C., and the presence of portions of Enoch among Qumran documents confirms their pre-Christian date. The portion of Enoch, however, that can be drawn upon to compare with the New Testament and that is required to justify the assertion that Jesus borrowed the title "Son of Man" from Jewish apocalyptic, is not to be found in the Qumran documents. The Similitudes or so-called parables occur only in Ethiopic Enoch. The attempt to date these "before 64 B.C." has been replaced by Klaus Beyer's dating of the document to "between 4 B.C. (67:8 refers to the death of Herod) and A.D. 70 (56:5–8 speaks only of Jerusalem's seizure by the Parthians in 40 B.C.)"[17] These two proof-texts, however, cannot bear the burden of proof for Beyer's later dating, any more than the evidence advanced for previous theories supported earlier dates. Enoch 67:8 speaks generally and says nothing about either death or Herod. Nor can 56:5–8 be related to the Parthian conquest of Jerusalem; its wording does not permit this. Jerusalem cannot be seized by the Parthians; they begin murder among themselves; they are swallowed up by Sheol before the eyes of the elect. But what happened in 40 B.C. was this: The gates of Jerusalem were opened for the Parthians, who attacked alone; they plundered it and withdrew with their booty. The Enoch text fits what we expect to find in the Bar-Kochba uprising (A.D. 132–135).

Thus, no proof has been brought forth that shows that either the title "Son of Man" or the apocalyptic sections in the New Testament have been preconditioned by Jewish apocalyptic. If one abides by extant writings and does not rely on alleged traditions, then it is the New Testament that is earlier, not the apocalyptic writings.

It is worth noting that a number of the verdicts of so-called "modern" theology formed part of the arsenal of the most ancient foes and detractors of the Christian faith. Two examples:

Criticism of the Book of Daniel and the attempt to place it in the second century B.C. rather than the sixth, go back to the Greek philosopher Porphyry (A.D. 233–304). His motive for this redating was to reduce the already fulfilled promises found in Daniel to *vaticinia ex eventu*—"prophecies" concocted after the events had already occurred.[18]

Lessing's remarks on the literary dependence of the Synoptic Gospels are a rather precisely detailed repetition of what Celsus (ca. A.D. 178), a sworn enemy of Christianity, stated long ago. He was roundly refuted by Origen (ca. A.D. 185–254) in the following century.[19]

These are just two examples. This number could probably be increased through more intensive study of the sources.

The "results" of historical-critical theology mentioned above are calculated to call in question the alleged "scientific" nature of such theology. "Scientific theology" is a colossus with clay feet.

We are not, of course, maintaining that historical-critical theology, which has produced thousands of researchers over the years, has no results whatsoever to show for its labors; certainly a number of useful detailed investigations have been produced. Since, however, the most basic underlying data informing this theology are wrong, it is understandable that the individual results, among which are to be found sober scientific labors, are impaired, because they are closely connected with the erroneous underlying data.

2. Evangelical theology and the claim to scientific character

a. The effort to show that it is scientific, too:

The claim to exclusive validity, the claim to be scientific, which historical-critical theology makes, exerts a powerful pressure on evangelical theology to conform. Since there is widespread failure among evangelicals to see through both the doubtful presuppositions of this alleged scientific character and the questionable nature of its results, a high premium is placed on being regarded as scientific just as the historical-critical thinkers are. After all, one is thoroughly prepared, willing, and in a position to pursue full involvement in scholarly work. Unfortunately, however, there is no possibility of evangelicals succeeding in this enterprise. For what is deemed "scientific" receives that recognition only from historical-critical theology, which—in spite of its numerical minority in the entirety of Christendom—occupies all the key positions The situation takes on the unfortunate appearance of the fatal footrace between the hare and hedgehog, because historical-critical theology can step forth at any moment and exclaim: "I'm already here."[20]

b. The procedure:

This breathless competition has an unfortunate outcome. Evangelicals give little consideration to which crucial questions need distinctively evangelical answers. Instead, they are essentially consumed with giving evangelical answers to historical-critical questions, as far as this is possible. Much good, sound effort is expended that, strictly speaking, has little relevance for the evangelical context, but rather only furnishes more stones for building up academia's ivory tower. Much-needed investigations that would correspond to direct felt needs among evangelicals are not taken up. Evangelical scholars are so much accustomed to the manner in which historical-critical theology places questions that the topics evangelicals choose to work on are often little more than an echo of what the historical-critical agenda has already established.

c. The result:

The situation sketched under a) and b) above has an unfortunate outcome. From the historical-critical point of view, evangelical books and articles often fail to measure up to expected scientific standards (as defined by historical-critical theology). At the same time, from an evangelical vantage point, the same writings fall short of a thoroughgoing fidelity to the Bible. Work designed to do justice to two worlds of thought is fully claimed by neither. Ought this situation to persist? Or could it be time to undertake foundational deliberations in the hope of glimpsing alternatives to this state of affairs?[21]

C. A new beginning

1. Theological thinking rooted in God's Word and oriented toward the triune God

Such thinking should be aware that an inexhaustible source of knowledge stands at our disposal in what God has revealed. In most areas of life and knowledge we have not even begun to draw from this source. All too obediently we have submitted to the separation between faith and knowledge that philosophy has argued for and historical-critical theology has observed for centuries. Even evangelicals have reduced the infallibility of the Holy Scriptures to that which is necessary for faith and practice. They fail to notice that in making this reduction they have made a false turn.

2. Scholarly labor as brotherly service

Theological work that is faithful to the Bible has a different value than "theological science" in historical-critical theology. It does not exist "to research whatever admits of investigation"; it is rather to be a service-performing activity intent on the Lord's commission to furnish help for fellow-believers. Ivory tower scholarship and theological work that is faithful to the Bible are mutually contradictory entities.

In historical-critical theology the principle of "the initiated" reigns: people privy to the assumptions and findings of historical-critical theology. Prior to the Second World War there was only a small elite of such "initiates," in keeping with the erstwhile Semler's counsel. In the 1950s and 1960s there was a gradual opening up of the ranks of the initiated to include those who were academically trained. We may liken these initiates to clergy who have taken holy orders. They have knowledge of lore of which the average person is unaware. But within the spectrum of religious initiation there are "lower orders," too: since the late 1960s, these lower orders have come to include initiation into the synoptic problem and source criticism of the Pentateuch, critical theories that are now dished up in every deacon and lay training seminar. Since the 1980s, at the latest, these theories have also been thrust on school children. The principle of "the initiated," however—the differences between the initiated of various levels who talk the same language, on the one hand, and those who are content to let such matters lie, on the other—is still in effect, despite the expansion of the dissemination of such theories.

Theology that is faithful to the Bible, in contrast, must never forget that all who believe in Jesus Christ our Lord are taught by God. The Holy Spirit has been poured out in our hearts and will lead us into all truth. Indeed, our Lord Jesus thanks his Father in heaven that he has hidden this from the wise and knowledgeable but revealed it to infants. Woe to us when we set ourselves up as an intelligentsia who dictate to the so-called layperson what he may and may not derive from his reading of God's Word.

Theology that is faithful to the Bible, as already stated, is a service-performing activity. That does not mean, however, that it should take its cues from short-term (and perhaps shortsighted) needs of the moment. The Lord gives instructions for the work that needs doing; but brotherly fellowship aids in hearing what he is saying. "Unless the Lord builds the house, its builders labor in vain" (Ps. 127:1) holds true also for theology that is faithful to the Bible.

The brotherly service of theology that is faithful to the Bible should grow out of faith and love. "Whatever is not from faith is sin" (Rom. 14:23). "Do everything in love" (1 Cor. 16:14).

The theologian who is faithful to the Bible is free, thanks to redemption in Jesus Christ, from the demand that he make a name for himself. "My Father will honor the one who serves me," says our Lord Jesus (John 14:26). That is sufficient. True, we are admonished to pursue love earnestly (1 Cor. 14:1), but we are not under pressure to compete with each other. The promise of James 1:5 applies to theological work, too: "If any of you lacks wisdom, he should ask God, who gives generously to all without finding fault, and it will be given to him." What a glorious, relaxed, and fruitful task is ours under such auspices!

3. Theological work that is faithful to the Bible is independent in the way it poses its questions as well as in its methods

The way questions are posed emerges from what is needful and not out of the complex of traditions that comprise the disciplines of theology. The methods employed are not simply those already present in the historical-critical nexus. With the help of God-given wisdom, methods should rather—to the necessary extent—be newly developed in connection with the respective tasks at hand and in a way commensurate with the object.[22]

Also in need of new development—or transformation—are the forms in which the fruits of scholarly labor are transmitted. An example here would be the commentary.

In historical-critical theology, commentaries have the function (among other things) of bringing the recalcitrant biblical text into line with the hypotheses that the critic uses. Exegesis thereby takes on the function of explaining away those data that count against the pre-decided hypotheses, or of adjusting those data in the course of interpretation so that they conform to the perspective the critic has adopted. Since the exegete follows the critical consensus in *Tendenz,* but wishes his work to be original in detail, individual explanations of the same passages in various commentaries often contradict each other. The large number of details requiring explanation, given the presuppositions of this approach, makes it necessary to use a commentary; the differences between explanations mean that any one commentary will not be sufficient.

A commentary that is faithful to the Bible, in contrast, has the task of making specialist knowledge available as a brotherly service. This knowledge is not absolutely essential to a profound understanding of the Word of God, but it can render essential aid in that direction. Such a commentary can help in at least five ways:

1. Support can be given through a clear grammatical analysis of the original text based on thorough knowledge of the original languages. Such an analysis could also pass along possible alternative translations, weighing the presuppositions behind and consequences of each one and setting forth the preferred translation in a fair and responsible manner.

2. The meanings of words can be illuminated through concept analysis (i.e., through the relaying of results of this field of investigation along with references to the relevant literature). The basic

meaning of words should constantly be passed along, since this will shed light on many variant meanings. Here etymological derivation and important variations of a word in its semantic history also have their place.

3. Also helpful are: findings regarding the cultural environment of the Old or New Testaments; relevant research summaries of archeology, illustrated where appropriate; insights from the extrabiblical history.

4. The course of thought and organization of the Scriptures can be opened up more effectively on the basis of intensive study of them.

5. An overview of God's Word can be made available through adducing parallel passages for those with little Bible knowledge. The basic insight that Holy Scripture interprets itself must receive due weight in the composition of a commentary that is faithful to the Bible. Every biblical writing is a part of the entirety of God's revelation; the commentator must bear this in mind, even as he seeks diligently to do justice to each individual portion, correctly handling the Word of Truth (2 Tim. 2:15).

A commentary that is faithful to the Bible should do all of the above. Yet the fact remains: God's Word is not dependent on some formal process of interpretation. It is directly accessible to every child of God through the Holy Spirit. For this reason, the use of commentaries remains an option for consultation when one has need; it should never be overplayed as a moral necessity. All children of God are taught by God. We ought never overlook that fact.

4. Theological work that is faithful to the Bible as critical assessment of historical-critical theology's supporting pillars

Although theological work that is faithful to the Bible should and can grow out from its own basis, it must still, for the sake of orientation, perform the service of staying abreast of historical-critical theology.

Considering the nature of historical-critical theology, it would not be difficult to refute all its fundamental tenets. We are, indeed, dealing with presuppositions and prejudgments having no solid foundation in God's Word. But we must be quite clear on this point: it will be a battle with a twelve-headed hydra that replaces each head that is lopped off with two more. New arguments are likely to be advanced constantly, as one can already observe in the area of the synoptic problem. We should probably expect a general turning away from historical-critical theology just as little as we expect a similar disavowal of the untenable theory of evolution—barring God's direct intervention. We need God's leading, therefore, to recognize those points where we should take up the battle so as not to dissipate our energies unwisely. A few examples will probably suffice to point the way for the evangelical camp toward a more decisive disavowal of historical-critical theology. Many have not yet seen fit to bring themselves to this disavowal, long called for by God's Word, because they regard historical-critical theology as "scientific" and regard its alleged scientific character to be indispensable.

D. A new concept

Once the fundamental incompatibility between historical-critical and biblically faithful theology has come to light, we must decide whether we want to dismiss the state of affairs we have uncovered, or whether we are finally willing to draw the obvious conclusions. Do we want to continue clinging to the fiction that there is only one theology, albeit with differences of degree? Do we want to continue to help erect the structure of historical-critical theology, possibly even just at points where the anti-Christian agendum does not stand out quite so clearly? Or do we wish to summon ourselves to a consistent "Come out from among them"?

Under the present circumstances that would certainly be a call for an exodus leading first into a desert, away from the fleshpots of Egypt. Isn't such a call, however, really our only alternative, so that God's Word does not continue to be abused—both by those who don't know any better as well as by those who could know better?

It is not enough for the individual researcher who is faithful to the Bible to take up his work, to the extent this is possible, according to the basic principles enunciated above. We need a concept that will enable us effectively to organize and institutionalize theological work that is faithful to Scripture. Historical-critical thinking has in large measure succeeded worldwide in taking over the key positions in ecclesiastical oversight boards and theological education centers, and it is clearly continuing its forward march. We must finally respond to it effectively.

1. Solidarity and division of labor

We cannot permit ourselves to fragment our theological resources, which are already too limited. Solidarity and division of labor must, therefore, become the foundational structure of evangelical theological work. Among God's people there is sufficient place and opportunity to qualify oneself carefully, but in the life of a child of God there should be no room for acquiring status in competition with others (especially not at their expense, or in any detrimental manner). Such fleshly aspirations are to be renounced.

We should therefore—as far as possible—take a common look at the research work needing to be done and try to carry out a worldwide division of labor. True, we will immediately encounter the objection that no researcher will or can allow his work to be prescribed for him, since creative work is fueled by the outworking of inner compulsion. But we can respond to this with the incentive that arises from clear insight into a broad spectrum of recognized necessities. Within this spectrum many can find a fruitful research opportunity that is appropriate for them. Let us not forget the large number of pending masters and doctoral projects whose themes only rarely go back to the initiative of those who produce them.[23] *What a wealth of fruitful and necessary work could be performed if we evangelicals really pooled our resources in order to aid the birth of an independent theology that is true to the Bible.*

2. Weighing research projects and considering priorities

In view of our limited resources we must set priorities. The necessary instrument for this would be an international research structure that could be worked at through focused inquiries or polls, professional conferences, and interdisciplinary international theological symposia. It is important, however, that clear standards for a theology that is faithful to the Bible be set from the beginning to avoid any later frustrating, endless tugs-of-war over what can be accepted in this research structure and what cannot. The international research structure for biblically faithful theology is not there to monopolize research or even regulate it politically; it should rather furnish orientation regarding which research projects have priority for a theology that is faithful to the Bible. It does not, therefore, have to accept everything that one could—with some good will—still accept despite its being borderline. To be any less discriminating would gradually blur the boundaries. Such a research structure must hew to a clear and unambiguous line. It can also be discriminating in its editorial policies without questioning the right of other positions to exist.

The international research structure should consolidate for every discipline the most urgent research tasks. Here the conventional dividing lines among the disciplines are not the law of the Medes and Persians to which we are bound no matter what.[24]

The research structure of a discipline is not there to list all possible research projects and to name every subject that could be investigated in that discipline, assuming that resources and means are available. It *should* rather *highlight those projects that are*, given the current conditions, pressing, in order to constitute an independent theology that is faithful to the Bible. The research structure should furnish orientation for the allocation of themes for dissertations appropriate to licentiate-, masters-, and doctoral-level research. It can also provide publishers with criteria for selecting those titles that they should incorporate into their publication lines. Along with the choice of theme, of course, the quality standards remain decisive and may not be undermined because of the urgency of the theme.

The research structure requires further leadership and reworking at appropriate time intervals. This needs to be overseen by the same kinds of persons who established the research structure at the outset: experts who are faithful to the Bible, engaged in an internationally coordinated joint effort. The research structure lists urgent, contemporary research projects; there is accordingly need to join together in getting on with the task so that its fruit can begin to be realized as soon as possible.

3. *Personal contribution to the international research structure*

In order to move beyond abstractions, I would like to set forth a set of suggestions as to what I see as priority subjects and procedures for such a research structure. This contribution is conditioned by the circumstances of my own situation, which involves an intimate knowledge of historical-critical theology along with a limited familiarity with evangelical scholarship. It also involves theological work across a broad spectrum rather than intensive specialization. Finally, my outlook reflects the German scene. It goes without saying that my views are in need of supplementation and correction.

a. General

1. At least in the German-speaking world, no first-rate, comprehensive, biblically faithful theological reference work exists that covers related areas (archeology, creation research, history of pedagogy as well as of philosophy and literature in biographical articles). I have in mind something comparable in level and scope to RGG (*Die Religion in Geschichte und Gegenwart*).

2. True of all theological disciplines is this: their history needs to be written anew, since the existing histories—at least in the German-speaking world—are by no means objectively written. In historical-critical theology, the history of the disciplines that has been effectually passed along consists essentially of the line of ancestors that well-known theologians have constructed for themselves.[25]

3. Research that is faithful to the Bible is in need of coming to its own independent conclusions regarding questions of dating. Dating within the framework of historical-critical theology is to a considerable degree not neutral but rather determined by critical hypotheses. In addition, important findings from archeology and dates stemming from the history of groups and movements faithful to the Bible are not passed along. For these reasons the presently accepted

dates in individual specialized areas need to be investigated. We are also in need of an overall framework within which to work out dating.

b. Biblical theology

(1) Attaining independence in dating

Urgently needed is inquiry into the biblical dating framework, the systematic investigation and correlation of all dates which God's Word itself gives. Studies that already exist should be consulted and evaluated toward that end. Synchronic chronologies (Velikovsky), which integrate biblical references with the flow of the whole of ancient history, should also be consulted, along with archeological data. Sources from ancient history should also be used in order to arrive at a complete picture. Biblical references, however, have priority.

Individual questions arising out of the above must be given fresh treatment. Dates established on historical-critical premises are to be investigated according to such considerations as the following:

- Where do historical-critical biases affect dates?
- Where are dates *influenced by historical-critical hypotheses*? Examples of problem areas here: dates based on the temporal sequence of biblical books when that sequence is the result of claimed literary dependence or use of sources; dating based on literary-critical operations that assume secondary enlargement; dating established in connection with alleged inauthenticity of biblical books as a whole or in part.
- Where have dates been established in connection with *alleged history of religions dependencies*?

(2) Basic investigation into questions of introduction

There is need to scrutinize where assertions (including those made by evangelicals) are marked by historical-critical prejudgments:

- with respect to dating
- with respect to questions regarding authorship

- with respect to determining and describing the original readership
- with respect to the question of literary unity
- with respect to questions of history of religions relationships
- with respect to the value placed on traditions passed on by the postapostolic church
- with respect to judgments made in the area of textual criticism

Everything is to be investigated from the ground up. Nothing is to be accepted without close inspection, not even from evangelical literature, since it has been dependent to no small extent on historical-critical research, which has represented its prejudices as facts.

(3) New Testament

There is need for commentaries on the three synoptic gospels under the assumption that each of them is equally original. This assumption accords with their self-testimony and ancient church tradition as well as the unambiguous data they contain.

There is need for incorporating John's gospel as the gospel that rounds out the others. Are there valid reasons for holding that the author could not have been the disciple of Jesus? Here consideration should be directed to his youthful age at the time of his actual discipleship and his advanced age at the time of authorship. Also to consider are the addressees (Gentile Christians) as well as the time of writing subsequent to the destruction of the Jerusalem temple. Bultmann's argumentation is to be examined as well as theories that John's gospel shows dependence on Gnosticism or Qumran. John's alleged dependence on sources is to be investigated in connection with thoroughgoing reconsideration of the whole matter of how literary dependence is established.

Also to be explored are the alleged pre-Pauline traditions that have been gleaned from his epistles by literary criticism. The criteria for such an investigation have yet to be established. Historical-critical bias had an especially large hand in this area.

We still lack an investigation that takes all evidence and arguments into account regarding the alleged pseudonymity of Ephesians, Colossians, 2 Thessalonians, and the Pastorals, it seems to me, although respectable individual investigations are available. On the

one hand, the question regarding pseudonymity in ancient literature needs to be taken up, and on the other the input of word statistics should be adduced, which by no means supports the current
critical consensus. Negative arguments should not only be scrutinized with respect to every document individually; they should also
be categorized, tabulated, and weighed as a whole. The object of
such investigation is not the question of "genuineness" but rather
the criticism thereof. For this reason such a study would need to contain a history of declarations of inauthenticity. Perhaps it would be
meaningful to include the question of dependence between 2 Peter and
Jude in the investigation; if not, one would need to devote a sepa-
rate investigation to them in order finally to rid the world of this fairy
tale spread by criticism.

(4) Research of comparative material
from the history of religion

Urgently necessary would be a systematic study of foundational
principles that would illuminate the presuppositions and conclusions
of the history of religion's dissolving of God's revelation into the religious environment of the Old and New Testaments. Such a move
would also expose the evolutionary thought at work.

The dating of comparative material used in history of religion work
is to be investigated. In connection with this, untenable allegations regarding dependence are to be exposed. Here the key allegation in need
of demythologizing is the claim that alleged history of religion parallels that are demonstrably later than the biblical books to which they
are being compared go back to (improvable) traditions that predate the
biblical books. Here investigation must focus on what conditions ob-
tain in the formation and transmitting of religious traditions. A further
question is whether the rise of syncretistic traditions is possible and
whether such appearances can be demonstrated.

The way that the scientific study of religion stylizes and schematizes
religious phenomena should be investigated, for it is this stylizing and
schematizing that makes the phenomena comparable in the first
place. The question should be raised and probed regarding the scientific study of religion: has it not first of all oriented itself to the

Old and New Testament and then brought mythical fables to bear on the religious concepts it investigates—all in order to place the resulting literary creations, considered to be comparative material from the history of religion, ahead of the biblical writings? To put it another way: are the works of R. Reitzenstein, Ernst Michel, Hans Jonas, and the like really dealing with history of religion material, or do they rather amount to a creative cooking-up of such material, which then, for example through "existential interpretation," creates the very parallels that the New Testament is claimed to be dependent on? Is this not how the New Testament is brought into view as a "syncretistic phenomenon"?

Also in need of study are the extra-biblical creation and flood myths. The question needs to be posed whether these are pre-Abrahamic traditions, preserved in pure form in the Bible and modified and secondarily mythologized elsewhere.

The Bible-Babel dispute needs to be taken up again under different premises, and mankind's early degeneration into polytheism needs to be exhibited.

Urgently in need of investigation are the so-called apocalyptic sections of the gospels in connection with the evidence that there was never any such thing as a pre-Christian Jewish apocalyptic, since its whole corpus, including the Similitudes of Ethiopic Enoch, arose at a time when the gospels were already extant. In this context belongs also:

- the (in my view not yet decisively settled) question of the dating of Daniel;
- the question of Zoroastrian influence on the Old Testament and first-century Judaism, since these are made use of in theories of the rise of Jewish apocalyptic;
- the question whether a connection between John the Baptist and Jewish apocalyptic can clearly be shown;
- the question whether a connection between Qumran and Jewish apocalyptic can be proven.

It needs to be investigated whether Jewish apocalyptic, as portrayed in the relevant writings stretching from the 90s to the 130s, is not a competing movement, affected by Christianity, which arose after the destruction of the temple in A.D. 70 and played its greatest role in the decades before the Bar-Kochba uprising.

Bultmann's claim should be examined that miracles were commonplace in the history of religion environment of the New Testament. An urgent wish is the translation of the documents he cites in his favor into German and English. Then each person could finally determine for himself what these documents contain: the one only a collection of ancient ghost stories—not comparable in either form or content with the New Testament miracles stories—and the other (Weinreich's *Antike Heilungswunder*) miracles attributed primarily to the Caesars who lived *after* the rise of the gospels, making it impossible for the gospels to have been influenced by such miracles stories.

In the German-speaking realm, at least, there is an urgent necessity for intensive investigation of studies that have established that there was no pre-Christian Gnosticism, contributing to a new comprehensive presentation of Gnosticism. (As far as I know, the book already mentioned above has not yet been translated into German: Edwin M. Yamauchi, *Pre-Christian Gnosticism*.) In this connection, Hans Jonas's argumentation in his *Spätantiker Geist und Gnosis* must be sifted; it has exerted decisive influence on historical-critical theology.

In addition, however, the arguments for a pre-Christian Gnosticism in introductory literature should be tabulated and examined. Further, the occurrence of the word *gnosis* and its derivatives in the New Testament should be studied to determine where there is usage as a Gnostic *terminus technicus* and where not. Other passages that are regarded as allusions to Gnosticism also need to be scrutinized.

The classification by the church fathers of Gnosticism needs to be pursued and the question explored whether Gnosticism was perhaps the product of speculative minds that brushed up against the Christian faith and then turned aside from it (Simon Magus).

In a word, the issue is whether Gnosticism was a general spiritual mood of late antiquity that included a form impacted by Christianity; or whether it was an enterprise competing with Christianity and furnishing it with its starting point. In the former case, Christianity precedes Gnosticism; in the latter, the reverse is true. To the best of my knowledge, no one has explained at all to what degree Gnosticism has the various periods of Christianity's tolerance to thank for its dissemination.

c. Church history

Although it is preeminently church history whose presentations possess the aura of neutrality and objectivity, these presentations are by no means free of bias. In various areas we must reckon with negative, non-, and deficient coverage. We must investigate the standard church-historical presentations alert for

- negative, non-, or deficient coverage in the area of missions
- negative, non-, or deficient coverage of baptizing sects and churches in Reformation and post-Reformation times
- negative, non-, or deficient coverage of Pietists and other groups faithful to the Bible in the eighteenth, nineteenth, and twentieth centuries
- negative, non-, or deficient coverage of Lutherans and Catholics during the so-called Protestament Scholastic era, as well as of Methodists, Baptists, Plymouth Brethren, Pentecostals, and other groups

Along with the above areas, one notes a strong tendency to focus too narrowly on national church entities; this leads to failure to grasp the church's universality as the unity of the body of Christ does not come into consideration.

Urgent needs, as I see them include:

1. A comprehensive history of the church, perhaps in eight to ten volumes. This would scrutinize the various angles of approach in church history writing and furnish a comprehensive presentation of the entirety of church history. It would be readable for the untrained as well as for the specialized historian.

2. A detailed compendium of church history in one volume (like that of Heussi, but from an evangelical point of view).

3. The overemphasis of rationalistic-philosophical theological circles in the ancient, medieval, and modern church calls for a fresh treatment. Why is the incorporation of philosophy in the history of the ancient church seen as positive, as openness to the world which preserved the church from degenerating into a sect, when at the same time it appears (rightly!) legitimate, from the standpoint of the Reformation, to speak of the "stifling of theology by philosophy" (to quote Link)? Are the apologists the ones who should really be seen as furnishing the model of what it means to be a theologian?

4. Regarding assessment of the conflict over the Trinity, several sub-fields need treating:

   • The false presupposition needs refuting that the New Testament, while it contains triadic formulations, says not a word about the Trinity in the proper sense.
   • The negative assessment of Irenaeus's doctrine of redemption is to be investigated and the question answered: to what extent is this doctrine identical with the Christological assertions of the New Testament when the New Testament is taken at face value rather than attenuated through historical-critical operations?
   • It is probable that the treatment of Athanasius's theology needs investigation.
   • The positive valuation of the left-wing Origenists needs reexamination.

5. The subject of "Luther and the peasant farmers" needs nonpartisan investigation.

6. Calvin's idea of a Christian-civic polity should be explored to determine whether it is "legalistic" as often charged.

7. The claim that Pietists and Rationalists were actually kindred spirits should be investigated.

8. To my knowledge we lack a comprehensive treatment of the relationship between evangelical revival movements and state churches.

9. Outbreaks of the occult in the eighteenth, nineteenth, and twentieth centuries needs thorough research.

10. There is still lacking a dissertation on J. M. Goeze that assesses him rightly and gives a good analysis of his polemical writing.

In the execution of the above research topics, the need is for truly seminal research growing first of all out of exhaustive knowledge and utilization of the primary sources.

The above must suffice as a few personal contributions to the international research structure that we are discussing in these pages. These suggestions may serve to stimulate others in their respective areas of expertise. Most important is disciplined focus: the point is not to tabulate everything that could ever possibly be in need of research; it is rather to underscore that which is most urgent, under the given circumstances, in order to constitute a theology that is faithful to the Bible.

4. Realization of solidarity through transparency and information

When no one knows who is working on what where, misdirected effort is the inevitable outcome: some themes get repeated treatment, while others receive none. Joint effort in research that is faithful to the Bible is only possible when information is accessible regarding the work underway in various countries.

A pressing demand is evangelical central libraries in every larger country; these would be sites for collaboration with smaller countries or countries where Christians are in the minority. Such libraries should contain all new evangelical publications through obligatory delivery from evangelical publishers. That which is hardly accessible for linguistic reasons should be accessible in the form of abstracts. One should at least be able to borrow older evangelical publications from the central libraries.

The central libraries should also work together in cataloging and exchange of material. An orderly means of exchanging duplicates and other surplus materials would also need to be developed. The libraries should be optimally organized according to a unified system. Here also the principle must be: cooperation instead of competition.

The central libraries would be appropriate sites for information regarding ongoing research to be collected and made available. What is computerized here would already be the researcher's exclusive property, and the same protection would extend for the continuation of a work's basic theme through the completion of that work. Not until after the point of completion would any material that the work does not consider be cleared for treatment by others. Until then that sub-field of work is closed off so that no one has the possibility of turning work already done by someone else to his own advantage through robbery of ideas. At the same time, everyone would be in a position significantly to distance his own work area from that of others. The point here is to benefit from pooling of information (without contributing to thievery), yet to avoid needless duplication of research.

In this way the full effectiveness of scholarly work in brotherly collaboration could be—through information and transparency—attained.

May these reflections assist in consolidating a self-standing, biblically faithful, evangelical scholarship.

Endnotes

1. This chapter appeared in *Journal of the Advent Theological Society* 5, no. 2 (1994); *Fundamentum* 1 (1997); *Faith and Mission* 14, no. 2 (1997).

2. It is the service of Norman L. Geisler to have made this clear. Cf. his essays "Philosophical Presuppositions of Biblical Inerrancy," in *Inerrancy*, ed. Geisler (Grand Rapids: Zondervan, 1982), 303–34, 473–75; and "Inductivism, Materialism, and Rationalism," in *Biblical Errancy: An Analysis of Its Philosophical Roots*, ed. Geisler (Grand Rapids: Zondervan, 1981), 9–22.

3. Monism is the doctrine that explains everything from a single principle. The term "monistic world view" was given form by Ernst Haeckel at the end of the nineteenth century, but a one-dimensional world view had already characterized the whole of Enlightenment philosophy.

4. For these little-known utterances of Kierkegaard, see the references in Geisler (n. 2 above) to Kierkegaard's journals as they appear in R. G. Smith, ed. and trans., *The Last Years: Journals of S. Kierkegaard 1853– 55* (New York: Harper and Row, 1965).

5. Cf. Richard Wurmbrand, *Karl Marx und Satan*, 3d ed. (Uhldingen/ Kreuzlingen: Stephanusedition, 1978); also Willem J. Ouwenell, *Evolution in der Zeitenwende* (Hückeswagen: Christliche Schriftenverbreitung, 1984), 298–302.

6. Ernst Lerle has called attention to this: *Moderne Theologie unter der Lupe* (Neuhausen-Stuttgart: Hänssler, 1987), 97–100.

7. Cf. Eta Linnemann, *Wissenschaft oder Meinung?* (Neuhausen-Stuttgart: Hänssler, 1986), 125–37 (= *Historical Criticism of the Bible* [Grand Rapids: Baker, 1990], 130–41).

8. Cf. Linnemann, *Wissenschaft oder Meinung?* 106–17 (= *Historical Criticism of the Bible*, 114–23). Further support for this statement is found in the second half of chapter one of my *Gibt es ein synoptisches Problem?* (see English edition, *Is There a Synoptic Problem?* 43–66).

9. C. H. Spurgeon, *Auf dein Wort. Andachten für jeden Tag*, 2d ed., ed. Wolfgang Bühne (Christliche Literaturverbreitung e. V., 1986), 124.

10. The Barmen Declaration was a statement issued in May 1934 by church leaders in Germany. It renounced Christian complicity in and collaboration with the Third Reich. The "first thesis" cited above includes these words: "Jesus Christ, as he is testified to us in the Holy Scripture, is the one Word of God, whom we are to hear, whom we are to trust and obey in life and in death. We repudiate the false teaching that the church can and must recognize yet other happenings and powers, images and truths as divine revelation alongside this one Word of God, as a source of her preaching" (see John H. Leith, *Creeds of the Churches*, 3d ed. [Atlanta: John Knox, 1982], 520).

11. Cf. Linnemann, *Wissenschaft oder Meinung?* 125–32 (= *Historical Criticism of the Bible*, 130–37).

12. This phenomenon is abundantly in evidence in literature dealing with the synoptic problem. See my *Gibt es ein synoptisches Problem?* (n. 8 above).

13. Cf. Samuel R. Külling, *Zur Datierung der "Genesis-P-Stücke,"* 2d ed. (Riehen: Immanuelverlag, 1985), passim. Also informative are some of

the sources adduced in J. McDowell, *More Evidence That Demands a Verdict*, 12th ed. (San Bernadino: Here's Life, 1981), 17–184, 327–63.

14. See Immanuel Velikovshy, *Die Seevölker* (Ullstein, 1983), 229, as well as the multivolume *Zeitalter im Chaos*, passim (on the Ipuwer papyrus, see vol. 1, *Vom Exodus zu König Echnaton* [Frankfurt am Main: Umschau Verlag, 1981], 38–69). More recently numerous works have appeared that take up the question of the new chronology.

15. Cf. among other works J. Urquhart, *Die erfüllten Verheißungen oder Gottes Siegel auf die Bibel*, 9th ed. (Barmen: Emil Müller, 1924); J. McDowell, *Evidence That Demands a Verdict* (San Bernadino: Campus Crusade for Christ, 1972), 147–84, 277–36; Werner Gitt, *Das Fundament* (Neuhausen-Stuttgart: Hänssler, 1985), 118–48.

16. Cf. my *Gibt es ein synoptisches Problem?* (n. 8 above). See also Robert L. Thomas and F. David Farnell, eds., *The Jesus Crisis: The Inroads of Historical Criticism into Evangelical Scholarship* (Grand Rapids: Kregel, 1998).

17. Klaus Beyer, *Die aramäischen Texte vom Toten Meer* (Göttingen: Vandenhoeck & Ruprecht, 1984), 226.

18. See David C. C. Watson, *Fact or Fancy* (Worthing: H. E. Walter, 1980), 88f.

19. See Watson, ibid., 89: Celsus "'considered that the different Gospels were incorrect revisions of one original' (B. F. Westcott, *A General Survey of the History of the Canon of the New Testament*, 6th ed. [1889], 405 n. 2), which some believers remodelled and remolded in various ways to answer objectors. To which Origen replies: 'I know of no people who remodel the Gospel except the followers of Marcion and the followers of Valentinus and perhaps those of Lucian.'"

20. In this fable the hedgehog fooled the hare when they raced. He put his wife, whom the hare could not tell from the hedgehog, at the end of the course. At the end of every heat, the hare would find a hedgehog awaiting him and announcing, "I'm already here." So he lost every race until finally he collapsed and died.

21. Cf. my *Wissenschaft oder Meinung?* 125–37 (= *Historical Criticism of the Bible*, 130–41).

22. As an example I refer to the second and third chapters of my *Is There*

a Synoptic Problem? ch. 2–3, where a methodological apparatus is developed in response to the particular task needing attention.

23. I assume the present situation, in which such possibilities are part of the program that leads to academic degrees. I will not take up the question here whether acquisition of such a degree is desirable or necessary for theology that is loyal to the Bible.

24. The separation between Old Testament and New Testament science such as that introduced by historical-critical theology has, to be sure, the practical advantage of specialization. On the other hand, it is a hindrance to the investigation of God's Word. This separation in its negative effects should, therefore, at least be checked—if not even eliminated—at least through research projects whose purview would be the entirety of the Bible.

25. Outstanding contributions to a history of New Testament research may be found in *The Jesus Crisis* by Thomas and Farnell (n. 16 above).

Chapter Seven

RESULTS

AS A WORK OF New Testament apologetics, this book should serve to place biblical criticism on the witness stand. This criticism has established itself as "historical-critical theology" in our universities and makes the claim to have sole validity for scientific theology.

Biblical criticism did not pass the test.

The attempt to push our canonical gospels to the side with the allegedly oldest gospel, Q, was unmasked as a "cleverly invented tale" (cf. 2 Pet. 1:16).

It could once more be confirmed that a literary dependence among the three Synoptic Gospels is not demonstrable and that accordingly a synoptic problem doesn't even exist. The claim of literary dependence between Colossians and Ephesians, between the two Thessalonian letters, and between Jude and 2 Peter—a claim that is supposed to prove the inauthenticity of these allegedly dependent writings—did not stand up to scrutiny.

It turns out to be a ridiculous undertaking to dispute the genuineness of New Testament writings by drawing up lists of 7, 24, 88, or 112 words of Pauline vocabulary that are lacking, or allegedly non-Pauline words that ought not appear. As soon as the Pauline vocabulary and its structure are investigated with scientific care, it becomes clear how little uniformity there is between the individual Pauline letters. By the use of such lists, **every** Pauline letter can be declared inauthentic; therefore it is illegitimate to set off **a few** as non-Pauline.

It should be recalled that even Romans, whose authenticity was never disputed, lacks no fewer than 1579 of the 2645 words of the Pauline vocabulary. Further, the percentage of hapax legomena in Romans is substantially higher than in a whole series of those New Testament writings that have been declared inauthentic not least because of their high percentage of hapaxes.

The procedure of biblical criticism, by which ten New Testament writings are declared pseudepigraphic by means of historical placement or theological classification, does not stand the test either. No scientific results have been produced using their procedure.

For that reason, no one who reads this book should feel obligated any longer to heed the suppositions of biblical criticism just because it makes the claim—without justification—to convey scientific results. Its arguments were tested at hundreds of points, and not one of them passed muster. The colossus of historical-critical theology has clay feet.

Evangelical theology should as a result purpose to give up the fruitless enterprise of being recognized as scientific by historical-critical theology; it needs to ponder its biblical foundation. A biblically sound, learned toil as brotherly service is necessary and possible, and it will turn out to be fruitful in the discovery of new methodological starting points that point the way to a labor that can be characterized rightly as scientific.

But such work is not to be twisted into a quest for selfish ends. **All honor belongs to the Lord alone!**

BIBLIOGRAPHY

Additional literature is cited in individual chapters and accessible through the author index.

Aland, Kurt. *Synopsis Quattor Evangeliorum*. 15th ed. Stuttgart: Deutsche Bibelgesellschaft, 1996.

Beyer, Klaus. *Die aramäischen Texte vom Toten Meer*. Göttingen: Vandenhoeck & Ruprecht, 1986.

Bruggen, Jakob van. *Die geschichtliche Einordnung der Pastoralbriefe*. TVG 305. Wuppertal: R. Brockhaus, 1981.

Carson, D. A., Douglas J. Moo, and Leon Morris. *An Introduction to the New Testament*. 4th ed. Leicester, U.K.: Apollos, 1994.

Farmer, William R. *The Gospel of Jesus: The Pastoral Relevance of the Synoptic Problem*. Louisville: Westminster/John Knox, 1994.

Geisler, Norman L., ed. "Philosophical Presuppositions of Biblical Errancy." In *Inerrancy*, 303–34; 473–75. Grand Rapids: Zondervan, 1979.

———, ed. "Inductivism, Materialism, and Rationalism." In *Biblical Errancy: An Analysis of Its Philosophical Roots*, 9–22. Grand Rapids: Zondervan, 1981.

Guthrie, Donald. *New Testament Introduction*. 8th revised ed. Downers Grove: InterVarsity, 1996.

Harrison, P. N. *The Problem of the Pastoral Epistles*. London: Oxford University Press, 1921.

Kulling, S. R. *Zur Datierung der 'Genesis-P-Stücke.'* 2d ed. Riehen: Immanuel, 1985.

Mattila, Sharon L. "A Problem Still Clouded: Yet Again-Statistics and 'Q.'" *Novum Testamentum* XXXVI, no. 4 (1994): 313–29.

Mauerhofer, Erich. *Einleitung in die Schriften des Neuen Testaments.* 2 vols. Neuhausen-Stuttgart: Hänssler, 1995.

Morgenthaler, R. *Statistik des Neutestamentlichen Wortschatzes.* 4th ed. Zürich: Gotthelf, 1992.

Patterson, Stephen J. "Q—The Lost Gospel." *Bible Review* IX, no. 5 (1993): 34–46, 61–62.

Reiser, Marius. *Syntax und Stil des Markusevangeliums im Licht der hellenistichen Volksliteratur.* Tübingen: Mohr, 1984.

Schnelle, Udo. *Einleitung in das Neue Testament.* UTB 1830. Göttingen: Vandenhoeck & Ruprecht, 1994. English edition: *The History and Theology of the New Testament Writings.* Translated by M. E. Boring. Minneapolis: Fortress, 1998.

Stein, Robert H. *The Synoptic Problem: An Introduction.* Grand Rapids: Baker, 1994.

Stoldt, Hans-Herbert. *Geschichte und Kritik der Markushypothese.* 2d ed. Giessen/Basle: Brunnen, 1986.

Synnes, Martin. Vakthold om "den skjonne skatt og kommentar til forste Timoteusbrev Innforing i Pastoralbrevene." Oslo, 1996.

Thomas, Robert L. and F. David Farnell. *The Jesus Crisis: The Inroads of Historical Criticism into Evangelical Scholarship.* Grand Rapids: Kregel, 1998.

Verkaik, André. *The Tenability of Synoptic Independence.* Unpublished treatise, 1995.

Watson, David C. C. *Fact or Fantasy: The Authenticity of the Gospels.* Worthing, U.K.: Walter, 1980.

Wenham, John. *Redating Matthew, Mark and Luke: A Fresh Assault on the Synoptic Problem.* London: Hodder & Stoughton, 1991.

Zahn, Theodor. *Einleitung in das Neue Testament.* Vol. 2. Leipzig: A. Deichert'sche Verlagsbuchhandlung, 1899.

INDEX

Acts 23, 100, 104, 126, 128, 129,
    133, 134, 155, 156, 179
Africa 10
Antioch 22–23, 133
Apocrypha 49
Apollos 158
Aquila 49, 50
Aramaic 21, 22, 54, 55
Asia 10
Asia Minor 114, 154
Athanasius 204
Authenticity issue 12–13, 100–57

Bar-Kochba 187, 202
Barmen Declaration 183, 207
Barnabas 22, 156
Barth, Karl 178
Basic Vocabulary 44–47
Beatitudes 35
Beyer, Klaus 187
Bruggen, Jakob van 128
Bultmann, Rudolf 146, 178, 179,
    183, 199, 202

Caesars, Roman 202
Calvin, John 204

Carson, D. A. 13, 17
Celsus 188, 208
Christology 140, 142, 204
Church, European 10, 11
Colossians
    Authenticity of 101–10, 142–48,
        152, 162, 199–200
    Word occurrences 76
Common order 56–59
Common Synoptic Vocabulary 48
Complete 167, 168
Corinthians, First 76–90, 127, 145
Corinthians, Second 76–90

Daniel 59, 153, 188, 201
Dating issues 29, 187, 197–98, 200,
    201–2
Descartes, René 178
Didache 137
Discipleship 37, 199
Domitian 134, 135

Easter narrative 29
Ecclesiology 143–47, 156
Egypt 185, 194, 208
Enlightenment 18, 183, 206

Ephesians
    Authenticity of 101–6, 111–17,
        126–27, 140–42, 152, 161,
        199
    Word occurrences 76–90
Epiphanius 22
Eschatology 141, 143–44
Ethiopic Enoch 187, 201
Europe 10–11, 13
Eusebius 22
Evangelical theology 177–206
Exodus 184
Eyewitness writings in Gospels 28,
    55, 57, 109

Farmer, William R. 30

Galatians 76–90
Galilean narratives 37, 48, 58
Geisler, Norman L. 206
Gentile Christians 23, 132, 133
Germany 10, 15–16, 18, 207
Gnosticism 202–3
Goeze, J. M. 205
Gospel of Thomas 19, 28–31
Gospels. *See* Synoptic problem.
Great Commission 27
Greek language 19, 22, 25, 38,
    44–52, 54–55, 86–90, 156
Greeks 185, 188
Guthrie, Donald 13

Haeckel, Ernst 206
Hapax legomena 87–88, 90, 101–7,
    109, 146, 158, 165–68, 170, 211
Harrison, P. N. 79–86, 94–96,
    110–11, 163
Hebrew language 22, 23
Hebrews 100, 133
Hegel, Georg 178, 184
Heidegger, Martin 179
Hellenism 108, 109, 144, 154, 161

Herod 187
Historical-Critical Theology
    As science 10
    Effect of 214
History of church 19, 20, 22–23,
    30, 54, 154–55, 203–4
History of religion 200–3
Hobbes, Thomas 178
Holy Spirit 147–48, 179–80, 191,
    193
Hume, David 178

Inductivism 206
Irenaeus 22, 204

Jacobsen, Arland 19
James
    Church leader 132–34, 138
    Epistle of 101, 102, 132–34,
        154–56
Jerome 22
Jerusalem
    Council 22–23, 133
    Destruction of 199
    Parthian conquest of 187
"Jesus people" 20–21, 23
Jesus-sayings 23
Job 156
Johannine Epistles 100, 137, 165
John the Baptist 201
Jonas, Hans 201–2
Joseph and Mary 137
Joses 138
Judaism and Christianity 22–23,
    131, 132–34, 186–87, 201
Jude, Epistle of 101, 102, 104, 113,
    123–25, 133, 137–38

Kähler Martin 178
Kant, Immanuel 178, 183
Kierkegaard, Søren 178, 207
Kloppenborg, John 19

Koester, Helmut 19

Lachmann fallacy 24
Laodiceans, Epistle to the 127
Lessing, Gotthold Ephraim 178, 188
Lord's Prayer, the 33
Lucian 208
Lüdemann, Gerd 100–1
Luke
    Matthew comparison 24, 27, 28, 33–41
    Q in 33, 35–41
    Synoptic comparison 42–72
Luther, Martin 204

Mack, Burton 19, 20–21
Manetho 185
Marcion 208
Mark
    As source 24
    Formation of 21
    Synoptic comparison 42–72
    Vocabulary 168
Marsden, George 15
Marx, Karl 179
Matthew
    Formation of 21–22
    Luke comparison 24, 27, 28, 33–41
    Q in 26, 28, 35–41
    Synoptic comparison 42–72
Mia 87–88, 164–67, 168
Michel, Ernst 201
Monism 183
Mono 167
Moo, Douglas J. 13
Morgenthaler, Robert 12, 50, 51, 76, 92
Morris, Leon 13
Moses 35, 185
Multy 164–67, 168

Narrative order 52–57
Nero 134
Nestle-Aland 57, 58, 61–71
New Testament
    Historical-critical theology 209
    Introduction 100–1, 164

Oden Thomas C. 16
Old Testament 132–33, 156, 185, 201, 209
"Oracles" 21–22
Origen 22, 188, 208

Papias 21, 23
Parallel texts 26–27, 42–44, 60–61, 113–25
Parenthetical material 52, 59–61
Parthians 187
Partial 168
Particles 27, 44–47, 50–51, 80–86, 96–97, 110–11, 162–63
Passion narrative 29
Pastorals 76–90, 93–97, 101–11, 128–32, 150–51, 153–54
Patterson Stephen J. 19–21
Paul 22–23. See also Pauline Epistles.
Pauline Epistles
    Eschatology 78
    Vocabulary 51, 75, 77, 79–81, 93–95, 110, 161–63, 169–76
    Word occurrences 74–90
Peter
    Apostle 22
    Epistles 101, 105, 108–9, 122–25, 134–37, 156–57, 161
Philemon 76–77, 109–10
Philip 126
Philippians 76–90
Pietists 203, 204
Pneumatology 147–48
Poly 89

Porphyry 188
Prepositions. *See* Particles.
Pronouns. *See* Particles.

Q 18–31, 35, 38, 113, 210
  Apocalypse 36
  Lost gospel of 18–19, 21–23, 25
Quantitative Analysis 26–28, 42,
  71, 164–76
Quelle source. *See* Q.
Qumran 187, 199, 201

Rationalism 204, 206
Reformation 203, 204
Reitzenstein, R. 201
Revelation of John 100,
Robinson, James M. 19
Roman Empire 135–36
Romans 76–90, 110–12, 139

Sayings source. *See* Q.
Schlatter, Adolf 18
Schleiermacher, Friedrich 23–24,
  74
Schnelle, Udo 50, 74, 75
Schulz, Siegfried 19, 25
Septuagint 47–50, 55
Simon Magus 202
Single 168
Solo 168
Spinoza, Benedict 178
Stein, Robert H. 52–61
Strecker, G. 50
Symmachus 85–50
Synchronic 195
Synoptic Problem 18–72

Theodotion 49–50
Theological education 10, 195
Thessalonians, First 76–90, 148,
  153

Thessalonians, Second
  Authenticity of 105, 106–6,
    118–22, 148–49, 152–53
  Word occurrences 76–90

Third Reich 207
Thomas, Gospel of 19, 28–31
Timothy, First. *See* Pastorals.
Timothy, Second. *See* Pastorals.
Titus. *See* Pastorals.
Trinity 204
Two-source theory 18
Tychicus 114, 127, 140

Valentinus 208
Velikovsky, Immanuel 198
Verkaik, André 44
Vocabulary statistics 74–99

Weisse Christian Hermann 24
Westcott, B. F. 18

Yamauchi, Edwin M. 202

Zahn, Theodor 18, 22
Zoroastrianism 201